SRI VID

THE TRUTH OF SANATANA DHARMA

SRI SAI VENKATESH

Contents

CHAPTER ONE

Introduction

Once heavily guarded and protected as a secretive esoteric tradition, Sri Vidya is now a household term, so much that one can find hundreds of people claiming to teach it, and thousands more claiming to practice it. This does not however reduce in any way, the real power and might of Sri Vidya, which is always available for the one that seeks the real truth amidst the ocean of misunderstood and miswritten texts.

In very simple terms, Sri is a term indicating Divinity and Vidya means know-how, basically meaning that Sri Vidya is that wisdom that makes a person transcend the normal human life of misery and pain, and lead us to a Divine Life living with God in a lifestyle of purity, bliss and love. However, there is no more direct manifestation of Divinity than Mother Nature existing all around us, and for this reason, Sri Vidya revolves around the Universal Mother Goddess, called Sri Lalitha, the name indicating Her gentle loving nature as a Mother called Amma, playfully entertaining us, Her infants.

Universally, it is a very strongly established fact that the oldest existent literature of any form, are the Vedas, which are believed to be Apaurusheya, or authored by the Divine itself, and compiled by seers or Rishis. In fact, any spiritual tradition derived from the Vedas, is claimed to be Sanatana Dharma, meaning it is the way of life that exists eternally, without a beginning or an end.

Sri Vidya finds mention in the Vedas in several places, the most noteworthy being the Sri Devi Atharva Shirsham, a text found in Rig Veda 10th Mandala, 10th Adhyaya, 125th Sukta, Verses 1 to 8, and borrowed also into the Atharva Veda. In this text, the verse starting Kaamo Yoni Kamalaa Vajra cryptically encodes the central Mantra or chant of Sri Vidya called Shodashi, and the same is also crpyptically mentioned elsewhere in Rig Veda as a wheel or Mantra with four "Ee" sounds.

In particular, Rig Veda 5.47.4 reads चत्वार ईम बभ्रिरति कषमेयन्तो दश गर्भ ंचरसे धापयन्ते |तरधिातवः परमा अस्य गावो दविश चरन्ति परिसिद्यो अन्तान || which translates rougughly as the Four Ee sounds bear him up and give him rest and quiet, and the ten wombs (referring to the nine Avaranas of Sri Chakra and tenth being Sumeru) invigorate the infant, referring to the Self, for travel. His kine most excellent, of threefold nature denoting the Trividha Upasanas, pass swiftly round the boundaries of heaven. This verse basically mentions the Sri Vidya Mantra, particularly with the four ईs, which is a reference to the 15 lettered base Mantra to Shiodashi Mantra of Amma in Sri Vidya, which contains one ई and three more within the ह्रीं Maya Bija.

Thus, from this it becomes clear that Sri Vidya the tradition is as old as the Vedas itself. Indeed one must understand that the entire purpose of Sanatana Dharma and the Vedas is simply to give us the wisdom of Sri Vidya, in the manner best possible, even while keeping the root wisdom coded from going into the wrong hands. Every other wisdom or religious tradition given by the Vedas or other texts are merely to delude people, and this can be seen in the words of Adi Shankara Himself, in Saundarya Lahari, verse 31, where He states clearly how Lord Shiva as Pashupathi remains content after deluding the world by giving 64 different Tantras which give people small doses of psychic powers and worldly fulfilments. It is only on the insistence of the Mother Goddess Herself that Shiva revealed the real wisdom and Tantra to the world, independent of all others and capable of conferring every single objective on the practitioners. He follows this verse with verses 32 and 33, which then go on to cryptically describe the Shodashi Mantra.

Thus, it is clear that close to 99 percent of available information on spirituality today is nothing but a gient deluder of truth, while the real Sanatana Dharma, as the real wisdom of Sri Vidya, is hidden and protected heavily, and this is indeed the way to understand various terms given in Vedic literature such as Treta, Dvapara, Kali Yugas, described as periods of declining truth and darkness. However, among seriously advanced spiritual followers, the prevalent knowledge is that these dark ages have ended, and Satya Yuga, the age of truth, dawned precisely on September 16, 2020, a day following sighting of a comet as well as more than six of nine planets placed in their own houses and strong points. This means that the present age is one where the true Sri Vidya is available in one single source, in unambiguous terms, and that is what this book precisely is.

As per the Lalitha Sahasranamam itself, Sri Vidya broadly consists of three components, called Maha Mantra, Maha Yantra and Maha Tantra, and these will be explored now.

CHAPTER TWO

Mantra - Shodashi

The power of Sri Vidya comes from the fact that it gives a roadmap for the journey of life itself, all the way from the mundane lifestyle of normal people, called Samsara, all the way to a liberated divine lifestyle. In fact the Shodashi Mantra is composed of 16 letters, each of which denote a stage or milestone called Bhumika, in the path from Samsara to complete Divinity.

The Mantra itself runs as

Ka E I La Hreem

Ha Sa Ka Ha La Hreem

Sa Ka La Hreem

Shreem

This list of stages is obtained by understanding the Vedantic or Upanishad meaning of the Shodashi Mantra of Amma given by Varivasya Rahasya of Bhaskararaya. This is compared with the Bhumikas or stages of enlightenment given in the Varaha Upanishad, to give the following list.

I. Satsanga: Knowing about the Divine, listening to discourses, books, etc knowing about various qualities and deeds of God.

II. Yama-Niyama: Purifying the mind by performing various righteous acts, observing ethics and adhering to the do's and don'ts.

III. Viveka: Curiosity is roused in the now purified mind, about the nature of God, finally understanding that the One (God) is the one behind the many diversity of the world. God alone is worth seeking and not worldly qualities.

IV. Vairagya: The chains that tie one to the world, ie emotions, society norms etc, are severed through dispassion towards worldly things.

V. Yoga: Having decided to pursue only the Ishta Devata, the Kundalini or life force is raised, thereby raising the level of concentration, and meditating on the form of God, Savikalpa Samadhi is achieved, where the meditator loses himself blissfully into the form meditated.

VI. Mumukshu: Addicted to the bliss of Savikalpa, an intense thirst for liberation arises, to the rejection of everything else.

VII. Subheccha: With the thirst for liberation kindled, everything one observes around raises multiple questions, that are asked, leading to deep philosophical questions and the thirst for enlightenment.

VIII. Sathya: To quench the intense thirst of enlightenment, the Divine now reveals a crucial truth: the unreality of the world is realised. Thus, the non-existence of everything in the outside world, but rather existing in one's own consciousness is realised.

IX. Anantha: As much as the world is realized to be unreal, it is also realized in this stage to be perishable and transitory. In contrast, God is understood to be beyond birth and death.

X. Vichara: Along with unreality and transitory, the insentience of the world is realized now. With this, a deep inquiry into the question Who am I? arises, negating everything that is not found to be the Self.

XI. Tanumanasi: The results of the previous stage are consolidated. Having understood everything the Self is not, one enters meditation, slowly eliminating all thoughts as the non-Self. The end result is Nirvikalpa Samadhi, the Self alone remains, and shines forth in its blissful purity.

XII. Sattvapatti: Having achieved Nirvikalpa, and addicted to it, while also pushing aside the illusory world as the non-Self, one gets the fear of falling down from the Nirvikalpa state. This is solved by exposing oneself to God's Will and the purpose of His Will, in that He is the one that brought forth the Samadhi. Maintaining Spiritual progress is His responsibility, and this thought leads one to Sharanagathi.

XIII. Asamsakthi: Here one surrenders completely to God, out of intense love. God on the other hand, takes on the ego and fully kills it. For a person who has surrendered, and where Divine Will alone does everything, there is no ego, neither is the fear of losing the Nirvikalpa state.

XIV. Padarthabhavana: One understands the entire world to be a dream. All characters in my dream are essentially me. Thus, not only am I the Self, I am also every character in the dream, every creation. The only difference is, the former is real, the latter is not.

XV. Thuriyatheetha: With all Bheda or distinction removed, with the ego fully killed, and with the complete nature of reality known, one abides blissfully in one's own Self. Samadhi does not require effort, but eternally exists effortlessly, as Sahaja Samadhi.

XVI. Leela: With the nature of reality understood and bliss attained, and with life still continuing, and with nothing to lose, this stage is the blissful playing along with Universal Mother Amma, in this world itself, as Jivanmukthi, knowing very well that it is unreal, simply because this playing is an expression of the bliss along with Amma.

The three Samadhi stages of 5, 11 and 15 mark three Kutas of Shodashi. In broad terms, the perspective of reality in these stages respectively give the Dvaita, Bhedabheda (such as Vishishtadvaita) and Advaita views respectively.

Varivasya Rahasya of Bhaskararaya details the significance and meanings of the Panchadashi Mantra letter by letter. Once this is understood, the sixteenth can simply be seen as Samashti or aggregate of the first fifteen. Broadly the Mantra is understood in light of its three Kutas or segments- the Vagbhava, Kamaraja and Shakti Kutas consisting of 5, 6 and 4 Bija Aksharas respectively of the 15, and all three ending in the Maya Bija Hrim.

In this context, the first Kuta called Vagbhava Kuta, mapped to Rig Veda is read as KaE ILa Hreem, the meaning being one proceeds from creation (K), destruction (a), preservation (E) actions towards praising (ILa) Brahman (Hreem) and attaining spiritual progress. This represents stages pertaining to cultivating interest in Brahman and preparing oneself to attain the highest goal.

The second Kuta called Kamaraja Kuta, Yajur Vedic, is read as HaSa KaHaLa Hreem, the meaning being Brahman (Hreem) is of the nature of Bliss (HaSa), Truth (Ka), Infinite (Ha) and Wisdom (La). In this stage, one learns about Brahman, comparing the properties with what is observed in materialistic world.

The third Kuta called Shakti Kuta, Sama Vedic, runs as SaKaLa Hreem, meaning that everything (SaKaLa) is Brahman (Hreem) itself. This amounts to completely surrendering to divine Will giving up ego, and merging one's identity in Brahman. This is the state of simply being Brahman, which is one's true, pure and original state.

The three Hreems from the 3 Kutas are mapped to Atharvana Veda. Whatever is the learning of each stage, is consolidated and brought into practice, through these Hreems.

In post Vedic Puranic Era Sri Vidya traditions, the above mentioned 15 lettered Panchadashakshari Mantra is seen in two other variations. The above elaborated version is called Kaadi Vidya, named for its starting letter Ka. The second variation is Haadi Vidya, which replaces Ka E I La Hrim with Ha Sa Ka La Hrim. Here Ha Sa, translates to smiling or blissful Ananda, hence Hasa Kala means Ananda Kala or the phases of bliss, which is nothing bit progress in stages towards Liberation, distinguished by 1st 2 stages as absence of discrimination Viveka versus next 2 stages as presence of Viveka. The third variation is referred to as Saadi Vidya, as it starts with the letter Sa.

It is said that Haadi Vidya was propounded by Lopamudra, consort of Agastya, and is Rajasic or egoistic in nature, whereas Saadi Vidya, propounded by sage Durvasa is Tamasic or delusional in nature, with only Haadi capable of extending to sixteen lettered Shodashakshari, and not Saadi.

Kaadi Vidya, the Mantra explained in detail above, is the one propounded by Shiva Himself as Dakshinamurthi, followed by Vishnu as Hayagriva, Manmatha, Skanda or Subrahmanya and other great souls such as Adi Shankara, Bhaskararaya and Muthuswami Dikshitar. This Kaadi is Sattvic or in the mode of truth and goodness. The reason is that Kaadi version contains the letter Ee, which, as Adi Shankara in Saundaryalahari explains, is the Kamakala Bija or letter that denotes the union of male and female principles as Shiva and Shakti which are nothing but pure existence versus attributes. Haadi and Saadi conspicuously omit the Kamakala and hence have an inherent gender inequality in them, which is against the modes of nature. It is Kaadi alone that is Vedic, since, as explained, a verse in the Rig Veda mentions about the Mantra with four Ees, which is Kaadi and cannot be possible in Haadi or Saadi which omit the letter Ee.

Thus the term Moola Mantra or Maha Mantra denotes Panchadashakshari or Shodashakshari Mantra in Kaadi version alone.

Mantra as a term derives from Man, meaning mind, and refers to the mindset of a person that evolves through the sixteen Bhumikas. For a person who has completed the course, the Mantra is used as a daily chant, to not just remind oneself of the journey that one has covered but also to activate by extension the Yantra and Tantra as well. The superpower conferred by this Mantra is fierce independence, depending on Amma alone for everything physical or otherwise, and completely transcending dependence on any other human or other thing worldly.

Furthermore, the Lalitha Sahasranamam mentions how the Maha Mantra is the very form and body of Lalitha Herself, with the three Kutas in order representing the head, torso region and lower regions respectively of the Mother Goddess. Shreemadvagbhavakutaika svarupa mukhapankaja,

Kantadhah kati paryanta madhyakuta svarupinee, Shakti-kutaikatapanna katyadhobhaga dharinee.

The correct form of this Goddess Lalitha, is established in the temple town of Thirukodikaval, the same place where Bhaskararaya resided and composed the Varivasya Rahasya as well as the very first commentary on Lalitha Sahasranamam. In this Thirukodikaval temple enshrining Lalitha Tripurasundari, the Goddess, confirms Her real form by giving Darshan or manifesting as the form of Balaji or Venkatesha, with Shankha and Chakra and Kati Hasta, confirming how the real form of Lalitha referred in the Vedic Sri Vidya is Balaji itself. This form was known in the ancient submerged Kumarikandam continent as well as in Siddha tradition of present age as Chempa or Chempakavalli, and is enshrined as such in Thiruvananthapuram by the name of Chempazhanthy.

Venkateshwara as Chempazhanthy

CHAPTER THREE

Yantra - Sri Chakra

As much as Sri Vidya is a wisdom of the highest order, it is also strongly grounded in reality, physically on the planet we live. In particular, Sri Vidya as a tradition is centered around two specific places, considered the most holiest and powerful of all places that ever exist in the universe. These two places are found in the Lalitha Sahasranama that is composed on the Mother Goddess, in the following names: Sumeru Madhya Shringastha, and Srimannagara Naayika. While generally one assumes both to be the same place, it is not so. These are two different places.

Of these, Sri-man-nagaram can be translated in Tamil in the following manner. Sri means Thiru, man is the word "aar' as a mark of respect such as pillaiyar, ayyanar etc, and nagaram means Oor, the city. Putting these together, we get the term Thiruvarur, which is located in Tamilnadu, and is home to the most magnificient temple in the world that enshrines Thyagaraja, Kamalamba and hundreds of other shrines, with many other smaller temples surrounding it. This place, is mentioned in Skanda Purana, by the name of Naagara, in the section titled Naagara Khaandam. Furthermore, the two handed deity Kamalamba and Thiruvarur, famous for its red Paatali flowers is the focus of the Tripura Sundari Manasa Puja Stotram of Adi Shankara, even while in Carnatic Music, the pinnacle of all compositions by Muthuswami Dikshitar focuses entirely on Thiruvarur and Kamalambika, who is Lalitha Herself, in form of the Navavarana Krithis, which contain the highest wisdom and philosophy of Sri Vidya. As per mention in Skanda Purana itself, the place of Thiruvarur was called Haataka Kshetra where a giant tunnel going to the nether worlds, was covered up by Indra the King of Gods, using a mountain peak broken from the King of mountains, referring to the fact that the land of Thiruvarur is half of the original mountain Sumeru, and this is why both places are mentioned together.

The place untouched by Kali Yuga, or Kali Raahitya Nagara – this is how Skanda Puraana describes the temple of Thiruvarur, one of the biggest in the world at 35 acres in size, with the holy temple tank Kamalaalayam of another 35 acres, and having more than 300 shrines, believed to have been built by Lord Vishwakarma Himself. The Skanda Puraana dedicates the entire sixth of seven cantos, titled Naagara Khaandam, to describing the glory of Thiruvarur.

The temple of Thiruvarur

View of the Thiruvarur temple

1. Lord Shiva describes the Haatakeshwara shrine within the temple, to be the most important and powerful among 68 Shiva Temples all over the world.

2. The Thyagaraja shrine is very powerful and has the combined power of 24 Shiva Temples including Kashi, Kailash, Kedar, Chidambaram, Thiruvannamalai, Ujjain etc.

3. Lord Thyagaraja has enacted 364 Leelas or Divine Plays, much more than the 64 He did in Madurai.

4. Kamalaamba shrine established by sage Agastya is the very center and capital of Sri Vidya, and has the combined power of the 51 Akshara Shakti Peethas all across India.

5. Mooladhara Vinayaka is one of the oldest shrines for Lord Ganesha, and with over 40 shrines for various forms of Lord Ganapathi, Thiruvarur is called the Mooladhara Kshetra.

6. Lord Murugan killed the demon Tharaka Asura in the famous town of Tiruchendur, and after the Samhaara, the Shakti or Vel of the Lord finally landed within the Haatakeshwara shrine. One can see this even today in the form of a Shatkona Yantra.

7. Jalashayina Vishnu shrine within the Kamalamba temple is the sole residing place of Lord Narayana for the Chaturmaasa period of four months, between Ashada and Karthika Ekadashi days.

8. There is a majestic shrine of Pushpa Aaditya, where Lord Soorya combines the powers of all the 12 forms of Aaditya.

9. The Navagrahas here are in a straight line, as Anugraha Moorthis, and are without malevolent effects, due to an assurance given by them to Lord Shiva. A trip to Shaneeshwara temple in Thirunallar is considered incomplete without a trip to Thiruvarur first.

10. Haatakeshwara shrine is a Naaga Bila, with an underground tunnel leading to the world of Naagas in Pathala Loka.

11. The Sthala Vriksha is the Paatali or Sacred Trumpet Flower tree, the only one found in its species, which cannot be replanted or propagated elsewhere by any other means.

12. The holy tank of Kamalaalayam is surrounded by 64 Ghats, which have various effects and benefits upon performing certain rituals. The holy water has the combined power of many famous Theerthas such as Ganga,

Saraswathi, Gaya, Prayag, Pushkar and Sethu.

13. The temple and town is also called Kamalapuram, in honor of Goddess Lakshmi, who attained the position of Mahalakshmi here and is seen in a shrine in constant Dhyana or meditation.

14. The temple is seen to be the only fully planned Sri Vidya Kshetra, combining both aspects of Vamachara and Dakshinachara with the respective deities. Lord Shaasta is seen enshrined in the position of Guru, which is the basis for the Dakshinamurthi form developed in later days.

15. There are shrines for Lingas representing the Pancha Bhoothas (five elements of nature), 11 Rudras, 12 Jyotirlingas, 4 Vedas and Lingas established by the Sapta Rishis, as well as various other Kings, Devas, Rishis and other people.

16. The temple is surrounded on all sides by tall, colourful Gopurams, tall walls, and the Chariot or Aazhi Ther is world famous at a height of nearly 100 metres and 300 tonnes in weight.

17. Lord Yama is enshrined here as Chandikeshwara, the prime devotee of Lord Shiva, and it is believed that those who are born in thiruvarur, or merely utter the name itself, are granted liberation or Moksha, without the troubles by Yama.

18. The shrine of Runahareshwara is powerful and helps in clearing of long term debts and chronic illnesses. Raudra Durga is seen as the deity of Rahu Kala and helps in eliminating marriage delays and obstacles. Kapaleeshwara established by Lord Indra cleanses one of the Brahmahatti Dosha.

19. The shrine of Jwarahareshwara and Vaidyanatha is worshipped for good health and freedom from fevers and terrible ailments. Shankha Theertha also gives same benefit and also alleviates handicaps and deformities.

21. It is a tradition that while reciting the Thevaaram hymns of the celebrated Nayanmar saints, one begins and ends with the word "Thiruchitrambalam", as a mark of respect and honor to Chidambaam, the oldest and most powerful of the 274 Shiva temples all across the world including Thirunelveli, Madurai, Kashi, Rameshwaram and Ujjain. However, for hymns of Thevaaram praising Thiruvarur alone, this practice is not followed, since this temple is much more older and powerful than Chidambaram itself.

What happens in Thiruvarur, and why is it so powerful?

Basically, Sri Vidya if seen as a superpower, consists of two superpowers, as evident in the name itself – Sri and Vidya, and these powers are granted in Srimannagaram and Sumeru respectively. Sri means wealth, and is the ability to generate wealth on any given day, even if starting from scratch. This seems easy to tell, but is not an easy thing to achieve, since wealth is just a by product of a much bigger cycle. Wealth is merely a marker of resource availability to accomplish a certain task, which itself is generated through some desire that arises in our mind to do something, and that itself arises because of some trigger or stimulus, as in we see something and are impressed and then a desire arises to do something about it, and so on. Furthermore, the very doing of the activity must be guarded from obstacles, difficulties and threats, even while keeping out body and mind at its most productive and efficient capability to accomplish the task. Thus, this entire cycle of activity, is referenced by Sri, and the ability to generate wealth means that all parts of this activity cycle are taken care of. The energies and various forms that are responsible for this reside in Srimannagaram.

These energies, seen as forms of Lalitha, are often arranged in a cosmic map pattern called the Sri Chakra or Sri Yantra, and thus Srimannagaram is synonymous with Sri Yantra. The visual depictions of each form, as well as its Purana or story of how it came to be in Thiruvarur, tells us about the specific role and properties of each of these forms resident in Sri Chakra.

As a temple, Thiruvarur has seen periods of monumental growth and celebration, as well as periods of decline, and so too, the real Sri Vidya core practices eclipsed and veiled by layers and layers of Agamas, Shaiva practices and so on. This is not new to the temple, with Skanda Purana itself referencing one such major incident during the time of Vibheeshana, with lot of shrines replaced. However, the Sri Chakra energies themselves are Sanatana and beyond any cycle of growth and decline. So too, even in the present age, there have been demons active in play, trying to block real seekers from accessing the real Sri Vidya and Sri Chakra energies of Thiruvarur, and in this attempt, by using the survivor of Mahabharata times Ashwathama as well as various Mantrika associates including Samayachari followers of Sri Vidya settling as far as London with the headquarters in Ernakulam area of Pathalam, literally translated as the nether world, bearing the name of Kridhna as Rajagopala just to attempt defiling the divine name, the Sri Chakra and wealth of Thiruvarur were looted, creating an entire kingdom of Travancore just to hide the wealth and rule using the kidnapped power, as well as kidnap Veda Vyasa the author of the Brahma Sutras, so that by their royal influence they may wean people away from the truth, except the idiotic miscreants did not realize how the real Sri Chakra is infused in the land of Thiruvarur as well as each of the deity forms in the main and surrounding temples, and removing just the Yantra form of Sri Chakra achieves nothing. For this sole purpose, the evil miscreants had carried out the entire exercise of colonization, looting and pillaging the Indian subcontinent, through various European powers including the British, to try and brainwash the people away from Sanatana Dharam into Abrahamic religions, even as various Siddhas and Yogis propped up to replace the real Sanatana truth with incomplete and misinterpreted Agamas, Hindu and other Dharmic religions. So too, the miscreants have used the dead souls of people, who are themselves undergoing heel in earth by punishment of Yama, even as these souls are used for affecting people psychologically and through occult means, creating negative thoughts, emotions and confusions, and the attacks are more severe on any person the closer and closer they reach out to the real truth. Indeed, the incarnation of Kalki bearing the name of Thiagesha Shiva of Thiruvarur has manifest explicitly to rescue people from these unspeakable atrocities and punish the miscreants suitably, even as the onus is on each person to suitably defend themselves from this evil force, in their pursuit and journey towards the truth of Sri Vidya. For this purpose, the Sri Chakra forms are consolidated into two super forms, namely Dhumra or Jyeshta, representing all the inner triangles, and Varahi representing all the outer non-triangles, and these forms are themselves merged into a single Dhumravarahi, which is enshrined as the form of Mookambika in Kollur and derived from this form in Chottanikkara Bhagavathi in Ernakulam, the home of the nether worlds. The Dhumravarahi is invoked by chanting of a Mantra, which must be chanted as one focuses on the third eye area in between the eyebrows, and feels a vibration in the same. The mantra runs as

Om Dhoom Dhoom Mrithyu Dhoom
Dhoom Dhoom Kaala Dhoom
Dhoom Dhoom Dhoomravaaraahi
Hoom Phat Swaahaa.

The face of the Devi symbolizes the Maha Tantra as the Mother form, even as torso consisting of Shankha Chakra is identical to Balaji as Maha Mantra, and the lower part seated in a lotus denotes Kamalanagaram, which is Thiruvarur as Maha Yantra form, and together, the Goddess guards and protects all three as well as our journey towards these three.

Goddess Mookambika

The Purana and stories associated with each of these forms and reported in this book, must be understood symbolically, conveying intricate messages about the powers of these forms and relation with other forms, and this is the original purpose of Puranas. Thus, one must take Naagara Khaandam as the only true Purana and discard all other Puranas pertaining to other places such as Kashi, Badrinath etc to be merely given to create delusion and eclipse the real Purana which is Thiruvarur alone.

Thus, the role of Srimannagaram in Sri Vidya is to bestow the Sri or wealth related blessing of the Mother Goddess. As and when a person graduates through the Bhumikas, they are lead to the Sri Chakra, which is the highest wealth a person can ever have, with all the varieties of Amma in Her various forms in the cosmic pattern, each of these having its own power. As and when a person gets acquainted with the nature and strengths of these forms, his view on life also changes accordingly, and is able to recognize these powers in action as and when they appear in different situations pertaining to him and those around him.

The Sri Yantra is a complex geometrical pattern of interlocking triangles, which is a form of Amma Herself. It is the most complete map of the universe ever drawn. The tradition of viewing the Sri Yantra is as layers or Avaranas, going from outward to inward, each enclosure going more subtle than the outer. There are nine such Avaranas, and traditionally worship is done in an order from outer to inner, known as Samhara Krama, or inner to outer, known as Srishti Krama.

However, the formation of the Sri Yantra is explained as the interlocking between 9 triangles, five downward facing and four upward facing ,such interlocking creating a number of smaller triangles which constitute each enclosure. This means that the Yantra is simultaneous in nature, rather than progressive. For example, smaller triangles as components of the 7th and 4th Avaranas can both be traced to interlocking of the same big triangles. This means, 7th Avarana is in no way more or less progressive than 4th.

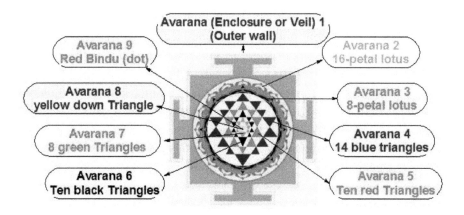

Avaranas of the Sri Chakra

Indeed one can derive the Yantra from the Shodashi Mantra, which also has been described in the Varivasya Rahasya. Briefly, the mapping is as follows:

The 7th and 8th Avaranas consist of a total of nine triangles, and these are mapped to the three Hreems. The 6th Avarana is mapped to the 9th Bija Ha, and 5th Avarana mapped to the 2nd letter E, with 4th Avarana mapped to 6th letter Ha. The 3rd Avarana is mapped to 12th letter Sa, while 2nd Avarana is mapped to 7th letter Sa. The first Avarana is mapped to the three La letters in Shodashi, while the 9th Avarana is mapped to the three Ka letters in Shodashi as well as the 3rd letter Ee.

For a person who has graduated through the Bhumikas, the Sri Chakra is a treasurehouse, residing with Him and running the universe as God, the power of the Atma itself. He venerates the Sri Chakra everyday using the ten Mudras or Dashamudra Aradhana, the first nine denoting the first nine Avaranas, and the tenth as a summary of all nine. The ten mudras in order are given as follows. Essentially, these Mudras are ways of regulating the five elements of nature, since little, ring, middle, index and thumb correspond respectively to earth, water, fire, air and space, even as the fingers correspond to psychological organs called Antahkaranas, with index, middle, ring and little fingers corresponding respectively to Ahankara, Chith, Buddhi and Manas, while the thumb maps to Atma itself. The ten Mudras are named Sarvasamkshobhini, Sarvavidravani, Sarvakarshini, Sarvavashankari, Sarvonmadini, Sarvamahankusha, Sarvakhechari,

Sarvabija, Sarvayoni and Sarvatrikhanda.

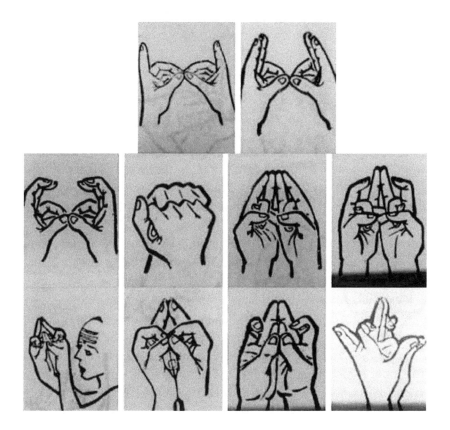

The Dasha Mudras

CHAPTER FOUR

Tantra - Vedanta

Tantra the word arises from the word Tan, meaning to hold, and refers to the world view of reality that one holds, since everything that one sees and does is based on this platform alone. Thus, Tantra is essentially an understanding of reality.

Essentially, one's own Self, is the Supreme Absolute. The entire creation of world is nothing but an illusion, Maya, much like a dream. Out of ignorance, taking the unreal world to be real, the Self sees itself as the individualised soul and experiences suffering, misery etc. Upon correct wisdom, the unreality is understood and the true nature of the soul as the Self is Realized. At which point, there is liberation from the sorrow etc. The soul simply then abides in the Self, which is of the nature of pure Bliss.

Creation, even through the unreal dream, is with a purpose, that is to create an illusion of separateness, so that while the Brahman by itself is bliss, the illusion of separateness and then joining back together, makes the resulting bliss feel more intense, similar to what Lord Krishna mentions as part of the Gopi Gita in Srimad Bhagavatam 10.32.20-21. Furthermore, the purpose is also to experience this intense bliss as enjoyment, in this same unreal creation, this being possible since there is no ignorance anymore to cause suffering. That intense bliss, as enjoyment in the unreal creation, is the state of Jivanmukthi. Thus, Brahman as the first cause of creation, proceeds with creation, well aware of the purpose, and to achieve it. This alone gives the complete picture of reality.

The knowledge of reality has been given in many texts throughout human existence, as philosophy forms a core of every major religion and faith. The Sanatana Dharma too has its own text, the Vedas and Upanishads, giving explanations of reality, yet these are such massive and vast that one may easily get lost in these statements, superficially finding contradictions and conflicts between various texts. It is to resolve all this that the grand text called Brahma Sutra or Vedanta Sutra has been consolidated and composed from the Vedas, and it reconciles all the vast points and understanding of reality into a single coherent stream by which one gains a correct perception of reality, even while realizing the apparent and inherent flaws in human designed systems, philosophies and religions in understanding said reality.

Thus, if the Atma or our Self is seen as a dreamer and the creation being a dream, then one asks where is the location of said dreamer, the bed on which he sleeps? That is, in thocean of all unreal places, there must be somewhere, a real place, that the Atma can call its real home. This place is called Meru or Sumeru.

This is why every single part and parcel of Vedic culture, ritual and text, always refers and positions itself in reference to Meru, and this is said to the a mountain which is the very center and primal axis of revolution of the entire universe. Indeed, this mountain exists physically on Earth, but its identity has been deeply hidden by Goddess from literally all people throughout the dark ages. However, with Satya Yuga being born, the real location and identity of Meru has been revealed to the author and this is seen in Tamilnadu among the Nilgiri Hills, in particular the hill adjacent to Valley View on the outskirts of Ooty and housing the temple of Rajarajeshwari, the Hanuman cave temple and the peak of the Hill enshrining Etha Temple.

The Peak of Mount Sumeru

The place is a true definition of paradise, and every heaven mentioned in every scripture matches exactly with the description of this Sumeru. For instance, Shaiva definition of Kailash includes a lofty mountain with the Lord meditating and looking over the world from there while assisted by His faithful mount Nandi, and true enough, in the forests behind the peak of Meru, the bison doews dwell. Vaishnavas describe Vaikuntam as an island surrounded by white milky ocean called Ksheera Sagara, and true enough, in days of absolute mist and fog, the meadow on the peak is surrounded completely by white clouds of fog, with the valley and neighboring hills becoming completely invisible, and exactly matching the description of Vaikuntam. The Shakta definition of an island Manidweepam or Shvetha Dveepam amidst an island of white nectar ocean, Sudha Saagara is the same idea. The Buddhist Pure Land of Amitabha as the Western heaven matches the location of Sumeru which is the western of the two places, Sumeru and Srimannagaram. The Jain definition of Siddha Loka, with all the pure enlightened Atmas dwelling here in subtle Videha forms match the description as one can see small particles of Prana in and around the peak of Meru floating about in space. The Abrahamic definition of heaven with the Throne of God, is easily seen in the meadow with the seat of God being the stone of Etha temple. The definition of Kadamba Vanam as full of fragrant trees and wild flowers completely match the trek path to the peak, full of fragrant eucalyptus and other trees. Sumer as the abode of the Gods and Devas, is attributed to the 27 different kinds of wild flowers seen to have unique and rare medicinal properties, seen in the location in the rainy season, which botanically identified to be spread far and wide in the world. Represent the Devas ruling over the 27 stars or Nakshatras, and by understanding one's own Nakshatra, one can map the properties of the flower to the nature of enjoyment in Meru.

The entrance to Meru

Route to the peak

The peak and Kadamba Vanam

Nakshatra Flowers - 1

Nakshatra Flowers - 2

Nakshatra Flowers - 3

As and when a person finishes graduating through the Bhumikas, He is lead to the various perspectives and intricacies of reality, and starts to understand the world and nature of creation, rebirth and so on, and when this understanding gets to completion, he is lead to the mountain of Sumeru, where he unlocks the superpower referred to by the term Vidya. This term Vidya means knowledge and information, and essentially defines not just the acquiring of knowledge, but the very creation of knowledge, as in whatever one says as a statement or Vaak, is made into reality unconditionally by the universe and Mother Goddess,. Thus, the person gets the power of creating and sculpting his own reality, simply by the power of speech, and since knowledge is simply based on what has happened, which now can be traced to the reality generated by the person. This power is known as Punasrishti, which is beyond the cycle of Srishti, Sthithi and Laya or creation, preservation and destruction of normal cycle of world.

For a person who has mastered all of the Bhumikas, the Maha Tantra of Meru simply becomes a powerful seven word statement that periodically reminds oneself of the correct perception of reality: "Enjoying this dream now with Vaalai Amma?" the context of this reaffirmation is that one perceives everything around oneself as being controlled and operated entirely by Amma, even as the self is viewed as a small infnant, seated on the lap of Amma, as She lovingly nurtures and cares for us, and gently and playfully entertains us using the entire world as Her toys.

Amma

The remaining portion of this book essentially deals with two topics. Sumeru Vaibhavam consisting of four parts is essentially a commentary and translation of the Brahma Sutra in the correct perception of Sri Vidya, in explaining the reality of the world, that can take a person to Sumeru ultimately. Srimannagara Vaibhavam consisting of nine parts is an exploration of the Sri Chakra, Avarana by Avarana, with the corresponding significance of deities of Thiruvarur.

CHAPTER FIVE

Metaphysics

ॐ अथातो ब्रह्मजिज्ञासा ॐ ॥ १.१.१॥

Atha-Now, Atah-Follows, Brahma Jigyasa - The inquiry into the nature of the Brahman.

The scope of Brahma Sutras and of Veda itself as philosophy is stated here. Gita 7:16-17 states Jigyaasa is the third of four types of devotees, and is second in quality to the Jnani. Gita 2:46 says Vedas are as useless to an enlightened Jnana, as a reservoir of water is for one immersed in the brink of water.

Vedanta and philosophy are neither for the afflicted and materialistic, nor for the enlightened Jnani, but for the curious one in between.

ॐ जन्माद्यस्य यतः ॐ ॥ १.१.२॥

Yatah- From Which, Asya - Of all this, Janmadi - Creation (as well as Preservation and Destruction) happens.

Brahman creates and destroys worlds out of nothing, just like a Dreamer spins forth a dream, for the purpose of enjoyment.

ॐ शास्त्रयोनित्वात् ॐ ॥ १.१.३॥

Shastra-Scripture, Yonitvat- Is the repository of the sought wisdom.

The importance of guidance in Realising the Truth is emphasised here. According to Tripura Rahasya, Nirvikalpa Samadhi, the trance state by which one merges into the Self in the absence of thoughts, occurs for all people at certain times, such as extreme happiness and extreme sorrow. Yet, all those who experience this state do not get enlightened immediately. One needs the guidance from Guru to understand that this is indeed the Real Self etc. In this context, Great, Enlightened Souls who have already undergone this process have given their wisdom as the Vedas, so that we do not have to reinvent the wheel.

ॐ तत्तुसमन्वयात् ॐ ॥ १.१.४॥

Tat- Brahman (is to be known from Vedanta), Tu- but nothing else, Samanvayat- Because it is the central focus.

As the only Reality, Brahman is the all that exists. Just like characters created in a dreamer's dream are essentially the dreamer himself, study of all creation that ever exists, in whatever subject, is study of Brahman alone. Thus, the central focus of every subject and text ever written is always Brahman alone, more so for the Vedanta which purport to the Brahman itself rather than its creations.

ॐ ईक्षतेर्नाशब्दम् ॐ ॥ १.१.५॥

Ikshathe- On account of thinking (attributed to the Brahman), Ashabdam- what is not mentioned in the scriptures, Na-cannot be the First Cause.

Brahman creates and destroys the world for the purpose of enjoyment. But for that, Brahman must have the ability to think, ie it must be sentient.

If Brahman is the dreamer and the creation is a dream, then only the dreamer is sentient, none of the dream characters can be sentient. Thus, there can be no other First Cause than Brahman, the One mentioned in the scriptures.

ॐ गौणश्चेन्नात्मशब्दात् ॐ ॥ १.१.६॥

Chet-If it is claimed (by anybody), Gaunah-in figurative sense (the word thinking is used), Na-we refute the claim, Aatmashabdat-on basis of the word Atma or Self that is used.

This again emphasises that the Atma alone is sentient, and is capable of thinking etc. Hence, the thinking cannot be attributed to any aspect of Brahman's creation.

ॐ तन्निष्ठस्य मोक्षोपदेशात् ॐ ॥ १.१.७॥

Mokshopadeshat-Because Liberaton is declared (to the one), Nishthasya-that is devoted to, Tat-that (Brahman).

On the one hand, this specifies that Brahman ie dreamer being capable of liberating must necessarily be outside the realm of creation ie dream, much like a person drowning in water cannot possibly rescue another person drowning in the same water.

ॐ हेयत्वावचनाच्च ॐ ॥ १.१.८॥

Cha-And, Na-There is no statement (in the scriptures), Vachana-mentioning that (Brahman), Heyatva-is something worthy of being abandoned.

As much as the previous Sutra spoke about liberation, the liberation itself means abandonment of those from which one desires to get liberated. Yet, Brahman is never cited as something that must be abandoned. In other words, everything except Brahman is abandoned during liberation.

ॐ स्वाप्ययात् ॐ ॥ १.१.९॥

Svapyayat-On account of merging with the Self.

Brahman creates and destroys the dream from itself. In the latter, the dream dissolves and merges into the Brahman, as the Self. If the waking state is itself taken as a dream spun forth by the Self, that dream vanishes when one enters deep sleep ie the universe has been withdrawn and merged into the Self.

ॐ गतिसामान्यात् ॐ ॥ १.१.१०॥

Gathisamanyath-On account of consistency between various Vedantic texts.

All Vedantic texts, no matter what their school or origin are consistent in one point, that is Brahman is the First Cause, the Self, and from whom creation arises.

ॐ श्रुतत्वाच्च ॐ ॥ १.१.११॥

Cha-And, Shruthathvath-Declared by the Shruthis ie Vedas.

With all this basis discussed in the previous Sutras as established, and refuting any other possibility, the Vedas finally declare the Srlf, Brahman as the first cause.

ॐ आनन्दमयोऽभ्यासात् ॐ ॥ १.१.१२॥

Anandamaya-of the nature of bliss, Abhyasat-repeated many times.

Scriptures do proclaim the Brahman as Bliss itself, as Sat-Chit-Aanandam. As much as the dream creation of the dreamer is the dreamer himself, what is created from Brahman is of the nature of Brahman. If Brahman is Ananda, then the creation is Anandamaya. In fact, it is for experiencing bliss and enjoyment through this creation, that creation happens in the first place. In Sri Vidya, Sri Yantra is the cosmos itself, and the Bindu, residence of Brahman as Amma, is Sarva Anandamaya Chakra, alluding to the same concept.

ॐ विकारशब्दान्नेतिचिन्नेन प्राचुर्यात् ॐ ॥ १.१.१३॥

Ithi Chet-If it be said that, Vikara Shabdat-On account of words denoting modifications or parts, Na-(Brahman is) not independent, Na-We refute it, Prachuryat-On account of abundance (of words mentioning parts or modifications).

Reference here is to Taittiriya Upanishad 2.1-5 referring to Brahman as the tail. Gita 9:5 says that while all creation does dwell in Brahman, Brahman does not dwell in any of the creation. This means that while every word denoting a component of creation is Brahman on account of it being a modification of the pure consciousness, Brahman itself neither is those parts nor dwells in them. Thus, being the One that Created the All, Brahman can never be a part or component of anything.

ॐ तद्धेतुव्यपदेशाच्च ॐ ॥ १.१.१४॥

Cha-and, Taddhethuvyapadishat-Because (Brahman) is declared to be the cause of it.

As mentioned already, Brahman is Ananda, while the creation is Anandamaya. The clear distinction as cause and effect is seen. Thus, as the Cause, Brahman cannot be the created ie Anandamaya.

ॐ मान्त्रवर्णिकमेव च गीयते ॐ ॥ १.१.१५॥

Cha-And, Mantravarnikam-that which is referred to in the Mantra portion of the Vedas, Eva-the same, Geeyate-is sung.

Here it is emphasised that the Brahman which was referred to by the Brahmana passages, is also referred to by the Mantra sections too.

ॐ नेतरोऽनुपपत्तेः ॐ ॥ १.१.१६॥

Na-not, Ithara-any other, Anupapatthe-On account of impossibility.

The possibility of Brahman being anything other than the Self has already been refuted in the context of Brahmana verses by the above Sutras. The same applies for the Mantra portions too.

ॐ भेदव्यपदेशाच्च ॐ ॥ १.१.१७॥

Cha-And, Bhedavyapadishat-On account of differences declared.

It has already been stated that Brahman, the Ananda, and Creation the Anandamaya are different in that One is real and the other is a dream. One is the viewer, the other is the viewed, and they cannot be the same.

ॐ कामाच्च नानुमानापेक्षा ॐ ॥ १.१.१८॥

Cha-And, Kamath-Due to the word desire, Na-it is not possible to, Anumanapeksha-infer (the non-Brahman).

Desiring to play and enjoy is again capable only by the sentient, which is the dreamer Brahman. Thus, on account of Vedanta mentioning the desire aspect, they refer only to Brahman and not to anything of the creation.

ॐ अस्मिन्निनस्य च तद्योगं शास्ति ॐ ॥ १.१.१९॥

Cha-also, Tadyogam-the merging of, Asya-the creation, Asmin-In Brahman, Shaasti-is taught by the Vedas.

The creation, which is Jiva, is part of the dream, and when the enjoyment is over, it is dissolved back in Brahman.

ॐ अन्तस्तद्धर्मोपदेशात् ॐ ॥ १.१.२० ॥

Anthah-(The Brahman) is within, Taddharmopadishat-Because its characteristics are mentioned thus.

Within here refers to both the seer and the seen, and is a reference to Chhandogya which states that Brahman is the One seen within One's eye. Again, earlier reference is made to Gita 9:5 where Brahman dwells in creation and not vice versa. Given that the seer is outside creation and the seen is within it, the same person inside both can only possibly refer to Brahman.

ॐ भेदव्यपदेशाच्चान्यः ॐ ॥ १.१.२१ ॥

Cha-Also, Anyah-there is a difference (between Brahman and creation), Bhedavyapadishat-On account of such distinction being mentioned.

The reference here is to Brihadaranyaka Upanishad, which says that the Brahman dwells in the sun and yet the sun does not know the Brahman. This yet again reinforces Gita 9:5.

ॐ आकाशस्तल्लिङ्गात् ॐ ॥ १.१.२२ ॥

Akasha-the word Akasha, Tat-refers to Brahman, Lingat-on account of its characteristics.

Reference is to mention of Akasha in Chhandogya. Gita 9:6 mentions that Brahman is the Akasha or space through which the moving air flows, all the while being unaffected by the latter. Brahman as the dreamer exhibits similar characteristic in that the dream with all its characters dwell inside Brahman, but all the while, the nature of Brahman as Ananda does not change.

ॐ अत एव प्राणः ॐ ॥ १.१.२३ ॥

Atha Eva-For the same reason, Prana-the word Prana (refers to Brahman).

Brihadaranyaka and Chhandogya Upanishad mention Prana, in which all Jiva merge, and also the Prana of Prana. Prana as such is the life force without which a body will be rendered motionless. Prana of Prana is that which renders the Jivas in motion. As the Jivas themselves are insentient dream characters, the only sentient One that keeps them running is Brahman, who then is the Prana of the Prana.

ॐ ज्योतिश्चरणाभिधानात् ॐ ॥ १.१.२४ ॥

Jyothi-Light (must be taken as Brahman), Charanabhidhanat-on account of mention of feet.

The reference here is to Chhandogya which talks in a verse about meditating on a light, while its preceding verse talks about Brahman as Purusha with one foot in Jivas and three others in heavens. From that context, one must take light too, to refer to Brahman alone and not physical light.

ॐ छन्दोऽभिधानान्नतेचिन्न तथाचेतोऽर्पणनगिदात्तथा
हि दिर्शनम् ॐ ॥ १.१.२५॥

Ithi Chet-If it is claimed that, Na-(Brahman) is not referred to, Chhandobhidhanath-on account of Gayatri the metre being mentioned, Na-this claim is refuted, Tatha-because in that way, Chethorpananigadath-the application of mind is implied, Thatha hi-in the same way that it had been in, Darshanam-other texts.

The mention of three feet in heaven and one foot in Jivas, in the above Sutra might give the impression that possibly the four footed Gayatri is mentioned. That impression is promptly refuted in this Sutra by first looking at other verses in the same Chhandogya text and understanding that it is the Brahman alone that is consistently praised there. Second, all creations of the dream are essentially the dreamer himself. Thus, even through Gayatri, one sees Brahman alone.

ॐ भूतादिपादव्यपदेशोपपत्तेश्चैवम् ॐ ॥ १.१.२६॥

Cha-Also, Evam-only in this manner, Upapathe-it is possible to conclude, Bhutadi-the representation of beings, Padavyapadesha-as feet.

The metre Gayatri is a mere collection of syllables and cannot possibly contain beings and other creation as its feet. Such an allegory is possible only in the case of Brahman.

ॐ उपदेशभेदान्नतेचिन्नोभयस्मन्निनप्यवरिोधात् ॐ ॥ १.१.२७॥

Ithi Chet-if it is claimed that, Upadeshabhedat-on account of varying descriptions and specifications, Na-(The same Brahman) cannot be possibly referred to in the above mentioned texts, Na-the claim is refuted, Avirodhath-because there is no contradiction, Ubhayasmin Api-in either description.

In the above Sutras, one was a mention of Brahman of light while the other was of Gayatri - two conflicting and completely unrelated descriptions of Brahman, leading one to possibly doubt if both refer to the same Brahman. This Sutra assertively answers it in the sense that in the case of light, Brahman was viewed as the one providing sentience to creation while being external to it, while in the case of Gayatri, the essence of dream characters being the dreamer was emphasised.

ॐ पुराणस्तथान्गुमात् ॐ ॥ १.१.२८॥

Thatha-In the same manner, Prana-the word Prana, Anugamat-must also be comprehended to mean Brahman.

The reference here is Kaushitaki Upanishad in which it is stated that knowing Indra as Prana is the most beneficial boon possible to a man. The text mentions Prana as undecaying and immortal, which is enough evidence that Prana here refers to Brahman, and not the transitory dream creation.

ॐ नवक्तुरात्मोपदेशादति चिदेध्यात्मसबन्धभूमा
ह्यस्मिन् ॐ ॥ १.१.२९॥

Ithi Chet-If it be claimed that, Vaktu-the speaker's, Atmopadishat-Instruction was about himself, Na-the claim is refuted, Hi-because, Asmin-in this, Adhyatma Sambandha-the references to Self the Atman, Bhuma-is abundant.

The reference is again to the previous Sutra, in that Indra is not referred to as the object that must be known, since Indra, a character in dream is neither immortal nor undecaying.

ॐ शास्त्रदृष्ट्या तूपदेशो वामदेववत् ॐ ॥ १.१.३०॥

Tu-However Upadisha-Indra's instruction is justified, Vamadevavat-Like Vamadeva's, Shastradrushya-through realisation of the truth confirmed by the scriptures.

The reference here is to Brihadaranyaka where Vamadeva states that whoever knows Brahman becomes Brahman. On that account, Indra having realised Brahman is justified in referring to Himself to be known.

ॐ जीवमुख्यप्राणलङ्गिान्नेति चिन्नोपासत्रैवैद्यादाश्रितत्वादहि
तद्योगात् ॐ ॥ १.१.३१॥

Ithi Chet-If it be claimed that, Na-Brahman is not referred to, Jivamukhyapranalingath-on account of characteristics of Jiva and Prana, Na-the claim is refuted, UpasaVaividyat-because it will enjoin threefold meditation, Ashritatvat-and on account of Prana accepted elsewhere as Brahman, Iha-here too, Tadyogath-Prana is referred to as Brahman.

Essentially, this Sutra builds upon many earlier Sutras to emphasise that Prana mentioned in the texts is indeed Brahman.

ॐ सर्वत्र प्रसद्धिोपदेशात् ॐ ॥ १.२.१॥

That which consists of the mind is Brahman, because, there is taught that Brahman which is the cause of everything.

Reference to Chhandogya 3.14.1-2, as to meditate on that which consists of the mind, which is Brahman on the basis that the text itself starts by saying, all this is Brahman.

ॐ वविक्षतिगुणोपपत्तेश्च ॐ ॥ १.२.२॥

Moreover the qualities desired to be expressed are befitting only of Brahman.

Reference quoted above mentions qualities of Akasa and light, of nature of truth, omnipresent and invisible - all these well known to be Brahman.

ॐ अनुपपत्तेस्तुन शारीर: ॐ ॥ १.२.३॥

On the other hand the individual soul is nor referred because these qualities do not apply to it.

ॐ कर्मकर्तव्यपदेशाच्च ॐ ॥ १.२.४॥

And on account of mention of the word attainer and attained.

Reference to Chhandogya 3.14.4 saying I will attain Him when I depart from here, meaning that He who consists of the mind is something to be attained, which is Brahman.

ॐ शब्दवशिषात् ॐ ॥ १.२.५॥

Because of difference indicated by case endings.

Reference to Satapatha Brahmana 10.6.3.2, where mention is of that Being the Self residing in the individual soul, with nominal and locative case endings used respectively.

ॐ सुमतुनेश्च ॐ ॥ १.२.६॥

From Smritis also.

Reference to Gita 18.61 of Self residing in the heart. Again, it must be remembered that Brahman alone is sentient, is the first cause, with the purpose of bliss and enjoyment, created the dream creation. Everything except Brahman is insentient, while Brahman alone is sentient and capable of experience. Thus, the soul that experiences pleasure and pain is undoubtedly Brahman and not different from it. Difference can only occur as long as the knowledge of dream is not yet realized fully, and unreal dream characters are superimposed on the real soul.

ॐ अरुभकौकसुत्वात् तदुव्यपदेशाच्च नेति चिनेन नचिाय्यत्वादवे
व्योमवच्च ॐ ॥ १.२.७॥

The claim that Brahman is not referred due to smallness of abode ie heart, and also mention as minute, we refute, as such characterization is for the case of contemplation, and is similar to Akasa.

Reference to Chhandogya 3.14.4 that says Self is smaller than rice within the heart. This is because contemplation in all pervading Self is difficult, just like all pervading Akasha is seen in the eye of a needle.

ॐ संभोगप्राप्तिरिति चेन्न वैशेष्यात् ॐ ॥ १.२.८॥

The claim that being connected with the hearts of all due to omnipresence, the Self would experience pleasure and pain, we refute, on account of the difference between the two.

It is already said that the apparent difference between the Self and soul, is the superimposition of the unreal dream characters and events on the Self, due to lack of complete knowledge that creation is a dream. However, Brahman does not experience pain since Brahman does not lack knowledge of dream creation, on account of Brahman itself being the very cause of that creation.

ॐ अत्ता चराचरग्रहणात् ॐ ॥ १.२.९॥

The eater is Brahman, because entire universe, both movable and immovable are taken as its food.

Reference to 1.2.25 in mentioning He to whom Brahmins and Kshatriyas are food and death is a condiment. As the dreamer, just as entire dream resides inside the dreamer and dissolves in him upon waking, or is Brahman alone that consumes the entire universe upon dissolution.

ॐ प्रकरणाच्च ॐ ॥ १.२.१०॥

And because Brahman is the subject of discussion.

Reference to Katha 1.2.14,15,18 establishing Brahman as the main subject.

ॐ गुहां प्रविष्टावात्मानौ हि तद्दर्शनात् ॐ ॥ १.२.११॥

The two that have entered the cavity of heart are soul and Brahman, as has been seen.

Heart reference in Katha 1.3.1. Already established that the Self enters and dwells in the heart, and given that only similar things may be grouped together, two, or another can only refer to another such thing as the Self, sentient and intelligent, which is the soul.

ॐ विशेषणाच्च ॐ ॥ १.२.१२॥

And from the distinctive qualities.

Reference to Katha 1.3.3,9, which mentions the soul as charioteer that reaches the abode of the Self as Vishnu.

ॐ अन्तर उपपत्तेः ॐ ॥ १.२.१३॥

The person inside eye is Brahman on account of the attributes mentioned being appropriate.

Eye reference in Chhandogya 4.15.1. Qualities of immortal, fearless etc apply to Brahman and not the individual soul.

ॐ स्थानादिव्यपदेशाच्च ॐ ॥ १.२.१४॥

And because abode, name and form ate attributed to it for the sake of meditation.

The same explanation as earlier, in that it is difficult to contemplate on an all pervading Brahman.

ॐ सुखविशिष्टाभिधानादेव च ॐ ॥ १.२.१५॥

And verily on account of distinguishing reference to bliss.

Chhandogya 4.10.5 refers to the Brahman as bliss and further elucidated as being within the eye.

ॐ श्रुतोपनिषत्कगत्यभिधानाच्च ॐ ॥ १.२.१६॥

Also on account of statements of the path after death, knowers of Brahman take.

Knower of the person of the eye takes the Devayana path, as per Prashna 1.10, the path applying only to the knowers of Brahman thus again making the person in the eye Brahman alone.

ॐ अनवस्थितिरसंभवाच्च नेतर: ॐ ॥ १.२.१७॥

Person in the eye cannot be soul, as it does not always exist, neither matches the attributes given such as immortality, fearlessness.

ॐ अन्तर्याम्यधिदैवादिषु तद्धर्मव्यपदेशात् ॐ ॥ १.२.१८॥

The ruler of Gods etc within is Brahman on account of qualities being mentioned therein.

Reference to Brihadaranyaka 3.7 which speaks of an Internal Ruler ruling wm various organs, and at the end of the text the section mentions that the Ruler is immortal and identical with the soul, which applies only to Brahman.

ॐ न च स्मार्तं अतद्धर्माभिपिलात् ॐ ॥ १.२.१९॥

And neither is the ruler the Pradhana of Smriti, since its attributes are contrary to what is mentioned.

Reference to Brihadaranyaka 3.7.23 if the internal ruler seeing, hearing etc cannot apply to the Pradhana on the Sankhya doctrine, which is inert and non intelligent.

ॐ शरीरश्चोभयेऽपि हि भिदेनैनमधीयते ॐ ॥ १.२.२०॥

And the individual soul is not the internal ruler, for both are read differently by the Kanwa and Madhyandina Sakhas.

The two Sakhas variously read Brihadaranyaka 3.7.22 as He, the Brahman dwelling in knowledge, and the self, the latter referring of course to the individual soul, as Brahman is already the subject of the discussion. Again as clarified earlier, the difference between Brahman and soul is only a superimposition due to ignorance.

ॐ अदृश्यत्वादिगुणको धर्मोक्तेः ॐ ॥ १.२.२१॥

The possessor of qualities like invisibility us Brahman on account of qualities being mentioned.

Invisibility reference in Mundaka 1.1.6, while 1.1.9 mentions all perceiving or all seeing, which rules out the inert Pradhana.

ॐ विशिषेणभेदव्यपदेशाभ्यां नेतरौ ॐ ॥ १.२.२२॥

The other two, soul and Pradhana are not mentioned because of characteristics of Brahman and difference from other two.

Reference to Mundaka 2.1.2 of birthless, pure, heavenly, referring to Brahman alone, and also higher than the high Imperishable the latter referring to Pradhana.

ॐ रूपोपन्यासाच्च ॐ ॥ १.२.२३॥

And because its form is mentioned.

Reference to Mundaka 2.1.10 mentioning the form of knowledge, which is Brahman.

ॐ वैश्वानरः साधारणशब्दविशेषात् ॐ ॥ १.२.२४॥

Vaisvanara is Brahman because of the qualifying adjuncts.

Reference to Vaisvanara in Chhandogya 5.18.1-2, mentioned as the Self and to be meditated as identical with one's own self, making the former Brahman and the latter the soul.

ॐ स्मर्यमाणमनुमानं स्यादिति ॐ ॥ १.२.२५॥

Because the form described in the Smriti is an indicatory mark.

Reference of Vishwarupa form in Gita as Vaishvanara.

ॐ शब्दादिभ्योऽन्तः प्रतिष्ठानान्नेति चेन्न तथा
(पाठभेद प्रतिष्ठानाच्च नेति चेन्न)
दृष्ट्युपदेशादसंभवात्पुरुषवधिमपि चैनमधीयते ॐ ॥ १.२.२६॥

The claim they Vaisvanara is not Brahman on account of the word meaning gastric fire and existing inside it, we refute, because neither is the gastric fire a person as per Satapatha Brahmana 10.6.1.11, nor is it possible for it to have heavens as head etc, and moreover instruction is given to contemplate of Brahman as Vaishvanara.

ॐ अत एव न देवता भूतं च ॐ ॥ १.२.२७॥

For the same reason, Vaisvanara is neither the deity nor element fire.

ॐ साक्षादप्यवरोधं जैमिनिः ॐ ॥ १.२.२८॥

Even if by Vaisvanara, Brahman is taken as the object of meditation, there is no contradicton, says Jaimini.

The meaning of Vishwa Nara as universal man is to be taken, referring to Brahman as the all pervading Self.

ॐ अभिव्यक्तेरित्याश्मरथ्यः ॐ ॥ १.२.२९॥

On account of manifestation, said Asmarathya.

The point is that even though all pervading and formless, the form from heavens to Earth is taken for the purpose of devotees.

ॐ अनुस्मृतेर्बादरिः ॐ ॥ १.२.३०॥

For the purpose of constant remembrance.

This is reinforcing why the Self is meditated within the heart, eye etc.

ॐ सम्पत्तेरिति जैमिनिः तथा हि दर्शयति ॐ ॥ १.२.३१॥

Because of imaginary identity, says Jaimini, as the scriptures declare so.

This mentions the practice of Sampat Upasana, where something is meditated as something else, on account of similarity.

ॐ आमनन्ति चैनमस्मिन् ॐ ॥ १.२.३२॥

Moreover the Jabala teaches to meditate the Lord between the head and the chin.

Reference to Jabala Upanishad, viewing the Lord as Pradeshamatra, extending to a span, for the purpose of meditating.

ॐ द्युभ्वाद्यायतनं स्वशब्दात् ॐ ॥ १.३.१॥

The resting place of heaven, earth etc is Brahman on account of the word Self.

Reference to Mundaka 2.2.5 and Chhandogya 6.8.4. Essentially, the entirety of creation is a dream, and m while as much as a dream wholly is created within the dreamer, the resting place of all creation is within the dreamer, ie the Self ie Brahman.

ॐ मुक्तोपसृप्यव्यपदेशात् ॐ ॥ १.३.२॥

Because of the statement that it is to be attained by the liberated.

Brahman as the goal of the liberation is evident in Mundaka 2.2.9 and 3.2.8.

ॐ नानुमानमतच्छब्दात् ॐ ॥ १.३.३॥

The abode is not that which is inferred owing to lack of terms mentioning it.

Mundaka 1.1.9 mentions terms indicating intelligence. Apart from that, there is no mention of that inert first cause, ie Pradhana as claimed by some philosophies.

ॐ पुराणभत्रच ॐ ॥ १.३.४॥

Nor also the individual soul.

Though the individual soul is an intelligent principle, it is not the resting place of the world. This isbecause from the individual soul one cannot discern a Cause driving creation.

ॐ भेदव्यपदेशात् ॐ ॥ १.३.५॥

On account of difference being mentioned.

The individual soul and the Self are differentiated as the knower and the thing to be known.

ॐ प्रकरणात् ॐ ॥ १.३.६॥

On account of subject matter.

Reference to Mundaka which starts with the question What is that, and ends with the answer, the knower of Brahman becomes Brahman. Thus the entire subject of the Upanishad is undoubtedly Brahman.

ॐ स्थतियदनाभ्यां च ॐ ॥ १.३.७॥

Also on account of remaining unattached and eating.

Reference to Mundaka 3.1.1, to the tale of the two birds, with the individual soul represented, indulging in eating the fruit while Brahman represented, unattached. Of course, since creation is all a dream, the only one capable of eating the dream food is an equally real dream character, which is of course the individual soul Jiva, and not Brahman.

ॐ भूमा सम्प्रसादादध्युपदेशात् ॐ ॥ १.३.८॥

The Bhuma is Brahman because it is taught after deep sleep.

Reference to Chhandogya 7.23-24, where mention of Bhuma as the highest principle, where one sees and hears nothing else. A claim is made that this mention is of the state of deep sleep, where the only thing that continues is the vital force Prana, and thus Bhuma is that life force. However, this is refuted on the basis of reference such as Chhandogya 7.24.1, and on the basis that mention of Ativadi or one surpassing all arguments arises only on realizing the truth.

ॐ धर्मोपपत्तेश्च ॐ ॥ १.३.९॥

And because the qualities mentioned are appropriate.

The qualities referred to such as truth, bliss, non duality, all pervading, the knowing of which removes misery etc, all this is indeed about Brahman.

ॐ अक्षरमम्बरान्तधृतेः ॐ ॥ १.३.१०॥

It is imperishable because it supports everything upto Akasha.

Reference to Brihadaranyaka 3.8.8 and 3.8.11 where Akshara is mentioned. The reference can be only about Brahman and not sound, since it is mentioned as the supporter of Akasha, further showing that it is devoid of all qualities.

ॐ सा च प्रशासनात् ॐ ॥ १.३.११॥

This also because of the command attributed.

Reference to Brihadaranyaka 3.8.9 as the Akshara directing the position of the sun and moon, which proves that this Akasha is an intelligent principle, and can thus be only Brahman and not the Pradhana.

ॐ अन्यभावव्यावृत्तेश्च ॐ ॥ १.३.१२॥

And because the qualities of anything other than Brahman have been negated.

The means by which the qualities of Brahman are referred, and how Pradhana or individual soul being a possibility is negated, has been explained in the above Sutras.

ॐ ईक्षतिकर्मव्यपदेशात् सः ॐ ॥ १.३.१३॥

Brahman, because of his being mentioned as the object of the act of seeing.

Prashna 5.5 mentions about the meditating on Om, as the meditating on the Highest person. In a possible doubt that this could probably refer to Brahma or Hiranyagarbha, is refuted here since the act of seeing is referred to here, which is possible only on an actual entity, and not an imagined one, such as Hiranyagarbha, which is yet another dream creation.

ॐ दहर उत्तरेभ्यः ॐ ॥ १.३.१४॥

The small Akasha is Brahman because of subsequent texts.

Reference to Chhandogya 8.1.1,3,5 which mentions the word small Akasha, within the heart, but also clarifies rust the small Akasha is as big as the external big Akasha, and both heaven and Earth contained within it, showing how this Akasha is indeed Brahman.

ॐ गतिशब्दाभ्यां तथा हि दृष्टं लिङ्गं च ॐ ॥ १.३.१५॥

Small Akasha is Brahman on account of the word going in, and mention of Brahma Loka, it is likewise seen and going is an indicatory mark.

Reference to Chhandogya 8.3.2 saying all creatures everyday in sleep go to Brahmaloka, and yet do not know it. Reference also to Chhandogya 6.8.1, clarifying that Brahmaloka, small Akasha and Brahman are all the same, since, deep sleep is a sort of intermission, in the absence of dream creation, where Brahman is the only thing that exists.

ॐ धृतेश्च महिम्नोऽस्यास्मिन्नुपलब्धेः ॐ ॥ १.३.१६॥

Moreover on account of supporting the world, since its greatness is seen in Brahman alone.

Reference to Chhandogya 8.4.1 and Brihadaranyaka 3.8.9. Yet again, the dream resting inside the dreamer is how Brahman supports Akasha within it.

ॐ प्रसिद्धेश्च ॐ ॥ १.३.१७॥

Because of the well known meaning of Akasha.

Reference to Chhandogya 8.14.1 and 1.9.1 indicating Akasha is indeed Brahman.

ॐ इतरपरामर्शात् स इति चेन्नासम्भवात् ॐ ॥ १.३.१८॥

The claim that Akasha is soul on account of reference to complementary passage, we refute on account of impossibility.

The passage referred is Chhandogya 8.3.4, where one gets a possible doubt if the individual soul, mentioned in deep sleep if Akasha. Yet they assumption would entail mapping something limited such as soul to something infinite such as Akasha. Thus, the comparison is absurd.

ॐ उत्तराच्चेदाविर्भूतस्वरूपस्तु ॐ ॥ १.३.१९॥

The claim that small Akasha refers to Jiva on account of subsequent references, we refute on that real nature as non different from Brahman is manifest.

References to Chhandogya 7, 8.7.4, 8.10.1, 8.11.1, refers to whom is seen qualified by the terms immortal, fearless and free from evil, all these clearly referring to the Brahman alone and not the individual soul.

ॐ अन्यार्थश्च परामर्श: ॐ ॥ १.३.२०॥

And the reference is for a different purpose.

The references above stating the name Jiva, while all the while clearly mentioning the nature of Brahman, its aimed at showing the ultimate real nature of Jiva, as non different from Brahman.

ॐ अल्पश्रुतेरिति चेत्तदुक्तम् ॐ ॥ १.३.२१॥

The claim that Sruthi declares limitedness of small Akasha, we refute as reference to devout meditation has been referenced in 1.2.7.

This is to say again that, the small Akasha within the heart is to be meditated upon, which is when one comes to the realisation that it is indeed Brahman.

ॐ अनुकृतेस्तस्य च ॐ ॥ १.३.२२॥

And Because of the acting after.

Reference here is to Mundaka 2.2.11 where mention of It shining, everything else Shines after it, and by Its light everything is lighted. This shows that the light referred to here is Brahman, and not any material light since one does not see such a source from which everything can be lighted. The reference is to Brahman alone as intelligence and enlightenment, the realisation that creation is but a dream.

ॐ अपि स्मर्यते ॐ ॥ १.३.२३॥ पाठभेदे अपि च स्मर्यते

Moreover the Smriti states.

Reference is to Gita 15.6 and 15.12 stating that the light even inside the sun and moon is Brahman alone.

ॐ शब्दादेव प्रमितिः ॐ ॥ १.३.२४॥

From the very word Lord, the being measured by thumb is Brahman.

Reference to Katha 2.4.12, as a being if the size of thumb residing within the body. Since the verse refers to this being as the Lord of the past and future, it is clearly the Eternal Brahman, since the individual soul neither knows the future nor is the Lord having the entire dream creation under its control.

ॐ हृदयपेक्षया तु मनुष्याधिकारत्वात् ॐ ॥ १.३.२५॥

But with reference to heart, and because man alone is entitled to study the Vedas.

The measure of a thumb is because of the space within the heart, which is of the same size, and again, it is man alone who is entitled to Self knowledge, as the highest evolved creature. For these reasons, the above references give a means for man to know the Self through meditation within the heart.

ॐ तदुपर्यपि बादरायणः संभवात् ॐ ॥ १.३.२६॥

Beings above men are also entitled to Vedas for it is possible to attain knowledge, as per Badarayana.

Reference to Chhandogya 8.11.3 and Taittiriya 3.1, where there is mention of Varuna having attained the knowledge. Thus, according to Vyasa, Devas too are corporeal beings with desire of liberation and thus, entitled to knowledge.

ॐ वरिोध: कर्मणीति चिदेनकेपुरतपित्तरेदर्शनात् ॐ ॥ १.३.२७॥

The claim that corporeality of Devas contradicts sacrifices, we refute, because we find the assumption of Gods in many forms at the same time.

Reference to Chhandogya 7.26.2, stating that Gods do manifest in multiple forms simultaneously through Yogic powers, and would do so especially if they are worshipped or called in multiple sacrifices in different places at the same time. In essence, Gods too are dream creations, and serve merely to execute the script leading to enjoyment of Brahman, and if multiple forms is necessary for that, then it will so happen.

ॐ शब्द इतचिन्नातः पुरभवात्पुरत्यक्षानुमानाभ्याम् ॐ ॥ १.३.२८॥

The claim that corporeality of Devas contradict Vedas, we refute because of mention of creation of worlds from Brahman, along with Devas.

The Sutra clarifies the principles of Vedantic philosophy. First, while it is indeed true that every word referred in Mimamsa and used in Yajnas are eternal, the names like Indra, Varuna etc are eternal only as positions and not as individuals. Furthermore the creation, being a dream, has its basis in mental thoughts, and only from there physical creation proceeds. That is the reason Brahma is depicted as having created everything from the Vedas. So too, the Devas like Agni, Varuna are physical forces of nature, having similar mental basis.

ॐ अत एव च नतियत्वम् ॐ ॥ १.३.२९॥

From this very reason results the eternity of Vedas.

If the Devas even as positions are eternal, and if they arose from Vedic words, then even the Vedas are obviously eternal. The Rig 10.71.3 mentions such eternal Vedas being revealed to the Rishis.

ॐ समाननामरूपत्वाच्चावतूतावप्यवरिोधो
दर्शनात्समतृश्च ॐ ॥ १.३.३०॥

And because of the sameness in band and form of every cycle, there is no contradiction even in the revolving of world cycles.

Again, with creation as a dream, even Pralaya or the entire destruction of all creation and recreating is nothing but withdrawing and emergence of a new dream, with the dreamer Brahman not having changed even a bit. Still from Rig 10.190.3, there is evidence that everything such as sun, Moon etc was created as before ie as in previous cycle.

ॐ मध्वादष्विसंभवादनधकिार जैमिनिः ॐ ॥ १.३.३१॥

On account of impossibility of Gods being qualified for Madhu Vidya, Jaimini states that Devas are not qualified for Upasana or knowledge of the

Self.

Vidyas such as Madhu Vidya instruct to meditate the sun as honey. Such Upasana would be impossible for the sun, says Jaimini, since it is absurd for the worshipped and worshipper to be one.

ॐ ज्योतिषि भावाच्च ॐ ॥ १.३.३२॥

And the Gods are bit qualified since words like sun, Moon etc are used in context of balls of light.

Reinforcing the above claim the Gods are stated as mere elements of nature, and not as something with hands, legs etc and thus are not eligible for Vidya.

ॐ भाव ंत्ुबादरायणोऽस्ति हि ॐ ॥ १.३.३३॥

But Badarayana maintains the existence of qualification due to presence of desire, body etc exist in the Gods.

Badarayana maintains that the deities have a form with hands, legs, desires etc qualifying them for knowledge, apart from the luminary celestial bodies that they preside over.

ॐ शुगुस्य तदनादरश्रवणात्तदाद्रवणात्सूच्यते हि ॐ ॥ १.३.३४॥

Janasruti's grief arose from hearing the contempt words of Rishi in the form of Swan, owing to his approaching Raikva, the latter calling him Sudra, because the grief is referred to by Raikva.

The reference is to the narration in Chhandogya 4.2.5, where King Janasruti approaches sage Raikva for knowledge about the Self. The first time, the sage calls the king Sudra and sends him away while in the second, he still calls him Sudra but agrees to teach. This is cited as a claim entitling Sudras to Vedic knowledge.

The Sutra refutes this citing Chhandogya 4.1.3 citing that Janasruti was a king and thus a Kshatriya. What is clear from this narration is that, the king, even though a Kshatriya, was not only denied knowledge the first time, but also called a Sudra. Thus, caste affiliations must only be taken through the context of mental state and definitely not by birth. Even the purest caste by birth, as long as mentally unfit, is nothing but a Sudra. And by this context, Sudras, in the context of the mentally impure, are never entitled to the knowledge of Brahman. On the other hand, a Sudra or even an unknown caste by birth, such as Satyakama, with the correct mindset, is not only eligible for knowledge, but is also valued as a prize student.

ॐ क्षत्रयित्वागतेश्चोत्तरत्र चैत्ररथेन लिङ्गात् ॐ ॥ १.३.३५॥

And because Kshatriyahood of Janasruti is known later by an indicating sign mentioned along with descendant of Chitraratha, also a Kshatriya.

As a rule, equals alone are mentioned together, and if Abhipratarin, descendant of Chitraratha was a Kshatriya, then so was Janasruti.

ॐ संस्कारपरामर्शात्तदभावाभिलापाच्च ॐ ॥ १.३.३६॥

Because purification ceremonies are mentioned in the case of twice born, and their absence declared for Sudras.

The reference is Manu Smriti 10.12.6. Those without purification rites lie Upanayanam are not entitled to the study of Vedas.

ॐ तदभावनिर्धारणे च प्रवृत्तेः ॐ ॥ १.३.३७॥

And because of inclination of Gautama to impart knowledge is seen only on ascertaining absence of Sudrahood of Satyakama.

Reference to Chhandogya 4.4.5 that Gautama made sure that Satyakama was not a Sudra before accepting him. Now since the father was not known, the caste by birth definitely could not have been known. What Gautama did ascertain was the mindset and mental purity of Satyakama.

ॐ श्रवणाध्ययनार्थप्रतिषिधात् स्मृतेश्च ॐ ॥ १.३.३८॥

And because of prohibition in Smritis of hearing, studying and knowing the meaning of Vedas,and performing rituals to Sudras.

Again the emphasis here is that mental state is crucial for taking up the study of a deep philosophy such as Vedas, and in the absence of that, ie a Sudra by mental state, cannot grasp the complete import of truth, and will likely misinterpret statements, causing harm to Himself. We already see this in cases like Bauddha and Jaina philosophies, who, fearing ill treatment, have done away with caste in all aspects, even the mental. Consequently, in addition to a few capable souls of tough logic and rigor, their own teachings of Buddha etc have been taken up by those of lesser capacity as well, on which account, have been grossly misinterpreted, leading to absurd understanding of reality and creation, as will be shown in the forthcoming sections.

ॐ कम्पनात् ॐ ॥ १.३.३९॥

On account of vibration.

Reference is to Katha 2.6.2, mentioning the whole world trembles in the Prana. It has already been established how Brahman the dreamer is the abode of all creation, and on this account, Prana is taken to refer to Brahman.

ॐ ज्योतिर्दर्शनात् ॐ ॥ १.३.४०॥

Light is Brahman on account of being seen as the subject.

Reference of highest light in Chhandogya 8.12.3, standing for Brahman, which is the central subject of the whole section, as well as liberation being mentioned to one who is one with this light.

ॐ आकाशोऽर्थान्तरत्वादिव्यपदेशात् ॐ ॥ १.३.४१॥

Akasha is Brahman because it is declared to be different than things with names and forms, and yet their revealer.

Reference to Chhandogya 8.14.1, Akashas the abode of everything with names and forms, which as earlier clarified is Brahman, and also the revealer of all these, as intelligence.

ॐ सुषुप्त्युत्क्रान्त्योरभेदेन ॐ ॥ १.३.४२॥

Because of the Self shown as different in states of deep sleep and death.

Reference to Brihadaranyaka 4.3.21, mentioning absence of knowledge in deep sleep, which can refer only to individual soul and also tone of death in Brihadaranyaka 4.3.35, where Brahman is mentioned as intelligence.

ॐ पत्यादिशब्देभ्यः ॐ ॥ १.३.४३॥

On account of words like Lord.

Reference to Brihadaranyaka 4.4.22 to words like Lord and Ruler assigned to the Self, since Brahman is not only beyond bondage, but also, is the Primary Cause, ie enjoyment, and ordains the dream creation to that purpose.

ॐ आनुमानिकमप्येकेषामिति चेन्न शरीररूपकविन्यस्तगृहीतेर्दर्शयति
च ॐ ॥ १.४.१॥

The claim that Pradhana is mentioned in some Sakhas, we refute on the basis that Avyaktha is a simile referring to the body.

Reference to Katha 1.3.11, mentioning Avyaktha the Unmanifest beyond Mahat. Comparison of 1.3.3-4 and 10-11, reveals similarity of Atman with Purusha, Mahat with cosmic intellect, thus leading to Avyaktha with the body.

ॐ सूक्ष्मं तु तदर्हत्वात् ॐ ॥ १.४.२॥

But the subtle cause of the body is meant by, Avyakta because it can be so designated.

In the context of body, Avyaktha refers not to the gross body, but its immediate cause, ie the elements of nature, since in the context of physical nature, it is Unmanifest.

ॐ तदधीनत्वादर्थवत् ॐ ॥ १.४.३॥

On account of its dependence on the Lord, it fits in.

With the image of first cause being Brahman with the aim of enjoyment, the immediate cause of body, Avyaktha as elements is ultimately traced as cause to the Lord and the power of Maya, but is not an independent cause since neither the elements nor its immediate cause, have sentience or knowledge of the prime cause.

ॐ ज्ञेयत्वावचनाच्च ॐ ॥ १.४.४॥

And because it is not mentioned that the Avyaktha is to be known.

This is because Sankhya holds that the difference between Purusha and Prakriti and thus Avyaktha is to be known. But such mention is not given in the Sruthis.

ॐ वदतीति चेन्न प्राज्ञो हि ॐ ॥ १.४.५॥

पाठभेदे 1.4.5 and 6 combined

ॐ प्रकरणात् ॐ ॥ १.४.६॥

The claim that Sruthi states Avyaktha to be known, we refute since it is the Self, the main topic that is mentioned.

Reference is to Katha 1.3.15, instructing to meditate on that beyond the Mahat, which, in line with the main subject matter, is Brahman alone.

ॐ त्रयाणामेव चैवमुपन्यास: प्रश्नश्च ॐ ॥ १.४.७॥

And thus the question and elucidation with respect to the three alone is consistent.

The subject matter is Yama's response to Nachiketa's three questions, which only involve the Self and Pradhana.

ॐ महद्वच्च ॐ ॥ १.४.८॥

And Like Mahat.

Reference to Katha 1.3.10, showing the Mahat to be greater than intellect, thus referring to Brahman.

ॐ चमसवदविशेषात् ॐ ॥ १.४.९॥

Aja cannot mean Pradhana, for want of special characteristics, like the bowl.

Shvetashvatara mentions one Aja, if three colours producing the offspring of the same colour. The Sutra says that in absence of special Characteristics I've cannot infer Aja as Prakriti with the 3 Gunas as colors, just as one cannot infer the shape of a bowl vaguely mentioned in Brihadaranyaka 2.2.3.

ॐ ज्योतिरुपक्रमात् तु तथा ह्यधीयत एके ॐ ॥ १.४.१०॥

But the elements beginning with light are referred to as Aja, some read.

Chhandogya 6 2, mentions the three colours standing for fire, water and earth.

ॐ कल्पनोपदेशाच्च मध्वादविदवरोधः ॐ ॥ १.४.११॥

And instruction having being given through the imagery of goat, there is no incongruity, just as in honey standing for Madhu Vidya for the purpose of devout meditation.

ॐ न सङ्ख्योपसङ्ग्रहादपि नानाभावादतिरिकाच्च ॐ ॥ १.४.१२॥

Even from the statement of the number fivefold five,it is not the Sankhya categories because of their difference in nature and also the excess over the Sankhyan number.

Brihadaranyaka 4.4.17 mentions Atma as the abode of the five groups of five and Akasha. On account of the total including Akasha being 26, and on account of the fact that the Sankhyan 25 cannot be divided as five groups of five, the latter is not mentioned.

ॐ प्राणादयो वाक्यशेषात् ॐ ॥ १.४.१३॥

The five people referred to are the 5 vital forces, as found from the subsequent text.

Brihadaranyaka Madhyama 4.4.21 enumerates the five as vital force, eye, ear, food and mind.

ॐ ज्योतिषैकेषामसत्यन्ने ॐ ॥ १.४.१४॥

In the Kanwa Sakha, food not mentioned, is replaced with light as per reference Brihadaranyaka 4.4.16.

ॐ कारणत्वेन चाकाशादिषु यथाव्यपदिष्टोक्तेः ॐ ॥ १.४.१५॥

Although regarding created things or Akasha, texts differ, there is no conflict of Brahman being taught and represented as the first cause.

Again it is reinforced that no matter how many things are created or what their order, all belong to the unreal dream creation, and are insentient, and as the only sentient One, Brahman alone is the first cause.

ॐ समाकर्षात् ॐ ॥ १.४.१६॥

And on account of connection.

Non existence mentioned in Taittiriya 2.7 is just Unmanifest existence and not absolute non existence, since such a possibility is denied in Chhandogya 6.2.2. So to the word undifferentiated in Brihadaranyaka 1.4.7 cannot imply spontaneous creation since the same reference mentions the Ruler present even in the finger nails. Thus, there is consistency among texts regarding Brahman as the first cause.

ॐ जगद्वाचित्वात् ॐ ॥ १.४.१७॥

He of whom all this is work denotes Brahman since work denotes the world.

Work reference in Kaushitaki 4, refers to Brahman as the maker of all that is the world, since the text declares its objective to be teaching about Brahman.

ॐ जीवमुख्यप्राणलिङ्गादिति चेत् तद्व्याख्यातम् ॐ ॥ १.४.१८॥

The claim that on account of characteristics of soul and Prana, Brahman is not mentioned, we refute in that it has been explained earlier, in Brahma Sutra 1.1.

ॐ अन्यार्थं तु जैमिनिः प्रश्नव्याख्यानाभ्यामपि चैवमेके ॐ ॥ १.४.१९॥

Moreover, as per Jaimini, reference to individual soul is due to questions and answers, even as some Sakhas read so.

Reference to Kaushitaki 4.19-20 asking the abode of individual soul and answering it is Brahman. Brihadaranyaka 2.1.16-17 calls the soul Vijnanamaya to distinguish from the self.

ॐ वाक्यान्वयात् ॐ ॥ १.४.२०॥

On account of the connected meaning.

Reference to Brihadaranyaka 2.4 with the Self as the main subject, and thus the common theme running between the verses, as the Self alone knowing which everything is known.

ॐ प्रतज्ञासिद्धेर्लिङ्गमाश्मरथ्यः ॐ ॥ १.४.२१॥

That the soul is taught as object of Realization in Brihadaranyaka 2.4.5 is an indicatory mark as proof of the proposition, so Asmarathya thinks.

It is well known that the individual soul is limited. Then, how can knowing the soul result in knowing everything? Thus, this is proof that the individual soul is the same and non different as the Self, when it comes to complete knowledge. Yet, the reason Sruthis clearly differentiate the soul and Self is the experience of sorrow and misery of the soul, due to its superimposition of insentient things onto itself. Thus, as long as this ignorance or lack of complete knowledge persists, the soul must be held different from the Self. This is the basis of the Bhedabheda view of Vedanta. In this view, the soul being one with the Self is given as much importance as the soul being different from the Self. Yet, the former is in the context of reality, while the latter is in the context of unreality. Such a view of Vedanta is thus most applicable in cases where the first cause, ie dream is in its last stages, ie nearing completion, but yet not fully complete, ie full knowledge is not yet attained. That is, the soul understands his nature as the

Self, through Vichara, and says Aham Brahmaasmi, I am the Self alone, and not this illusive world.

On the contrary, the Abheda or Advaitic view, which occurs with further knowledge, is that, I am the Self. This world is Maya which is my creation, ie my dream. Characters in my dream are essentially me. Thus, the soul is Brahman, as well as all this world, except that the former is real while the latter is not. With the reality of the entire world denied, the experience of sorrow etc too is denied in Advaita, and consequently there is no means to distinguish the soul from the Self - both are one.

Returning back to Bhedabheda, while the knowledge of the truth is indeed there that the soul is the Self, in that it is sentient. Yet the statement that I am not this Maya results in the fact that there is something ie world, apart from the soul, even though unreal. This makes the soul limited in capacity and thus different from the Self. This is the essence of Bhedabheda - non difference as far as nature of soul is concerned and difference as far as nature of world is concerned. There are many types of Bhedabheda, the most popular being Visishtadvaita, but others too such as Upadhika, Dvaitadvaita, Shuddhadvaita and Achintya.

In even earlier stages of knowledge, the world is not yet understood to be unreal and dream. In that case for the world to be real, there must exist many souls as well as the Brahman or Self as the first cause. Thus, due to limitation between soul and Brahman, as well as variation of experience such as sorrow and misery. This will result in complete difference between soul and Self, and this is the Bheda or Dvaita doctrine of Vedanta. Even in Bhedabheda doctrines, some may posit the world being real, in so much as it does not alter the position of soul seen different as Self due to declaring the world as not mine.

As long as the world as unreal is not understood, the nature of soul as limitless is not understood. Thus, Bheda, Bhedabheda and Abheda doctrines all represent the Vedantic view from various perspectives from earlier to later.

However even with that Advaitic perspective as the relatively most matured, there still is no understanding of the purpose of creation. This results in two deficiencies. First, the cause being Brahman, and the effect, if taken as the world, as ignorance, does not match in quality. Second, even if the cause is given as pastime, such as Shankara Bhashya of the Brahma Sutra, the Advaitic bliss arises in fully realizing the identity with the Self. If that be the case, and if that be the ultimate Cause of Brahman, why then does the created world continue in its same unreal state even after liberation? One cannot give for an answer the Prarabdha Karma, since, just as Ramana Maharshi mentions, once the liberation is achieved, there is no more agency of the soul ie there is no more Karta. Then, just like the three wives of a deceased man are all rendered widows, all three Karmas, Prarabdha, Sanchita and Agami, cease. On the same lines, the doctrine of Ajatavada, stating that there is no creation, no bondage, no liberation, does not hold, since while the reality of created things can certainly be negated, there is no denying of the dream experience itself, since it is as obvious as the Self itself.

Thus, the solution to the deficiencies mentioned above, is Sri Vidya Vedanta, which progresses one step further to the Advaitic view. Creation, even through the unreal dream, is with a purpose, that is to create an illusion of separateness, so that while the Brahman by itself is bliss, the illusion of separateness and then joining back together, makes the resulting bliss feel more intense, similar to what Lord Krishna mentions as part of the Gopi Gita in Srimad Bhagavatam 10.32.20-21. Furthermore, the purpose is also to experience this intense bliss as enjoyment, in this same unreal creation, this being possible since there is no ignorance anymore to cause suffering. That intense bliss, as enjoyment in the unreal creation, is the state of Jivanmukthi. Thus, Brahman as the first cause of creation, proceeds with creation, well aware of the purpose, and to achieve it. This alone gives the complete picture of reality, which, when seen in perspective of different stages of knowledge, one gets the various schools mentioned earlier, such as Advaita, Dvaita, Visishtadvaita and so on.

ॐ उत्क्रमिष्यत एवं भावादति्यौड्लोमिः ॐ ॥ १.४.२२॥

Statement at the beginning identified the soul with Brahman because of this nature ie one with Brahman at the time of release, thus thinks Audulomi.

ॐ अवस्थितिरिति काशकृत्स्नः ॐ ॥ १.४.२३॥

The statement of made because of existence of Brahman as individual soul, as per Kashakrutsna.

ॐ प्रकृतिश्च प्रतिज्ञादृष्टान्तानुपरोधात् ॐ ॥ १.४.२४॥

Brahman is the material cause also, due to contradiction not arising with respect to the Sruthis.

Chhandogya 6.1.3-4 asserts this, just as how when one lump of clay is known, all that is made of it is known.

ॐ अभिध्योपदेशाच्च ॐ ॥ १.४.२५॥

Also on account of the statement of will.

In Chhandogya mentioning Brahman's desire to be many, the fact that a desire existed proves efficient cause, while the desire to become many indicates material cause.

ॐ साक्षाच्चोभयाम्नानात् ॐ ॥ १.४.२६॥

On account of Sruthi stating both.

Reference to Chhandogya 1.9.1 and Taittiriya 3.1, showing that creation arising and re absorbing in Brahman makes it the material cause.

ॐ आत्मकृतेः परिणामात् ॐ ॥ १.४.२७॥

Because it created itself by undergoing modification.

In the absence of any other cause, Brahman creating itself means that it undergoes modification. However, such modification is real only from the dream standpoint, that is within the dream creation, just like a Dreamer getting wounded in the dream.

ॐ योनिश्चि हि गीयते ॐ ॥ १.४.२८॥

And because it is called the origin as in Mundaka 1.1.6.

ॐ एतेन सर्वेव्याख्याताव्याख्याताः ॐ ॥ १.४.२९॥

By this same explanation, all other doctrines contrary to the Vedanta are refuted.

CHAPTER SIX

Philosophy

ॐ स्मृत्यनवकाशदोषप्रसङ्ग इति
चेन्नान्यस्मृत्यनवकाशदोषप्रसङ्गात् ॐ ॥ २.१.१॥

The claim that Brahman is the First Cause would render certain Smritis having no scope, is refuted on account of that, by rejecting the doctrine of Brahman as First Cause other Smritis would have no scope.

The Smritis, written in the Second Wave, pertain to wisdom as has been revealed by the Divine. Thus, in being consistent with the original Cause, they too are to be taken as authoritative sources of wisdom. Yet, Smritis written in a Divided cultural world reflect the lack of such completeness, that one sees in the Shruthi, which arises from a unified Vedic world. Thus, Smritis are subject to misinterpretation, Shruthis are not.

If the idea that Brahman is not the First Cause, if taken as a claim from (mis)interpreting certain Smritis is denied, then those Smritis would be rendered wrong. Yet, if such a claim is accepted, they would render other Smritis based on Shruthi like Manu Smriti, which do claim Brahman as the first cause, wrong.

ॐ इतरेषां चानुपलब्धेः ॐ ॥ २.१.२॥

With there being no mention of the other entities in the scriptures.

If Brahman as not the first cause be accepted, then one must find reference to something else, some other category Sankhya, as the first cause in the scriptures, which does not happen. That is, it is the dreamer alone that is in control of the First Cause, and thus of the Universe.

ॐ एतेन योगः प्रत्युक्तः ॐ ॥ २.१.३॥

By this, Yoga too is refuted.

Since the previous Sutra rejects any other entity as the first cause, it means that there is no entity but Brahman capable of deciding the course of events. Thus, there are no two entities to join Yoga, as there is no separating

Viyoga in the first place. The doctrine of Yoga is only to be taken as an Upasana to realise the reality as dream while in it.

ॐ न वलिक्षणत्वादस्य तथात्वं च शब्दात् ॐ ॥ २.१.४॥

Brahman is not the Cause of the world, on account of the world being a nature contrary to Brahman, its being so known from the Shruthis.

All earlier Sutras spoke of Brahman as the First Cause. But what exactly is the First Cause? The Cause is enjoyment alone, that creating an illusion of separateness and then joining together, intensifies the bliss even more. That alone is the First Cause. The Cause here is Brahman who is Bliss, and the Effect here is more bliss, making the Cause and Effect of the same nature. On the other hand, Brahman is of the nature of sentience while the created universe is insentient, and for the reason that Cause and Effect cannot be of different nature, Brahman is not the Cause of the Universe.

ॐ अभिमानिव्यपदेशस्तु विशिषानुगतभियाम् ॐ ॥ २.१.६॥

However, reference is to presiding deities of organs mentioned in scriptures and being given that special status as deities.

Here a claim is made that since Deities ie Devas like fire and air are mentioned in scriptures such as Kaushitaki and Brihadaranyaka 6.1.7, to be presiding over the organs, may be the organs are sentient. However, this claim is refuted, because while the Brahman proceeds with a certain Cause, which is in agreement of how the creation works, no such sentient cause can be discerned from individual organs or physical forces of nature.

ॐ दृश्यते तु ॐ ॥ २.१.५॥

However it is seen.

The claim of the previous Sutra is refuted here, that Brahman cannot be the Cause of the Universe since they are of different nature.

There are examples of life such as scorpion coming out of non life such as cow dung, and of non life such as hair and nails coming out of life such as human. Therefore, just the simple fact that Brahman and Universe being of different nature doesn't completely preclude one as cause of another. In the examples of life and non life, there was commonality - nutrition in cow dung became nutrition absorbing scorpion while inertness in human body became dead cells such as hair and nails. In the same way, there is bliss in Brahman and experience of bliss in created world, which means that Creation is indeed Effect of Brahman as Cause, though indirectly, through the concept of bliss.

ॐ दृश्यते च ॐ ॥ २.१.७॥ पाठभेदे दृश्यते तु

ॐ असदिति चिन्न प्रतिषिधेमात्रत्वात् ॐ ॥ २.१.८॥

The claim that world, the effect is non existent before the cause, is refuted as a negation without basis.

If the world is seen as an effect of the Cause Brahman, then it is not possible for the world to have existed before creation, and that Brahman brings a non existent world into existence. That claim has no basis, says this Sutra. That is, first, the creation is as unreal as a dream. Second, the direct effect of Brahman the Cause is not the universe but the bliss experienced. Such bliss already resides in Brahman even before the universe creation, and thus no non existent thing is brought to existence.

ॐ अपीतौ तद्वत्प्रसङ्गादसमञ्जसम् ॐ ॥ २.१.९॥

On account of the fact that at time of dissolution, Cause becomes of nature of effect, the doctrine is absurd.

A claim is made that, just like a salt doll dissolving in water makes it salty, insentient world dissolving in Brahman will make it insentient and thus, the doctrine of Brahman being a sentient First Cause is absurd.

ॐ न तु दृष्टान्तभावात् ॐ ॥ २.१.१०॥

However it is not so on account of existence of illustrations.

The claim of the previous Sutra is refuted, since there are many examples such as a clay pot being dissolved back into clay, that illustrates how Brahman cannot get polluted with insentience. But even more importantly, the distinction must be understood, that Brahman is Real, while the world is not, unlike the case of salt doll and water, which are both taken as real in the example. As much as an unreal dream injury does not show up as a wound in the dreamer's body, the unreal creation cannot pollute Brahman on dissolving.

ॐ स्वपक्षदोषाच्च ॐ ॥ २.१.११॥

And because of objections cited being applicable to his own view too.

If the claims refuted above had been made by Sankhya or any other philosophy, that Brahman the Cause being a different nature than the Effect the universe could not have possibly created by it, then such claims equally apply to any other First Cause that the Sankhya claims. That is, whatever is claimed as First Cause by Sankhya, must be explained as to how it creates a variety of things in the Universe, and such an explanation is indeed given for Brahman in the previous Sutras.

ॐ तर्काप्रतिष्ठानादपि अन्यथानुमेयमिति
चेदेवमप्यनर्मिोक्षप्रसङ्ग: ॐ ॥ २.१.१२॥

Also because reasoning has no sure effect. Even if it is reasoned otherwise, there will result the contingency of the non release of the defect.

The scriptures have been written keeping in mind the First Cause and the ultimate objective of Brahman creating to enjoy. Reasoning out and trying to find that truth, independent of this fact, cannot give a sure or even homogenous answer. Because, even if another chain of thoughts can be given as reason for the fact that Brahman or anything else was the First Cause, still one would have to explain, how the insentient world, or even the variety of things in the world can be created from the singular Cause and how they can dissolve in the Cause without polluting it. The only solution to all this question is to properly understand the Cause and its direct Effect. Bliss of Brahman is the Cause, and Bliss as enjoyment is the Effect. They are of the same nature and there is no question of polluting at all.

ॐ एतेन शिष्टापरिग्रहाऽपि व्याख्याताः ॐ ॥ २.१.१३॥

On the basis of the same arguments, other views not accepted by the wise are explained.

That is, not just Sankhya but any other philosophy claiming a First Cause different than Brahman have been refuted by the above Sutras, on the same basis ie consistency between Cause and Effect when taken as Bliss and Enjoyment, as well as distinction between sentient Reality and unreal insentience.

ॐ भोक्त्रापत्तेरविभागश्चेत्स्याल्लोकवत् ॐ ॥ २.१.१४॥

The claim that, if Brahman is the Cause then there should be no distinction between the enjoyer and objects enjoyed, we refute on account that such distinction may exist, as is commonly seen around the world.

First, as means of knowledge, perception is stronger than Shruthi. The Sutra refutes the non distinction of Brahman and world being a necessary factor for enjoyment. This is done by giving examples like the sea and its waves, which, though the same in substance, are different in appearance, form and function. The same applies in the case of a person seeing his reflection in a mirror - the same person is seen in both, yet, any features of the mirror like dirt shows up as distortion, making the image appear different than the original. Either way, the important point is, the Cause is Brahman, and the Effect, is the creation, and both are of the nature of bliss, and may be experienced so upon attaining completeness in the spiritual path. Then, even by perception, the non difference between Brahman and creation will be apparent, and until such time, the incompleteness of the

Spiritual path is like the dirt of the mirror, which makes a difference of image, with the Brahman appearing blissful wisdom while its creation miserable.

ॐ तदनन्यत्वमारम्भणशब्दादिभ्यः ॐ ॥ २.१.१५॥

Non Difference from Cause arises due to words like origin etc.

The explanation of the previous Sutra is reinforced here. Unlike the sea and waves which can both be sensed, in the case of Brahman, the created world can be sensed, while Brahman can only be experienced in Samadhi etc. There can only be proper comparison, if the Cause of creation is fully understood, and experienced first hand, which happens only at the end of the spiritual process, at which point, the similarity of Brahman and universe, both as bliss, is experienced directly. Till such time, Brahman as bliss and world as misery are simply differences in name given, that too by those who have not correctly and directly experienced both, and neither does such difference align with the ultimate Cause of creation.

ॐ भावे चोपलब्धेः ॐ ॥ २.१.१६॥

And because on the existence of Cause is the Effect experienced.

Brahman alone is sentient. Thus, Brahman alone is capable of all action, either as the actions in the universe leading to bliss, or the action of experiencing the bliss, as Brahman itself.

ॐ सत्त्वाच्चावरस्य ॐ ॥ २.१.१७॥

And on account of the Effect coming to existence after the Cause.

Since before creation, the Cause as Bliss and Effect as enjoyment were both one, as only Brahman existed, or means that before creation, Cause and Effect were homogenous. Thus, even after creation, it is only reasonable that they continue to be homogenous.

ॐ असद्व्यपदेशान्नेति चेन्न धर्मान्तरेण वाक्यशेषात् ॐ ॥ २.१.१८॥

The claim that, on account of the effect being non existent before creation the previous Sutra is untrue, is refuted because of mention of another characteristic in the latter part of the text.

Chhandogya 3.19.1 states the view of non existence of creation ie universe in the beginning. The very succeeding says that creation became existent and it grew. This shows that the non existence mentioned is not absolute non existence, but just that the creation was very much existent inside Brahman, but in an undeveloped state, ie as simply bliss and not enjoyment.

ॐ युक्तेः शब्दान्तराच्च ॐ ॥ २.१.१९॥

From reasoning and another Sruthi text.

Chhandogya 6.2.1 states the view emphasised in the previous Sutra. That is, in any case of creation ever seen, like river from a glacier, or rain from cloud, or salt doll from salt, or clay pot from clay, the created exists in its source before creation albeit Unmanifest. Creation cannot happen out of nothing. Then, if Brahman is Bliss, then, creation as enjoyment exists inside that bliss, prior to creation.

ॐ पटवच्च ॐ ॥ २.१.२० ॥

And Like a piece of cloth.

Creation is like a cloth folded, when it exists Unmanifest in Brahman, and is like the same cloth spread out, when created. That is, what is seen as just enjoyment Unmanifest in bliss, after creation is manifest as various objects of enjoyment.

ॐ यथा प्राणादि: ॐ ॥ २.१.२१ ॥

And as in the case of different Pranas.

In Pranayama, all five Pranas are brought in control under the Prana, creation is all existent in Brahman, though Unmanifest.

ॐ इतरव्यपदेशाद्धिताकरणादिदोषप्रसक्ति: ॐ ॥ २.१.२२ ॥

On account of the individual soul claimed as non different from Brahman, the latter would incur the defect of not doing what is beneficial for itself, and the like.

If Brahman is taken as Direct Cause of the created world, then Brahman, being sentient and aware of the Cause, would have created a perfect world without misery, but since that is not the case in the observed world, one might accuse Brahman of doing harm to its own Self. However, the Direct Effect of Brahman as the Cause is enjoyment from the world, and thus, Brahman only ordains towards that objective, and not to ensure a perfect world, since Brahman is not its direct Cause.

ॐ अधिकं तु भेदनिर्देशात् ॐ ॥ २.१.२३ ॥

However on account of statements of difference between Brahman and individual soul Jiva, Brahman is something more.

The previous Sutra attempted to identify the actions of the individual soul, experiencing misery, on Brahman. That is refuted here since, there is something that is there in Brahman that is not there in Jiva. That is, Brahman is aware of the Cause of creation, as well as the unreality of Creation. Thus, not only is there no sorrow in the first place, but such sorrow itself is an illusion created by the equally unreal Jiva.

ॐ अश्मादविच्च तदनुपपत्तिः ॐ ॥ २.१.२४॥

And due to the case of stones produced from Earth of the same nature, the argument is untenable.

Valuable minerals and gems as well as worthless stones are produced from the same source, Earth. On this account, one can understand the possibility of joy and misery both arising from the same Brahman, even if the Creation is wrongly taken to be Real.

ॐ उपसंहारदर्शनान्नेति चेन्न क्षीरवद्धि ॐ ॥ २.१.२५॥

The claim that Brahman could not have created the universe without external aid, is refuted on account of similarity of milk changing to curd.

Shvetashvatara 6.8 mentions that Brahman has no instrument, nor is one necessary. Heat may accelerate the process of milk becoming curd, but the same heat cannot turn water into curd. Thus, all the requirements to create curd are inherent in the milk itself.

ॐ देवादिवदपि लोके ॐ ॥ २.१.२६॥

Like Gods and other beings in the world.

In most scriptures and sacred texts there are mentions of God creating the universe simply through their inherent power.

ॐ कृत्स्नप्रसक्तिर्निरवयवत्वशब्दकोपो वा ॐ ॥ २.१.२७॥

Brahman being the Cause involves either the entire Brahman being modified or violates the doctrine that Brahman is without parts.

A claim is made that if Brahman creates out of itself, then, Brahman must have beforehand those parts within itself, or atleast must undergo a modification.

ॐ श्रुतेस्तु शब्दमूलत्वात् ॐ ॥ २.१.२८॥

However not so on account of scriptures supporting both contradictory views and on account of Brahman based on scripture only.

On the one hand, Sruthis like Chhandogya 3.12.6 do claim that Brahman has one foot in Jiva and three in heavens. On that account, the scriptures taken as authority do imply Brahman being modified due to creation. However, there is always the overarching truth that Brahman is Real while the creation is unreal, as a dream. Does the dreamer get modified due to a dream? The modification of Brahman according to creation is but an illusion, and from the standpoint within the dream creation, it is true.

ॐ आत्मनि चैवं विचित्राश्च हि ॐ ॥ २.१.२९॥

And because in individual soul too diversity exists, the same in Brahman.

The example of dream cited above, as well as a magician, being the soul Jiva, producing magic even while he himself is not modified, reinforces the point of the Sutra.

ॐ स्वपक्षदोषाच्च ॐ ॥ २.१.३०॥

On account of this view applicable to the other philosopies too.

Any philosophy raising the claims refuted thus far, of Brahman being modified by creation, will also apply to what they themselves cite as First cause, too. More so, if a philosophy holds that creation is Real, then it will have tough time explaining how the first cause it proposes, does not undergo modification.

ॐ सर्वोपेता च तद्दर्शनात् ॐ ॥ २.१.३१॥

Because it is seen in scriptures, Brahman is endowed with all powers.

Reference to Shvetashvatara 4.10, Chhandogya 3.14.4 and 8.7.1 stating that Brahman is endowed with powers, especially of illusion or Maya.

ॐ विकिरणत्वान्नेति चेत्तदुक्तम् ॐ ॥ २.१.३२॥

The claim that devoid of organs, Brahman cannot create, we refute on account that it has already been explained.

Again, the Cause and Effect are merely bliss and enjoyment, for which purpose the only creation is knowledge or lack of it, for the purpose of which, illusion is the only power necessary. There is nothing else physically created, and no other organs are necessary as Shvetashvatara 3.19.

ॐ न प्रयोजनत्त्वात् ॐ ॥ २.१.३३॥

Brahman is not the creator of the world, on account of every activity having a motive.

A claim is raised that the world does not seem to have any motive, simply being created and destroyed, then Brahman cannot be its Cause.

ॐ लोकवत्तु लीलाकैवल्यम् ॐ ॥ २.१.३४॥

However, Brahman's Creative Activity is Leela or pastime, as seen from the world.

Brahman as Amma is called Lalitha, solely for the reason that Leela is its fundamental essence. The ultimate objective of bliss intensifying is the motive by which the world is created. Thus, on the basis of creation having a motive, the claim of the previous Sutra is refuted.

ॐ वैषम्यनैर्घृण्ये न सापेक्षत्वात्तथा हि दर्शयति ॐ ॥ २.१.३५॥

Partiality and Cruelty cannot be attributed to Brahman on account of taking into consideration, other factors, since the scriptures say so.

The direct Cause of creation is enjoyment alone, which happens through realising the unreality of the dream, which in turn happens through removing of Karma Vasanas or latent tendencies. That is the sole thing Brahman is concerned with, and definitely not a world where everybody is wealthy and there are no punishments etc. Thus, these are not the Direct Concern of Brahman, and the latter cannot be accused on that basis.

ॐ कर्मावभिागादिति चिनेन्नानादित्विात् ॐ ॥ २.१.३६॥

The claim that it is not possible for want of distinction before creation, is refuted, on account of world being without a beginning.

If every punishment is an attempt to change Vasanas, one may ask, what Vasanas did the earliest creations have? This Sutra refutes on the basis that the world does not have a beginning to start with, because the world has no reality itself to begin with.

ॐ उपपद्यते चाप्युपलभ्यते च ॐ ॥ २.१.३७॥

Also, that is reasonable and seen from the scriptures.

If the world did not have an existence before creation, then it would mean that something was created out of nothing, which is impossible. In that absurd case, there would be neither cause nor effect, and the created world would be nothing short of anarchy. Reference to Rig 10.190.3 states that the sun and moon was created as before, the before referring to their subtle Unmanifest existence in Brahman, as simply the Cause ie enjoyment.

ॐ सर्वधर्मोपपत्तेश्च ॐ ॥ २.१.३८॥

Also from the possibility of all attributes.

A claim is made that attributeless Brahman cannot be the cause for the material world. This claim is refuted on the basis that the world is not material to begin with, and that the only real attribute of the world is Bliss, which is the same attribute as Brahman. Yet, in the unreal perspective of a dream, all illusions of attributes can be created, owing to the power of Maya of Brahman.

ॐ रचनानुपपत्तेश्च नानुमानम् ॐ ॥ २.२.१॥

And that which is inferred cannot be taken as First cause, because it is impossible to explain the design of creation.

The claim by Sankhya or other philosophy that there is an inert first cause named Pradhana, cannot account for the creation of universe with all its variety. Such creation can be performed only by a sentient intelligent first cause, which is mentioned in scriptures as Brahman, and thus need not be known by independent inference.

ॐ पूरवतृतेश्च ॐ ॥ २.२.२॥

On account of impossibility of tendency to create.

Just as clay has not ever created a pot on its own, an inert first cause cannot and has no tendency to create.

ॐ पयोऽम्बुवच्चेत्ततत्रापि ॐ ॥ २.२.३॥

The claim that Pradhana spontaneously undergoes modification like flowing of milk and water, we refute on account that even there, intelligence is seen.

The fact that water flows spontaneously from higher to lower ground cannot be quoted as an example to show lack of intelligence. This is because, in every instance of spontaneous water flow, we only see flow from higher to lower level, not vice versa. Is it not intelligence that ordains this way? Is it not intelligence in sensing the levels and then flowing accordingly? Thus, in every action ever observed, there is intelligence, and an inert first cause cannot possibly create anything without intelligence.

ॐ व्यतरिकानवस्थतिश्चानपेक्षत्वात् ॐ ॥ २.२.४॥

And because of independence on anything, there being no extragenous agency beside it, its activity or non activity cannot be obtained.

Here again, with an inert first cause, and no external agency, one fails to answer the question, who started the process of creation? Or once created, who stops the process? This is created because the Pradhana is inert and cannot guide itself.

ॐ अन्यत्राभावाच्च न तृणादिवत् ॐ ॥ २.२.५॥

And spontaneous modification is also ruled out as in the case of grass becoming milk, because of its absence elsewhere.

Grass becoming milk requires the cow to eat it first. Thus, even to undergo spontaneous modification by the Pradhana, there must be an external aid, which contradicts the doctrine of the Pradhana.

ॐ अभ्युपगमेऽप्यर्थाभावात् ॐ ॥ २.२.६॥

Even accepting so, Pradhana cannot be first cause on account of lack of motive.

Even if we do assume that spontaneous modification is real just for the sake of argument, still, it is spontaneous and not guided. In that case, it does not have an end purpose or motive for creation. This violates the Pradhana doctrine that there is an end motive, that being liberation.

ॐ परुषाश्मवदतिचितेत्तथापि ॐ ॥ २.२.७॥.

The claim that Purusha directs Pradhana even as a crippled guiding the blind, or a magnet directing iron filings, even then, the claim cannot be accepted.

Pradhana is inert and independent, while Purusha isintelligent yet indifferent. If Purusha guiding Pradhana is similar to magnet attracting iron because of being near it, then Pradhana must be creating all the time without stopping or destroying. Similarly, Purusha is too indifferent to give directions unlike the crippled and blind case. Thus, creation requires Brahman to be indifferent but still intelligent.

ॐ अङ्गत्विानुपपत्तेः ॐ ॥ २.२.८॥

And owing to impossibility of relation between main and subordinate.

The theory that creation occurs when one of the three Gunas is set out of equilibrium, which cannot happen without an external intelligence or force, the Gunas themselves being insentient.

ॐ अन्यथानुमितौ च ज्ञशक्तवियियोगात् ॐ ॥ २.२.९॥

Even if inferred otherwise it is impossible on account of absence of intelligence power.

For argument sake, even if the role of Gunas is accepted, it still fails to explain the design of the creation. In summary, the first cause must be a sentient One full of intelligence, which can direct the actions of the universe, the start and stop of creation, as well as experience it, all aligned with a purpose. This is possible only by the dreamer who alone is sentient.

ॐ विपिरतषिधाच्चासमञ्जसम् ॐ ॥ २.२.१०॥

Also Is inconsistent because of contradiction.

Reference here is to inconsistent variations mentioned by Sankhyas such as number of senses quoted as seven or eleven and so on. What must be understood is that philosophies such as Sankhya, Vaisheshika etc have their roots in Smritis. That is, they arise from revelations by for example Lord Krishna of the Puranic era, the divided world of the second wave. From such basis, these philosophies attempt to understand the Vedas and try to synergise the Sruthi and Smriti. However, what is missing in their attempts is consideration of the scope of these philosophies. In Sankhya, the focus is on the various categories by which the various components of nature and the universe is understood. This pertains to one in the earlier stages of knowledge, who sees the world as real. For such a person, in order to understand the interconnectedness and presence of God in the world, the Sankhya has been proposed. Since it does not pertain to the view of one with complete knowledge, this cannot be used to interpret the nature of reality itself, and doing so will result in gross inconsistencies as shown till now. Yoga too is built from the same philosophy as Sankhya, with its objective being the proper maintenance of body and purification of the mind so as to prepare for further progress. To the Sankhya Base, it adds the concept of a personal God Ishwara, since that can be used by a purified mind to progress through Dharana, Dhyaana and eventually Savikalpa Samadhi, the 5th of the 16 stages. This too, like Sankhya gives the perspective of the earlier stages, and cannot be used to describe reality itself.

ॐ महद्दीर्घवद्धा ह्रस्वपरमिण्डलाभ्याम् ॐ ॥ २.२.११॥

World may originate from Brahman even as long may originate from short, and short from infinitesimal.

The view of certain philosopies such as Vaisheshika is such that, just as white thread weaves a white cloth, the nature of Cause and Effect are homogenous. It then proceeds to describe atom as the fundamental and ultimate Cause of the world, with two atoms forming dyads, three dyads forming triad, and so on, with gross elements created in this way. Even as per this theory of Vaisheshika their fundamental doctrine of homogeneity is violated, since the long triad is of a different nature than the short dyad which is further different than the infinitesimal atom.

ॐ उभयथापि न कर्मातस्तदभाव: ॐ ॥ २.२.१२॥

In either case, activity is impossible; hence its negation.

Furthering the Vaisheshika argument, begs the question, what causes and directs the combination of atoms? If it is a physical factor, then that would have not been existent before creation itself. If it is an unseen Adrishta, then it is inert and cannot act without anything intelligent directing it. In both cases, the fact that is obvious is that the purpose of Creation as enjoyment and its subsequent sentience as the First Cause has not been captured effectively in Vaisheshika.

ॐ समवायाभ्युपगमाच्च साम्यादनवस्थिति: ॐ ॥ २.२.१३॥

Also because of regression in infinitum on similar reasoning due to acceptance of Samavaya.

Samavaya is what Vaisheshika holds to be the connection between the dyad and its constituents since the constituent ie atom and composite ie dyad are of different qualities. Then, by that logic, Samavaya itself is of a different quality than either the atom and dyad, and to hold Samavaya with these two homogenously, another Samavaya will be required. In this manner one will keep requiring infinite Samavayas to keep the theory consistent.

ॐ नतियमेव च भावात् ॐ ॥ २.२.१४॥

And because of the permanent tendency to act of the atoms.

The atoms are mentioned as having a consistent invarying tendency. If that tendency is to create, then there can be no dissolution since the tendency does not change. The same holds for dissolution also. If the unseen Adrishta controls the atoms, then that Adrishta by their theory cannot have varying tendency. Then that Adrishta can only continuously create or continuously destroy alone.

ॐ रूपादमित्तत्वाच्च वपिर्ययो दर्शनात् ॐ ॥ २.२.१५॥

On account of possessing colour etc it is seen that the opposite of what Vaisheshika holds will be rendered true.

Anything that possesses qualities such as colour cannot be atomic and permanent since they are gross, and at the same time the Vaisheshika contradicts this view by saying that atoms are indeed permanent.

ॐ उभयथा च दोषात् ॐ ॥ २.२.१६॥

And because of defects in either case.

The theory holds that the fundamental elements earth, water, air and fire are created from respective atoms, and that they have varying number of qualities ie senses of sight, touch etc in them. If the atoms creating these four have varying number of qualities, that must show up as a difference in size. In that case, the bigger of the four atoms can no longer be called fundamental unit. In case the atoms are all of the same size, then the theory fails to explain how similar causes can produce variations in effects.

ॐ अपरग्रिहाच्चात्यन्तमनपक्षेषा ॐ ॥ २.२.१७॥

Because it is not accepted by authority, it is to be rejected.

No authoritative text such as even Smritis like Manu Smriti seems to accept the Vaisheshika doctrine. The fundamental problem, again like earlier Sutras clarified, is that the First Cause is taken to be inert, insentient and without intelligence. With that sort of basis, one cannot sufficiently explain the Cause and Purpose of Creation, or even the bliss that is experienced in it, as well as the nature of reality, as a dream.

ॐ समुदायोभयहेतुकेऽपि तदप्राप्तिः ॐ ॥ २.२.१८॥

Even the two kinds of aggregates proceeding from the two causes would lead to non formation of the two kinds of aggregates.

The Sutra pertains to the Realist Bauddha doctrine called Bahyartha Vaada followed mainly in Theravada tradition as Sautantrika and Vaibhashika variants, where the premise is that the external material world is formed by aggregates of atoms of earth, water, fire and air, while the mental world is formed by aggregates of five kinds of Skandhas - Senses, identity, pleasure, cognition and attachment. Both worlds are real, but only momentary. Here again, the contention is what causes these Skandhas to aggregate. If the Cause is not intelligent, then, there will be non stop creation or destruction. If the cause is intelligent then question is if it is momentary or stationary. If it is stationary then it violates the momentary doctrine. If it is momentary then, it would take time to come into existence and then aggregate, which would then be more than a moment.

ॐ इतरेतरप्रत्ययत्वादिति चेन्नौत्पत्तमात्रनमित्तत्वात् ॐ ॥ २.२.१९॥

The claim that formation of aggregates due to successive causality, we refute because they are merely the efficient cause of what comes subsequently.

The series as Nescience, Samskara, Vijnana, name, color, body and senses, contact, pleasure etc..., in this series each leads to the next as its Cause. Using this, a claim is made that an unceasing chain of cause and effect results, without the need of a directing principle or even by combining different types of atoms. The Sutra refutes by saying even in this case, as long as there is a lack of intelligence, causality can only explain the relation between an atom and what is immediately subsequent to it, but not combination into aggregates.

ॐ उत्तरोत्पादे च पूर्वनरोधात् ॐ ॥ २.२.२०॥

And because even in production of subsequent entities, the antecedent has already ceased to exist, it cannot be the cause.

A pot of clay can only be created from clay that exists, and not from clay that has been consumed somewhere else. Thus, the doctrine of the previous Sutra, that each entity creates the next subsequent entity in the series, cannot hold true if they only have momentary existence.

ॐ असति प्रतिज्ञोपरोधो यौगपद्यमन्यथा ॐ ॥ २.२.२१॥

Non existence of cause will contradict their own proposition. Otherwise there would result simultaneity of cause and effect.

The point of previous Sutra is reinforced. If momentary existence is held, then it would mean one entity being created while its creator is non existent, in which case one cannot say that the latter created the former.

If there is simultaneous existence of both entities, then the momentary doctrine will be falsified for the creating entity.

ॐ प्रतसिङ्ख्याप्रतसिङ्ख्यानिरोधाप्राप्तिः अवच्छिेदात् ॐ ॥ २.२.२२॥

Conscious and unconscious destruction would be impossible due to non interruption.

The theory mentions two kinds of destruction, conscious meaning thoughtful such as breaking, and unconscious meaning natural decay. In either case, the existence is always valued on causal efficiency - one thing leading to another. In such a context, the Sutra refutes the possibility of both types of destruction. This is because, if destruction has occurred, the last momentary existence should have had an effect or not - those are the two possibilities. If it did have its effect, then it means it was a Cause for something to exist in the next moment - that is, the series has not been destroyed. If the last momentary existence did not produce any effect, it means, its Cause ie the momentary existence before it did not produce any effect, and so on. Moreover conscious destruction is not possible, since in a moment when the thought to destroy comes, by the time the action is performed in the next moment, the thing to be destroyed no longer exists, due to momentary existence. Also in unconscious destruction, there is no real destruction at all, just like when a pot of clay is destroyed, there is clay in the pieces, and when water is heated, it becomes steam.

ॐ उभयथा च दोषात् ॐ ॥ २.२.२३॥

In either case, it is untenable because of objections.

While the previous Sutra discussed the impossibility of destruction, the same applies to nescience, which is a false idea of permanency in momentary things. This Nescience also must undergo destruction, for liberation to be achieved. However, as stated above, conscious destruction cannot be achieved. Unconscious destruction means that Nescience will eventually destroy itself and thus one doesn't need to put efforts into it by following the eightfold path etc. This violates the Bauddha premise of the path itself.

ॐ आकाशे चावशिेषात् ॐ ॥ २.२.२४॥

Akasha being non different from the twofold destruction, it cannot be a non entity.

The theory holds that Akasha is the absence of any occupying body. The fact that Akasha is experienced means that it does have its basis and attributes, namely sound, just like others such as earth. Just like the two kinds of destructions cannot be non entities described above, Akasa too cannot be a non entity.

ॐ अनुस्मृतेश्च ॐ ॥ २.२.२५॥

On account of memory.

This is a key aspect refuting momentariness, in that to have memory, an experiencer must have existed at the time of event, and at the time if remembering the event. Different people cannot have the same memory, for what is experienced by one person is not remembered by another unrelated person. This means, the same person must have existed for atleast two moments, in which case, monentariness is refuted.

ॐ नासतोऽदृष्टत्वात् ॐ ॥ २.२.२६॥

Existence does not arise out of non existence, because it is never seen.

The theory holds that anything that exists eternally cannot produce any effect, since there is no change in it. Thus, cause must undergo destruction before the effect is produced. If that happens, then the relationship of a thing causally creating another thing is rendered moot. In that case, anything might create anything else without an order or system. Mango seeds do not grow into apple trees.

ॐ उदासीनानामपि चैव सिद्धिः ॐ ॥ २.२.२७॥

And thus, attainment of goal even by the effortless.

If existence arising from non existence is posited, then it is possible that without any prior activity, anybody may get anything, even liberation. In that case, the eightfold path would be rendered irrelevant. Thus, the momentary doctrine is refuted.

ॐ नाभाव उपलब्धेः ॐ ॥ २.२.२८॥

Non existence of external things are not true, on account of being experienced.

The idealist Bauddha doctrine called Vijnana Vaada and followed as Yogachara in Zen as well as some traditions of Tibetan Buddhism such as Nyingma, while decreed subject to interpretations in Gelug, holds that external material things are non existent. If non existent, in the absolute idea, such as horns of a hare, are mentioned then that idea is refuted, since the external world is indeed experienced. If the claim is that external world is in internal consciousness, but appearing to be external, that too is refuted, since if the claim appearing like external is made, that means there is something external, to compare the consciousness to. That is like saying a rope looking like a snake, in which case, somewhere else there is a snake that has been seen, on basis of which this comparison is made.

ॐ वैधर्म्याच्च न स्वप्नादवित् ॐ ॥ २.२.२९॥

Owing to the difference of nature waking state is not like dreams etc.

The dream state is merely a result of memories, while the waking state involves real perception. What occurs in the dream state on one night is contradicted by waking state the very next day. Thus, the external experience cannot be written off as a dream using the Bauddha doctrine, where monentariness and thus absence of continued experience is held. It can be done though, in the Vedantic doctrine, on account of the fact that a sentient Primary Cause Brahman is acknowledged, who is also the experiencer of the dream.

ॐ न भावोऽनुपलब्धेः ॐ ॥ २.२.३०॥

Existence of Samskaras are impossible because external things are not experienced.

A claim is made that just like waking state leaves impressions in the dream state, the impressions of previous experiences on the mind may appear as external things. This is refuted, on the basis that to have Samskaras in the mind of external things, there must have been perception of those things sometime in the past, which violates the denial of external things by the idealist Bauddha.

ॐ क्षणकित्वाच्च ॐ ॥ २.२.३१॥

And on account of momentariness.

For Samskaras to be seen as external objects, they must first have entered the mind sometime in the past, and more importantly must have stayed there from that moment till the moment of Samskaras giving a false external experience. However, the momentariness principle does not allow for it.

ॐ सर्वथानुपपत्तेश्च ॐ ॥ २.२.३२॥

And as being illogical in every way.

The explanations of previous Sutras refuting Realist and idealist Bauddha views, must also be taken as refutal of the Nihilist view also, on the same basis as mentioned above. In addition to the above Bauddha views, the Nihilist or Shunyata, followed in Mahayana as the Madhyamaka introduced by Nagarjuna, followed in East Asia as well as parts of Tibetan tradition such as Gelug, literally takes the concept of Shunyata in that the reality of existence is completely denied both externally as well as images within consciousness. Thus, Shunyata views all experiences as momentary consciousness, and thus Nirvana to be the absence of the same. This means, only as long as the experience is taken to be real, the presence or absence of the same can be accorded reality, and thus, Nirvana is equally of the same nature of unreality. Except for the acknowledging of an eternal Brahman, Shunyata is similar to the Ajatavada doctrine of Vedanta which holds the principles of no creation, no bondage, no liberation. However, claiming momentary consciousness and its absence as Nirvana makes the state of liberation no different from death, in which case, the theory of rebirth is violated, and this is the reason the Sutra claims Shunyata to be wanting in logic.

The original essence of the emptiness principle in all schools, whether it be called Shunyata or Anatta or Anatma, is that there is no soul, no person, and that too is Maya. However, this is misleading in that, to even state that all this is Maya, somebody must be experiencing this Maya, as well as the Nirvana or bliss after enlightenment. This experiencer, which is one's own Self, is too obvious to deny. This we find in Buddha's own words, where the Aggivacchagotta Sutra records a conversation between the Buddha and an individual named Vaccha. In it Vaccha asks the Buddha to confirm one of the following, with respect to the existence of the Buddha after death: 1. After death a Buddha reappears somewhere else, 2. After death a Buddha does not reappear, 3. After death a Buddha both does and does not reappear, 4. After death a Buddha neither does nor does not reappear. To all four questions, the Buddha answers that the terms 'appear', 'not appear', 'does and does not reappear' and 'neither does nor does not reappear' do not apply. Thus, in all four statements, one is simply left with the terms, "After death, Buddha" - that is the pure existence of the Self that remains after the mistaken reality of the world has ceased. This is the true intent and meaning of emptiness. In the Alagaddupama Sutta, the Buddha describes how some individuals feared his teaching because they believe that their 'self' would be destroyed if they followed it. All things are subject to change and taking any impermanent phenomena to be a 'self' causes suffering. Nonetheless, his critics called him a nihilist who teaches the annihilation and extermination of an existing being. The Buddha's response was that he only teaches the cessation of suffering. The closest Buddhism has got, to explaining an eternal Self that stays even after Nirvana is the concepts of Tathagatagarbha the fundamental Buddha consciousness which has as its seat the storehouse consciousness carrying forward Karma across births, called the Alaya Vijnana, and Apratishthita of Mahayana, a "stateless" form in which a Buddha may be after Nirvana so as to bring enlightenment to others through compassion. However, this too is inconsistent in that the momentariness of world either externally, or internally, ie in consciousness itself, implies that there is no other person to liberate after one's Nirvana is attained.

Fundamentally, the momentariness proposed by the Buddha is a valuable guideline in understanding the unreality of the experience, as in, whatever is observed as external reality is all happening in internal consciousness itself, as a dream, and that, by realising reality as a dream the existence will vanish in a moment. Since that realisation can be achieved any moment, the creation itself has only momentary existence. This idea has to be taken as relative momentariness of creation with respect to eternal Self, the same repeated in Lalitha Sahasranamam by names such as Unmesha Nimishotpanna Vipanna Bhuvanavali, as well as the concept of Drishti Srishti, along with the understanding that there is a sentient First Cause Brahman who spins forth the dream with a particular objective ie Enjoyment, and is the experiencer of this dream. If the idea of momentariness is taken along with rejection of Vedic ideas, and thus of a sentient Brahman, then, trying to apply such momentariness to the nature of creation and world results in one illogical conclusion after another, resulting in a grossly absurd understanding of the Reality itself, as has been discussed thus far. Among the various Bauddha views, the closest to Reality and Vedantic view is Yogachara, in which the dream state is acknowledged, and the only incompleteness is its insistence of absolute momentariness of internal experiences, and this will be rectified if an eternal Self is accepted. Thus, it is not surprising that the future Buddha, Maitreya is said to adhere to this school of thought.

ॐ नैकस्मिन्निनसम्भवात् ॐ ॥ २.२.३३॥

On account of impossibility of contrary attributes in the same thing the doctrine is untrue.

The Jaina Anekantavada doctrine is addressed here, which states that everything is classified into seven categories which may either be soul, or non-soul. The existence of any thing is then described as all of the following possible at the same time: real, unreal, neither, both, indescribable. It is absurd to describe anything in such uncertain terms, for this leads to the conclusion that according to Anekantavada, one's own liberation, knowledge and heaven may be real, unreal, both or neither, in which case the relevance of effort in attaining liberation will be put in question.

ॐ एव॑ चात्माकार्त्सन्यम् ॐ ॥ २.२.३४॥

And similarly would arise non universality of the soul.

The theory holds that the soul is of the size of the body. Since the body changes, grows etc,this would render their theory of soul as eternal, untrue, since it would be limited. Further, an elephant reborn as an ant due to its Karma, could hardly fit its soul inside its body.

ॐ न च पर्यायादपृयवरिोध: वकिरादभिय: ॐ ॥ २.२.३५॥

Nor is there consistency, if the soul takes parts to suit different bodies, on account of the change therein.

As the body changes and grows, if the soul were also to adapt by adding and taking away, then such a soul undergoes modification and is non eternal. Eternal Liberaton cannot then be possible or predicated of such a soul.

ॐ अन्त्यावस्थतिश्चोभयनत्ियत्वादवशिषेत् ॐ ॥ २.२.३६॥

Because of permanency of size at the end, there follows permanency of the two preceding sizes, hence there is no difference in size at any time.

If the size of soul is permanent, then it could not have been created, since it exists permanently from the beginning of time. If it is not created, then it should have been permanent in size even as the body's size changed, on which case the soul cannot be the shape of the body. The Jaina doctrine of the soul being the shape of the body must not be taken literally, but figuratively, since the entire theme of Jiva is about Karma Vasanas, and latent tendencies which accrue of various actions done in the past, using the body. That is, as one grows in body, one performs actions, and the Vasanas keep accruing, increasing the figurative size of the soul. After all, it is through such Vasanas that the script of Creation as a Dream is executed. The variations of Jain faith ie Shvetambar and Digambar only differ in the stress on secluded asceticism as mandatory for liberaton, yet both schools equally adhere to Astikaya or maintaining that the world is real and is held so by five different categories of things. Yet, it has already been shown how this view creates problems in that one cannot account for the variation in experiences in wake, dream and sleep states of awareness. Saying dream world is false while awake has the reason Simply because one doesn't experience it while awake. There is no other basis. So on same basis, in deep sleep one doesn't experience wake world and there is no third person or way by which it can be proven real. Thus, that wake world is not real. Dream is on a non existent, and not simply unaware state while in waking state and thus tbere is No point in saying dream is unreal when one is out of it. One says so only because one doesn't experience it now. One can say same about wake world in deep sleep, and this disproves the mistaken belief of reality of the world.

The same holds of other religions such as Christianity, whose philosophy holds the world to be real, and where differences in sects such as Protestant and Catholic is merely a matter on emphasis on faith alone, or in rituals - this resembling the differences between Vedanta and Mimamsa respectively. So too, in Islam, Sufi is the only school that pertains to the Quran as spirituality, while Sunni and Shia remain in the realm of ritualistic religions, caught in a tussle of historic context.

ॐ पत्युरसामञ्जस्यात् ॐ ॥ २.२.३७॥

The Lord being efficient cause alone does not hold due to inconsistency of the doctrine.

In Nyaya, Vaisheshika, Yoga and Maheshwara doctrines, while the Lord is efficient cause, the material cause is either Pradhana or the atoms, while the Lord is the ruler of all these. This is inconsistent because, if the Lord has role in functionality, it would make Him partial to some and cruel to others on account of their experiences. This accusation is absent in Vedanta due to the fact that in the presence of Material Cause alone, that being enjoyment, the Lord ordains everything to that purpose alone.

ॐ संबन्धानुपपत्तेश्च ॐ ॥ २.२.३८॥

And because relation between God and Pradhana is not possible.

If Lord and Pradhana are taken to be both First Causes, efficient and material respectively, positing a relationship would mean that the Lord or Pradhana has parts, which violates their definition. Neither does an inherent relationship become possible, which predicates one as whole and other as parts. The only possibility is that, with creation being a dream, there can only be one dreamer, and that too a sentient One, but not inert.

ॐ अधष्ठिठानानुपपत्तेश्च ॐ ॥ २.२.३९॥

And on account of rulership being impossible.

For God to be a ruler and Pradhana His subject, it must be possible for some means of perception on the Pradhana to receive instructions from God. However, by definition, the Pradhana is devoid of perceptions.

ॐ करणवच्चेन्न भोगादिभिय: ॐ ॥ २.२.४०॥

The claim that Lord rules Pradhana just as Jiva rules senses, is refuted, because of enjoyment.

The Jiva rules sense organs and experiences their pleasure, passion etc. If similar analogy is applied, then it would lead the Lord to experience pleasure and pain etc of the Pradhana, which is not possible because the Lord would not inflict pain on itself.

ॐ अन्तवत्त्वमसर्वज्ञता वा ॐ ॥ २.२.४१॥

More so, the Lord being subject to destruction or non omniscience.

If Lord and Pradhana are both taken to be First Causes, then arises the question: does the Lord know the measure of Pradhana? If yes, then the Pradhana cannot be eternal and infinite. If no, then it means that the Lord is not omniscient. Both violate the definition of both Pradhana and the Lord. Thus, while understanding creation as a dream, there is no viable option but a sentient Lord to be seen as the First Cause of creation, both efficient and material. Then alone, can one talk of an intelligent progress of dream culminating in liberation and enjoyment in bliss.

ॐ उत्पत्त्यसम्भवात् ॐ ॥ २.२.४२॥

Owing to impossibility of origination.

The Bhagavata doctrine is addressed here, which states that from Vasudeva, the Material and efficient Cause of creation, fourfold forms or Vyuhas of Vasudeva, Sankarshana, Pradyumna and Aniruddha arise to perform acts of creation etc. Liberaton of souls occur by devotion, meditation, surrender etc to the Lord. All this is agreeable to Vedanta. What is not logical however is the claim that the Lord creates souls. If the soul be so created, then it is not eternal, and if it is something that is created and destroyed, then liberation cannot be predicated of it. The correct Vedantic view is not that Lord created the soul, but rather that the Lord is the soul.

ॐ न च कर्तुः करणम् ॐ ॥ २.२.४३॥

Nor is the instrument produced from the agent.

The doctrine states that mind arise from the Jiva soul, and from mind ego arises etc. Here again, while the Brahman or Vasudeva possesses a fixed cause ie of enjoyment for creation, the Jiva neither possesses a fixed cause, nor is the mind etc sentient enough to possess a Cause and work for it, by creating something else.

ॐ विज्ञानादिभावे वा तदप्रतिषिध: ॐ ॥ २.२.४४॥

If the four Vyuhas possess intelligence, there's no warding off of that.

On the one hand, if the four Vyuha forms are all the Lord itself and all equal to one another, then all of them are intelligent, which contradicts their own doctrine of one intelligent Lord. On the other hand, if all the

4 Vyuhas are equal, then one cannot have possibly been created from the other, since what is the creator ie Cause is always greater than the created ie effect. Furthermore, by the Bhagavata doctrine itself, the forms of Vasudeva cannot be limited to just four, as everything from Brahma to a blade of grass is a form of Vasudeva.

ॐ वपिरतषिधाच्च ॐ ॥ २.२.४५॥

And because of contradictions.

The doctrine sometimes mentions the 4 Vyuhas as qualities of the Atman, and at other times mentions these are the Atma itself, thus contradicting itself. The essence of Bhagavata doctrine in wholeheartedly accepting Vasudeva as both material and efficient cause of the creation shows accordance with Vedanta. However, the concept of surrender has undoubtedly been exaggerated to gross proportions by stating the soul to be a creation of the Lord, which has been proven illogical. The relationship between the Lord and the soul must be taken as a friend or father-son, as shown by numerous examples Prahlada, Dhruva, Hanuman, Sudama, Arjuna, Andal etc, where such a relationship must not demean either the Lord or His creation and Jiva, which are but His own forms. This is the only way by which one can reach the ultimate purpose of creation, which is enjoyment of bliss with the Lord Govinda, while in His own dream creation, realising that this is all a dream.

In the spirit of clarifying the positions of different religions, the following is an exposition of the three Abrahamic religions, which one may argue have emerged after composing Brahma Sutras, but the claim is refuted here, since the source narration of all three Abrahamic religions, namely that of Adam and Eve, is clearly derived from the Upanishadic story of two doves, Atma and Jiva, one watching while the other eats the fruit of sensory experiences.

This trio of philosophies, namely Bheda, Abheda and Bhdedabheda is not restricted to Dharmic philosophies alone, and one can find this even in Abrahamic religions. For example consider the universally famous Shahada of Islam - La Ilaha Illallaha. From the exoteric to the esoteric, three interpretations are given for this statement. The first is, there is nothing but God, as in there is nothing else worthy of worshipping, even though the world exists with a wide variety of things in it - this is Dvaita. Second, there is no thing but God, as in there is no substance or entity that exists independent of God and controlled by Him, and all the things that appear to exist now, will perish one day, leaving no entity but God remaining -

this is Vishishtadvaita. The third interpretation, characteristic of doctrines such as Wahdat ul Wujud, is There is not a thing but God, referring to the all inclusive view of entire creation within God, as the dream within the dreamer - this is Advaita. The complete surrender, and this destruction of the Ahankara or self, to merge fully in the Divine in nonduality is termed Fanaa. This is achieved by systematically collapsing the distinction perceived between oneself and one's Murshid or teacher, followed by that between oneself and the Rasool or messenger, and finally between oneself and God Allah.

Similarly, the trio can be seen in Christianity too. Statements of Jesus such as John 10:30: I and the Father are one, and also Ye are Gods in Psalms, indicate Advaita. Other statements in the Bible by Jesus, such as Luke 17:21: The Kingdom of God is within you, indicates how the Self and God are of the same nature, and yet are different in that The Kingdom is within you and not you itself - this is Visishtadvaita. Apart from these and similar instances, most of the other verses in Bible including Jesus' sermons, parables etc indicate a real world and thus, Dvaita. The mystical union of oneself with God, spoken of in terms such as Dark Night if the Soul, illustrates the stages crossing which one achieves liberation. The idea is closely connected with Henosis in Platonic traditions, which again seeks the union of the Self with the Divine through understanding the microcosm as a reflection of the macrocosm. Interestingly, the interpretation of the Holy Trinity given by Ramana Maharshi reflects its Advaita context - The Holy Spirit represents the Atman or soul, the Son represents Guru while the Father represents God. In Surrender the Son takes the body and its ego, represented by the Crucifix, onto Himself, and destroys it, merging the soul ie the Holy Spirit into God.

In Judaism, there is the mystic Kabbalah traditions that speak of concepts such as reincarnation Gilgul, and Yehodah which is one of the highest planes of consciousness where a soul can achieve union with the Divine. Popularised and reinforced in Hasidic Judaism, speaks about the Bitul Ha Yesh, ie negation of the existent, in which, through abandoning of material concerns in favour of spiritual ones, a devotee sees beyond the illusory facade if the world that meets the eye, and understands that there is nothing but God. Essentially one perceives himself as Ein, which is the name of God meaning both nothing as well as infinite, and that takes one to the highest ideal called Hitpashtut ya Gashmiyut, which is the removal of corporeality, since it is believed that this is the reversal of the contraction of the Divine which is what makes the worldly illusion possible. The Divine soul within one is called Nefesh Elohit, which is the sentience of the first cause in that it constantly craves this communion with the Divine.

ॐ न वयिदश॒रुतः ॐ ॥ २.३.१॥

Akasa is not created as it is not stated so in Sruthi.

A claim is raised with texts like Chhandogya 6.2.8 mentioning creation of fire etc but not Akasha.

ॐ अस्तति॒ॐ ॥ २.३.२॥

But there is a Sruthi text.

The claim is refuted using Taittiriya 2.1 saying Akasha sprang forth from Brahman.

ॐ गौण्यसम्भवात् ॐ ॥ २.३.३॥

Sruthi text dealing with Akasa is to be taken in secondary sense on account of impossibility of being created.

A claim is raised on the basis that Akasa has no parts, and is all pervading and thus may be interpreted as eternal.

ॐ शब्दाच्च ॐ ॥ २.३.४॥

Also from Sruthis Akasa is eternal.

Claim is furthered citing Brihadaranyaka 2.3.3 stating Vayu and Akasa are immortal.

ॐ स्याच्चैकस्य ब्रह्मशब्दवत् ॐ ॥ २.३.५॥

It is possible that sprang may be used in secondary sense like Brahman.

Reference to Taittiriya 3.2 and 3.6 using Brahman in secondary and primary context to refer to food and Bliss. In same way, sprang may have been used. This furthers the claim.

ॐ प्रतज्ञाहानिरव्यतरिकाच्छब्दभेयः ॐ ॥ २.३.६॥

Non abandonment of proposition ie by knowledge of which everything is known, can result only in non distinction of entire world from Brahman, this established from Sruthis.

The claim is refuted on the basis of Sruthis claiming that knowing Brahman everything will be known. This is possible only if everything has been created by Brahman. If Akasa is eternal and independent of Brahman, then knowing Brahman will still result in not knowing Akasa, which violates the statement that everything is known.

ॐ यावद्वकिरं त्वभिागो लोकवत् ॐ ॥ २.३.७॥

But in all effects whatsoever there is separateness as seen in the world.

Everything that is created such as a pot or cloth are different from each other. There is nothing that can have separateness about it and still be eternal. On this account, Akasa being different than Agni or earth, means it is created.

ॐ एतेन मातरिश्वा व्याख्यातः ॐ ॥ २.३.८॥

By this same explanation, the fact of air being an effect ie created is also explained.

ॐ असम्भवस्तु सतोऽनुपपत्तेः ॐ ॥ २.३.९॥

But there can be no origin of Sat, as it stands to reason.

Reference to Shvetashvatara 4.3 stating Brahman is born. But the claim that Brahman is created is refuted in that it is existence itself, and there is no cause for it to be the effect. Further existence cannot be possible from non existence. References to Chhandogya6.2.2 and Brihadaranyaka 4.4.25 about Self being birthless. Essentially, Brahman is the dreamer, the first cause, ordaining with a purpose ie enjoyment.

ॐ तेजोऽतस्तथा ह्याह ॐ ॥ २.३.१०॥

Fire is created from air, says Sruthi.

Reference to Taittiriya 2.1 as air creating fire while at the same time Chhandogya 6.2.3 saying Brahman created fire. The latter must be taken only as an indirect cause for fire, since Brahman is the direct or indirect cause and ultimate origin of everything.

ॐ आपः ॐ ॥ २.३.११॥

Water is produced from fire.

The same argument holds, with water created from fire and Brahman as per Taittiriya 2.1 and Chhandogya 6.2.3.

ॐ पृथ्विव्यधिकाररूपशब्दान्तरादभ्यिः ॐ ॥ २.३.१२॥

Earth is meant by the word Anna because of subject matter and color, and other Sruthis.

Taittiriya 2.1 says water created earth while Chhandogya 6.2.4 says water created Anna. Yet in Chhandogya 6.4.1 it is said that black colour in fire is Anna. Hence in these references, Anna refers to Earth and not food.

ॐ तदभिध्यानादेव तु तल्लिङ्गात् सः ॐ ॥ २.३.१३॥

But because of His reflecting only are subsequent elements created from previous element, hence Brahman is the creator of air etc, We know from indicatory marks.

Even though there were explanations that Akasa created air, air created fire etc, none of these elements are either sentient or have a Cause for creation, these elements being inert themselves. It is Brahman alone that is sentient and has a Cause for creation, while also intelligent. Thus it is Brahman alone that creates each element by dwelling on its previous element.

ॐ विपिर्ययेण तु क्रमोऽत उपपद्यते च ॐ ॥ २.३.१४॥

At Pralaya the elements are withdrawn into Brahman in the reverse order, and this is reasonable.

Just like ice melts into water, each element as an effect goes back into and merges into its immediate cause, all the way back to Akasha and Brahman.

ॐ अन्तरा विज्ञानमनसी क्रमेण तल्लङ्गिादिति
चेन्नावशिषात् ॐ ॥ २.३.१५॥

The claim that between Brahman and elements the intellect is mentioned and therefore that ought to be the order of creation and inverse in reabsorption owing to instructions on Sruthis, we refute on account of non difference between intellect and elements.

Reference is to Mundaka 2.1.3 which mentions mind, Prana and senses in between Brahman and the elements. This is refuted on that the Mundaka reference must not be taken as an order of creation. But still Chhandogya 6.6.5 mentions how mind consists of elements such as earth etc. This is because the intellect, mind and organs can all be an effect of the elements, and thus are created only after elements are created.

ॐ चराचरव्यपाश्रयस्तु स्यात् तद्व्यपदेशो भाक्तः
तद्भावभावित्वात् ॐ ॥ २.३.१६॥

But the mention of birth and death of soul is apt only with references to the body of moving and stationary beings. With reference to soul it is only secondary on account of those terms requiring existence of the body.

The impossibility of the soul dying is mentioned in Chhandogya 6.11 3 and Brihadaranyaka 4.3.8. This is because the soul is nothing but a reflection of the dreamer ie Brahman. It is the experiencer of the dream and is thus the dreamer himself who will continue even after the dream ends.

ॐ नात्मा अश्रुतेर्नित्यत्वाच्च ताभ्यः ॐ ॥ २.३.१७॥

Individual soul is not produced, for it is not mentioned so in scriptures. Also on account of it being external, as it is known from Sruthis.

Reference to Katha1.2.18 and Brihadaranyaka 4.4.25 mentioning the soul as eternal and birthless. It is indeed the Brahman, the Self that appears as the soul.

ॐ ज्ञोऽत एव ॐ ॥ २.३.१८॥

For this very reason, individual soul is intelligence itself.

It is already established that Brahman as the first cause is sentient and intelligent and capable of experience. Also it is known that whole of creation is a dream and is thus unreal. In that creation, every character that is created is an effect of Brahman and serves the cause of Brahman ie enjoyment of bliss. The dream characters are all insentient and incapable of experience. Given this, and given that the soul experiences pleasure, pain etc, the soul cannot be any dream character but is Brahman itself. Thus, the soul is that towards which the whole dream is oriented as the means of serving the first cause. As the orientation of the dream, the soul is eternal, since the dream itself is real. So too, the soul is the Self in that dream, despite associating itself with a certain character in the dream and imposing the pleasure and pain of that character onto itself. Yet these experiences of pleasure and pain are due to not properly realising the nature of creation as a dream.

Reference to Brihadaranyaka 4.3.22 saying that the soul does not see anything apart from itself, and even in deep sleep, although seeing, it does not see. But the simple fact that a person mentions that he slept well, shows that he must have been existent at that time. In short, the soul is assigned all experiences, which is possible only for a sentient thing, and thus the soul is intelligent.

ॐ युक्तशेच ॐ ॥ २.३.१९॥

ॐ उत्क्रान्तगित्यागतीनाम् ॐ ॥ २.३.२०॥

As Sruthis declare the soul's passing out, going to other realms and returning, the soul is not infinite in size.

Reference to Shvetashvatara 6.11 as the soul as all pervading and to Mundaka 3.1.9 mentioning soul as atomic, both contradicting each other. In that context, a claim is raised. For soul to go to other realms, it cannot be all pervading but atomic.

ॐ स्वात्मना चोत्तरयो: ॐ ॥ २.३.२१॥

And the going and coming connected directly with their agent.

Going and coming, as transporting from one place to another, is not possible for an all pervading entity which does not have a localised space.

ॐ नाणुरतत् श्रुतेरिति चिन्नेन इतराधिकिरात् ॐ ॥ २.३.२२॥

The claim that soul is not atomic due to all pervading mention, we refute, as Brahman is the subject of that reference.

This furthers the claim.

ॐ स्वशब्दोन्मानाभ्यां च ॐ ॥ २.३.२३॥

And on account of direct statements and infinitesimal measure.

Shvetashvatara 5.9 mentions the soul is part of a hundredth part of the tip of a hair divided by a hundred times. This furthers the atomic claim.

ॐ अविरोधश्चन्दनवत् ॐ ॥ २.३.२४॥

There is no contradiction like the sandal paste.

The soul even though atomic, occupying only one part of the body, experiences happiness and misery even throughout the body, just as how sandal paste applied to any one part gives pleasant feeling throughout the body.

ॐ अवस्थितिविशेष्यादिति चेन्नाभ्युपगमाद्धृदृद्धि हि ॐ ॥ २.३.२५॥

The claim that sandal paste location is just an analogy, we refute, on the admission by scriptures of the soul having a special location, ie the heart.

Reference to heart as location in Brihadaranyaka 4.3.7.

ॐ गुणाद्वाऽऽलोकवत् ॐ ॥ २.३.२६॥

Or owing to its quality as intelligence in this world.

Just like light in a corner of the room illuminates the entire room, the soul on account of intelligence pervades the whole body. This furthers the atomic claim.

ॐ व्यतिरेको गन्धवत् तथा च दर्शयति ॐ ॥ २.३.२७॥

Extension of intelligence beyond soul is like odour that extends beyond the fragrant object.

This furthers the claim using flower analogy, whose fragrance spreads far and wide than the flower size.

ॐ पृथगुपदेशात् ॐ ॥ २.३.२८॥

On account of separate teaching of Sruthi that the soul so pervades the body due to intelligence.

Reference is to Kaushitaki 3.6. Intelligence and soul are related as instrument and agent.

ॐ तद्गुणसारत्वात्तत्तद्व्यपदेशः प्राज्ञवत् ॐ ॥ २.३.२९॥

However, the declaration of atomic size is on account of its having for its essence qualities of that ie Buddhi, even as the intelligent Brahman which is all pervading is declared to be atomic.

The atomic claim raised and furthered in previous Sutras is refuted. Given that Brahman itself has entered the universe as the soul, which is identical with it, is all pervading, the mention of atomicity are on account of preponderance in the qualities of Buddhi etc so long as it is imagined to be connected with the latter and bondage. This is again, as mentioned earlier, the Self as soul superimposing the limited identity of an insentient dream character onto itself, and this mismatch of type, insentient imposed on sentient is bound to cause misery and sorrow. However, among the two entities involved ie soul and dream character, it is the soul that is sentient and experiences the misery.

ॐ यावदात्मभावित्विाच्च न दोषस्तद्दर्शनात् ॐ ॥ २.३.३०॥

And there is no defect in previous Sutra as the conjunction with intellect exists so long as soul exists in its relative aspect, because it is so seen in the scripture.

The connection of the soul with Buddhi lasts as long as the soul's state of Samsara ie individualisation, is not destroyed by knowledge and realising of creation as a dream. Reference to Brihadaranyaka 4.3.7 that soul moves with intellect even after death. Essentially, as long as the first cause ie enjoyment is not achieved, the creation ie dream does not cease. Different births are merely different scenes of the dream. As long as the script of the dream lasts, there will be continuity between scenes. In that case, the soul will continue with its conjunction of the dream creation ie Buddhi.

ॐ पुंस्त्वादिवत्त्वस्य सतोऽभिव्यक्तियोगात् ॐ ॥ २.३.३१॥

On account of manifestation of conjunction in waking state possible only on existing potentially in deep sleep, like virility.

If it is claimed that in deep sleep, when dream creation does not happen, then there is no connection between soul and Buddhi, that claim is refuted, since as long as the prime cause has not been served, neither has the dream ended, nor the connection severed, but is there in a subtle and fine state.

ॐ नित्योपलब्ध्यनुपलब्धिप्रसङ्गोऽन्यतरनियमो

वाऽन्यथा ॐ ॥ २.३.३२॥

Otherwise if intellect or mind be not accepted there would result either perpetual perception or perpetual non perception, or limitation of the power of either the soul or senses.

The basis of accepting an internal organ, of which the Buddhi is a mode, is as follows: If not accepted, with the senses always in contact with objects, there would be perpetual perception since all ingredients as soul, senses and objects are present. If this is denied then, no perception or knowledge can ever result. In that case one will have to accept the limitation of the power of the soul, which is not possible as it is changeless,or of the senses which given is not impeded in past or future, can be limited in the present. Thus, the internal organ and its modes, are a necessity, and are that part of the dream creation that are in control of the script of the dream, so that the Self as soul has experiences.

ॐ कर्ता शास्त्रार्थवत्त्वात् ॐ ॥ २.३.३३॥

Soul is an agent, on account of scriptural injunctions having meaning on that ground only.

The Sruthi enjoins various acts on the soul, such as He is to sacrifice etc, and this is possible only if the soul is an agent.

ॐ वहिारोपदेशात् ॐ ॥ २.३.३४॥

And on account of Sruthi teaching its wandering about.

Reference to Brihadaranyaka 2.1.18 showing that only an agent may perform activities like wandering.

ॐ उपादानात् ॐ ॥ २.३.३५॥

On account of taking organs.

The same reference shows that soul in the dream state takes the organs with it.

ॐ व्यपदेशाच्च क्रियायां न चेन्निर्दिशेवपिर्यय: ॐ ॥ २.३.३६॥

On account of mentioning soul as an agent by scriptures with respect to action. If it were not so, the reference would have been of different kind.

Reference is to Taittiriya 2.5, referring to soul as intelligence, and performing activities. The intelligence is soul and not Buddhi, otherwise the mention would have been By intelligence, as instrumentality.

ॐ उपलब्धवदिनयिम: ॐ ॥ २.३.३७॥

As in the case of perception, there is no rule here also.

The claim that if soul were an agent, wouldn't perform acts painful to itself, is refuted. This is because the activity the soul performs is not bound by rules, but by the limitation that it has imposed on itself, in conjunction with the Buddhi. Taken in another sense, to satisfy the prime cause of enjoyment, the Self, which is the only sentient One capable of experience gets in conjunction with the script of the dream ie Buddhi. Thus, free of Buddhi, the soul would not perform any actions. This means that various actions are performed primarily in accordance with the script ie Buddhi alone. This completely and outright negates and refutes the doctrine of free will, by stating that all actions that happen, do so by the script, ie Divine Will in alignment with the first cause. The only case of free will the soul has is to realise the creation as a dream, and abide in its real state, which it can when full knowledge is acquired.

ॐ शक्तविपिर्ययात् ॐ ॥ २.३.३८॥

On account of reversal of power of Buddhi which is inadmissible.

If Buddhi becomes agent rather than instrument, then some other thing must be taken as instrument.

ॐ समाध्यभावाच्छ ॐ ॥ २.३.३९॥

On account of impossibility of Samadhi.

Reference is to Brihadaranyaka 2.4.5 mentioning realizing of Atma through Samadhi, which would be impossible if soul is not taken as an agent. Neither will it be capable of hearing, comprehending and Meditation as the means to Samadhi nor will it be capable of liberation. Thus, the soul, and not Buddhi is the agent.

ॐ यथा च तक्षोभयथा ॐ ॥ २.३.४०॥

And even as a carpenter is both.

The Nyaya doctrine that agency is the soul's real nature, is refuted. Reference to Brihadaranyaka 4.3.15 saying that the soul is non attached, means that the soul takes up the role of an agent only when the dream creations are present including Buddhi ie the script. When in connection with Buddhi, ie even after death, the soul is still attached to the script, as ie dream continues. And while dream creations are manifest, such as body etc, the soul is attached to the body due to the script, which is when it experiences joy and sorrow. When through Realization, the soul has no attachment with the script, and is no longer an agent.

ॐ परात्तु तच्छ्रुतेः ॐ ॥ २.३.४१॥

But even that agency of soul is from the supreme Lord as per Sruthi.

Reference to Kaushitaki 3.8, and as already specified, as the sentient prime cause, Brahman alone ordains all actions, through the script. It is for these actions that the soul is an agent.

ॐ कृतप्रयत्नोपेक्षस्तु वहितिप्रतिषिद्धावैयर्थ्यादिभ्यः ॐ ॥ २.३.४२॥

But the Lord's making the soul act depends on work done by it, then only would injunctions and prohibitions be relevant.

It is already explained how Self ordains through the script. However, seeing the present actions with the soul as agent, leads to even seeing soul as agent for past actions, which are in reality, part of the same script. However, as long as the soul is deluded into thinking as the agent, injunctions will apply.

ॐ अंशो नानाव्यपदेशादन्यथा चापि
दाशकितवादित्विमधीयत एके ॐ ॥ २.३.४३॥

Soul is part of the Lord, on account of difference between the two being declared and otherwise also, as non different from Brahman. For in some Sakhas, Brahman is spoken of as being fishermen etc.

The relationship between soul and Brahman is the key factor on which the entire prime cause of creation and maximising bliss, is built. Thus, with Brahman always unchanging, and with the entire creation nothing but a dream, the only factor that changes throughout the process, minimising and maximising bliss, is this relation between soul and Self. As such, it must be taken in two parts. As much as knowledge of reality is not attained, the soul is a part of Self, whereas when such knowledge is attained, the soul and Self are one. In other words, as long as the dream is maintained as reality, the soul is a part of the Self. As long as the reality of the dream ceases to exist ie it is revealed as unreal, then the soul is the Self.

ॐ मन्त्रवर्णात् ॐ ॥ २.३.४४॥

Also from words of Mantra

Reference to Chhandogya 3.12.6 mentioning soul as part of Self.

ॐ अपि स्मर्यते ॐ ॥ २.३.४५॥ पाठभेदे अपि च स्मर्यते

As also in Smriti.

Reference to Gita 15.7.

ॐ प्रकाशादविन्नैव परः ॐ ॥ २.३.४६॥

Self is not affected by pleasure and pain like soul, even as light is not affected by the shape of things it touches.

It is already said how the entire creation is a dream. Just as a dream injury does not show up as a wound in the dreamer's body, so too, pleasure and pain do not affect the Self.

ॐ स्मरन्ति च ॐ ॥ २.३.४७॥

Smritis too state so.

ॐ अनुज्ञापरिहारौ देहसम्बन्धाज्ज्योतिरादिवत् ॐ ॥ २.३.४८॥

Injunction and prohibition are possible on account of connection of Self with body, as like light.

It is already said, how concept of agency is not the soul's original nature, and arises only on conjunction with Buddhi and the script. Only when agency arises, does the possibility of injunctions and prohibition.

ॐ असन्ततेश्चाव्यतिकिरः ॐ ॥ २.३.४९॥

And on account of non extension of soul beyond its own body, there is no confusion of results of actions.

Here again, individualized soul ie with agency has superimposed on itself a well defined limitation, that of the body. Then there is no question of the action of somebody else affecting the soul.

ॐ आभास एव च ॐ ॥ २.३.५०॥

And the soul is only a reflection of the Self

The analogy of sun reflecting in pots of water is reinforced here.

ॐ अदृष्टानयिमात् ॐ ॥ २.३.५१॥

There being no fixity about the unseen.

Reference to Sankhya, Nyaya and other schools which talk about a plurality of souls, all of them all pervading. In that case there would ensue terrible confusion about the fruits of action. The root cause for this confusion again is understanding of the world as real.

ॐ अभसिन्ध्यादष्विपर्चिवैम् ॐ ॥ २.३.५२॥

And even as regards resolve etc it would be so.

In the Sankhya resolve one makes to achieve anything will result in Adrishta allocated to the souls, when again the confusion of overlap will occur.

ॐ प्रदेशादतिचिन्नेन्नान्तर्भावात् ॐ ॥ २.३.५३॥

The claim that distinction of pleasure and pain arise from difference of location, we refute on account of the Self being in all bodies.

Again it is reinforced that the idea of many selves is nothing but an ignorance, which the soul undergoes due to attachment with the script ie Buddhi. In reality, neither the world nor its many selves and characters is real. All that does exist is Brahman alone.

ॐ तथा प्राणा: ॐ ॥ २.४.१॥

Likewise the organs Prana are produced from Brahman.

Organs are the primary means of enjoyment in the created world, which is an aspect of the objective by which Brahman created. Indeed, only the Effect can be produced from Cause and not vice versa.

ॐ गौण्यसम्भवात् ॐ ॥ २.४.२॥

A secondary sense of interpretation Gaunah is rendered impossible.

It is impossible to assume that organs existed before creation, since then there would be no explanation of how or what cause can lead to the creation of Brahman from the organs. Again the One creating the All view is also put on jeopardy due to the incorrect assumption.

ॐ प्रतज्ञिआनपुरोधाच्च ॐ ॥ २.४.३॥ पाठभेदे sUtra absent

ॐ तत्पुराक्श्रतुणेश्च ॐ ॥ २.४.४॥

More so because the Vedas Shruthi mentions Brahman as the first originated Prak, earlier to the organs.

Yet again the simple idea that cause must precede effect is invoked here. This is why the Brahman the enjoyer exists earlier to the organs, the enjoyed.

ॐ तत्पूर्वकत्वाद्वाचः ॐ ॥ २.४.५॥

On account of the organ of speech Vaacha being preceded by the elements of nature.

It is well mentioned in texts such as Chhandogya as well as common scientific nature that the organs are made of various elements since these are physical objects. In this account, the organs could not have occurred earlier than the elements themselves.

ॐ सप्त गतेर्वशिषितित्वाच्च ॐ ॥ २.४.६॥

It is known from scriptures that the organs are seven Sapta in number on account of their specifications.

Texts such as Mundaka and Taittiriya Samhita enumerate the seven organs as eyes, nose, ears, tongue, speech, touch and inner organ.

ॐ हस्तादयस्तु स्थितेऽतो नैवम् ॐ ॥ २.४.७॥

However, Scriptures mention hand Hasta too to be an organ, and since it is a fact, the total organs are much more than seven.

Since the hands are specialised body parts to perform specified tasks, they do qualify as an organ, and by this logic, one must add four more organs to the above enumerated seven. These are hands, legs, Excretory and Procreative organs, bringing the total to 11 organs.

ॐ अणवश्च ॐ ॥ २.४.८॥

The organs are minute Anava.

Minute in one context refers that they are finite in size, especially in relation with the entire size of creation itself. But more importantly, the fact that each organ can only sense at any given time, a tiny slice of the entire universe, is enough evidence of their minuteness.

ॐ श्रेष्ठश्च ॐ ॥ २.४.९॥

And the Chief Shreshtha Vital Force Prana is also produced from Brahman.

Brihadaranyaka already states how life is impossible without Prana, and as the sustainer of life, it is the chief vital force. However, the sustenance of life itself is to serve a certain cause, that of enjoyment of the creation by Brahman. Thus, as effect coming after cause, Prana is created from

Brahman.

ॐ न वायुक्रियि पृथगुपदेशात् ॐ ॥ २.४.१०॥

Bring separately mentioned Pruthag, Prana is neither air Vayu nor Kriya.

The argument that Prana is simply air that also exists outside the body begs the question, why then is life not there outside the body? Also, Prana is mentioned as a creation of Brahman, and thus cannot be an emergent outcome of other actions in the body.

ॐ चक्षुरादवित्त् तत्सहशष्ट्यादभिय: ॐ ॥ २.४.११॥

On account of being mentioned along with eye Chakshu and other organs, Prana too is subordinate to the soul.

The reference is that since organs already are subordinate to the soul and satisfying a certain cause of Brahman as enjoyment, Prana too follows suit.

ॐ अकरणत्वाच्च न दोषस्तथा हि दर्शयति ॐ ॥ २.४.१२॥

The scriptures teach that there is no objection on account of Prana not being an instrument Karana.

The earlier Sutras have already enumerated 11 functions, and thus 11 organs matching them. There is no room for a 12th organ, and thus the Prana cannot be an instrument of the soul.

ॐ पञ्चवत्तूतर्मिनोवद्व्यपदिश्यते ॐ ॥ २.४.१३॥

It is taught as having a fivefold aspect Panchavritti like the mind Mana.

The mind, has fourfold expansions, namely Chitta, Manas, Ahankara and Buddhi. Similarly there are five aspects of Prana as Prana, Apana, Vyana, Udana and Samana.

ॐ अणुश्च ॐ ॥ २.४.१४॥

Prana is minute Anu.

As a component of creation that enables life and thus enjoyment for Brahman, Prana is crucial. Yet, as much as there are millions of beings created, one Prana enables life only in one limited creation, and thus, it is minute in effect.

ॐ ज्योतिरिद्यधष्ठिान ं त् तदामननात् ॐ ॥ २.४.१५॥

But there is the presiding over of organs by fire Jyothi and others, as mentioned in scriptures.

This further reinforces the fact that Prana and other organs exist merely to satisfy a Cause, and to direct its activity properly, the Gods preside over them.

ॐ पूराणवता शब्दात् ॐ ॥ २.४.१६॥

From the scriptures, the organs are connected with the one possessing them.

Fundamentally, the one who controls the organs, and experiences the results would have to be a sentient One, and that is the soul, and for this reason, the organs and functionality are connected only with the soul, and not with Gods like fire, who themselves are insentient creations.

ॐ तस्य च नतियत्वात् ॐ ॥ २.४.१७॥

More so on account of permanence Nithyathva of the soul in residing in the body.

The soul, to satisfy the purpose of enjoyment, would of course exist continously in the body, while the Gods, themselves here only to serve the purpose would not be capable or entitled to such enjoyments.

ॐ त इन्द्रयिाणि तिद्वय्पदेशादन्यत्र श्रष्ठात् ॐ ॥ २.४.१८॥

Except the chief Shreshtha, the other Pranas are designated as organs Indriya, on account of being designated thus by the scriptures.

The Mundaka mentions Prana and organs separately as arising from Brahman, which implies that the organs are different from Prana.

ॐ भदेशर्तुे: ॐ ॥ २.४.१९॥

On account of differentiating portions in texts.

This is to emphasise that texts like Brihadaranyaka mentions Prana and organs in separate sections.

ॐ वैलक्षण्याच्च ॐ ॥ २.४.२०॥

ॐ संज्ञामूर्तकिल्पूतसित् तुरवितृकरूवत उपदेशात् ॐ ॥ २.४.२१॥

But the apt arrangement of names and forms is the work of Him who makes the triple agglomeration.

Reference to Chhandogya 6.3.2 making each of these three deities of fire, water and earth. The claim that this is done by the Jiva is refuted on account that this is tied with the first cause and thus, possible for Brahman alone.

ॐ मांसादि भौम ंयथाशब्दमतिरयोश्च ॐ ॥ २.४.२२॥

Flesh returns back to Earth, as also with regards to fire and water.

Essentially all organs of the body are produced by the aspects and elements of nature, and will subsequently return back upon death.

ॐ वैशेष्यात्त् तद्वादस्तद्वाद: ॐ ॥ २.४.२३॥

On account of preponderance is given the special name.

Names of fine elements fire, water and earth, are used for a gross element on the basis of which one is most dominant in it.

CHAPTER SEVEN

Epistemology

ॐ तदन्तरप्रतिपत्तौ रंहति सम्परष्विवक्तः
प्रश्ननरूपणाभ्याम् ॐ ॥ ३.१.१॥

From question and answer it is known that the soul goes out of the body enveloped with subtle tendencies Samparishvakta, in search of a new body.

It is already emphasised how the entirety of creation is but a dream. Every dreamer realizes the wrongly assumed reality to be a dream upon waking up. Yet, to realise that it is a dream while dreaming itself is a challenge. That comes with wisdom and surrender alone, at which stage one's involvement in the dream world taking it to be real, ceases. The subtle tendencies, called Vasanas are nothing but one's involvement in the dream. As long as these last, dreams will not cease. Death and rebirth in a new body are in reality nothing but a location and settings change in the dream, sometimes even as a new dream, one better suited to the Vasanas remaining at death.

ॐ त्र्यात्मकत्वात्तु भूयस्त्वात् ॐ ॥ ३.१.२॥

In spite of water containing all three elements Thrayathmaka, water alone is mentioned considering its preponderance in the body.

The reference is to Chhandogya which explains the biological process as a Yajna or sacrifice where Sraddha, Soma, Rain, Food and Seed are given in oblations to five kinds of fires, from which result respectively heavens, rains, earth, man and woman. In this, the fifth oblation calls man as water. Scientifically, the human body is indeed composed of all elements of nature, yet three quarters of the human body is undeniably water, hence the mention of water as man.

ॐ प्राणगतेश्च ॐ ॥ ३.१.३॥

And because of the going of sense organs.

As mentioned earlier, so long as the Vasanas last, dream after dream ie birth after birth will be generated. The Vasanas are all about involvement and enjoyment in the world, which is possible only through the sense organs. Thus, every life, from birth to death will contain the senses. In death even as the body is destroyed, the next birth opens with all sense organs, with the same Vasanas seen at time of death. Thus, one can effectively say that sense organs too go along with Vasanas in search of a body. Yet, for sense organs to go, their bases as the subtle elements must go too, and this is what texts like Brihadaranyaka claim.

ॐ अग्न्यादगितशिरुतेरेति चिनेन भाक्तत्वात् ॐ ॥ ३.१.४॥

The claim quoting scriptures that organs enter into fire Agnyadi and thus do not go along with the soul, we refute on the basis that the scriptures are to be taken in a secondary sense. Bhaktatvat.

It is again emphasised here that one birth is nothing but a dream, and death simply means the end of that dream. If the dream ends, all characters in the dream end, along with the deceased body, relatives, surroundings etc. Then there is no question of cremation or of organs burning there. Any cremation of any other human witnessed is nothing but an illusion, just like everything else in the dream. In reality, all that happens is, a new dream is generated, maintaining the Vasanas.

ॐ प्रथमेऽश्रवणादति चिनेन ता एव ह्युपपत्तेः ॐ ॥ ३.१.५॥

The claim that water is not mentioned in the first oblation, we refute on the basis of Sraddha meaning water alone on the appropriateness of interpretation.

Taittiriya Samhita clarifies this point saying water is indeed Sraddha. As already mentioned, the subtle elements like water are mentioned as going with the soul only to account for the continuity of Vasanas. That is, physical entities have their basis in mental entities, and not vice versa. In that context, water, as an instrument for propagating Vasanas has its basis in desire, a form of which is Sraddha.

The concept of Sraddha can be understood scientifically as follows. If Vedic injunctions are strictly followed, then a person typically follows all 4 Ashramas and in the last few days, enters Sanyasa Ashrama. In the Diksha or initiation process, one invokes Praisha Agni and internally burns the body and all the defects associated with it (The author can personally attest to this fact by virtue of extreme body heat with temperatures as high as 103F experienced in the three days immediately following Diksha). Typically bodily defects are present in the body so as to exhaust Karma Vasanas through it. In the Sanyasa stage, a person enters the spiritual path which means the task of driving one's mind to the correct destination is achieved, and hence bodily defects are no longer required, and thus Praisha Agni. For this reason, Sanyasis are buried and not burnt upon death, and their body returns back to nature, its original source from which the body had been formed all these years through food. For a person not yet undertaken Sanyasa, and thus with bodily defects present, the body cannot be buried upon death, since all creatures that feast upon this body and decompose will carry forward these defects. For this purpose, the practice of Cremation upon death is performed. However, in that case, one cuts off the supply of food to the many organisms which are decomposers and scavengers like crows, dogs, vultures, ants and many more. As a compensation to this, the ritual of Sraddha is performed yearly, where the Pinda or ball of rice along with water is given to nature, since it is this rice that sustained the body as staple food. In doing so, one does Sankalpam specifying the particular person and his lineage, for whom Sraddha is performed. Pronouncing the Aksharas or syllables that make up the person's name invokes the same pattern of sound energy that was invoked when the person was alive, due to people calling out his name. Kanchi Mahaperiyava has mentioned the role Aksharas and sound plays in the formation of clouds and rain. Thus, by and large, Sraddha is a systematic tradition followed, to give compensation for violating nature. There is also the practice of offering greens to cows, to get relief from Pitru Dosha originating from ancestors, and this too pertains to the same context. The use of various products originating from the cow spiritually in Yajnas etc, and ecologically as manure etc needs no introduction.

ॐ अशरुतत्वादिति चेन्नेष्टादिकारिणाि प्रतीतेः ॐ ॥ ३.१.६॥

The claim that scriptures do not mention the soul departing enveloped with water, is refuted on the basis of scriptures mentioning that only performers of sacrifices Ishtadikarinam go to heavens.

Purity of mind is an essential requirement for a person to sufficiently understand reality as a dream, while in it. The removal of worldly involvement can only occur through the spirit of sacrifice and readiness to give up. This is why scriptures mention the one performing sacrifices and good deeds alone as one going to heavens ie progressing spiritually. Thus, while the mention of five oblations do refer to water eventually becoming man, it is possible only in the subtle form, on the basis of soul getting purified successively.

ॐ भाक्तं वाऽनात्मवत्तित्वात् तथा हि दर्शयति ॐ ॥ ३.१.७॥

However, the souls being mentioned as a food for the Gods, must be taken in a secondary sense on account of the souls not knowing the Self Anathmavithvath.

It is already emphasised how the Gods, also being insentient creations of the dream, do not have the capability to experience enjoyment. On that basis, one can comfortably say that the souls being the food ie enjoyment of Devas ie Gods, cannot possibly be literally taken. What does happen of course, is, as long as the Self is not realized, the soul Jiva is in the mercy of the dream creator, and has no freedom of its own, but has to follow the script of the dream. The Gods are mere instruments in executing the script.

ॐ कृतात्ययेऽनुशयवान् दृष्टस्मृतृभ्याम् ॐ ॥ ३.१.८॥

As per both Shruthi and Smriti, the soul, having exhausted the merit of its good deeds Krithathvaye, possessed of residual Karma Anushayavan, takes a different path.

The reference here is to the soul descending back to Earth, having exhausted the fruits of its previous good Karmas. A clear distinction is made here on the concept of Punya-Papa and Karma Vasanas. Punya, the good deeds done in one's life time, have their merits which are enjoyed in heaven, while the Karma Vasanas stay on, to the next birth on Earth. This alone explains why babies born on the same day in the same region have varying features and varying experiences of misery and joy. In the context of dream however, the Earth is as much a dream as the heavens. Both are dream creations spinning out of Brahman, and both serve the common purpose of causality ie the law of Karma.

पाठभेदे 3.1.8 and 9 combined

ॐ यथेतमनेवं च ॐ ॥ ३.१.९॥

ॐ चरणादिति चिन्नोपलक्षणार्थेति कार्ष्णाजनिः ॐ ॥ ३.१.१०॥

The claim that, rebirth is based on conduct Charana only and not Karma Vasanas, is refuted on the basis that conduct indirectly Upalakshana refers to these Vasanas, thus thinks the Rishi Karshnajani.

The difference between Punya and Karma Vasanas have already been elucidated. There are reference in texts like Chhandogya that state that a good conduct leads to a good birth. But that does not happen directly, since a good conduct purifies the mind and thus alters the Karma Vasanas, which are nothing but tendencies and preferences of a person toward certain things and away from others.

ॐ आनर्थक्यमिति चिन्नेन तदपेक्षत्वात् ॐ ॥ ३.१.११॥

The claim that conduct is irrelevant Anarthakya since only Karma determines next birth, is refuted, on account on the latter depending on the former.

The point explained in previous Sutra is further reinforced here.

ॐ सुकृतदुष्कृते एवेति तु बादरिः ॐ ॥ ३.१.१२॥

However, conduct is merely good and bad deeds, Sakrutha Dushkrutha, as per sage Badari.

As much as the direct effect of Karma Vasanas and the indirect effect of conduct on a new birth has been explained, it is also understood that, what is defined as conduct is ultimately one's own good and bad deeds, which are again Karma, which in turn, arise from the Vasanas - all this is a cycle, one leading to another.

ॐ अनिष्टादकिारणिमपि च श्रुतम् ॐ ॥ ३.१.१३॥

The scriptures declare that those who do not perform sacrifices Anishtadikarinam, also go to heaven.

Again it is emphasised here that heaven is a dream creation, just like Earth, but with a different setting. The simple fact that Karma Vasanas of a person remain, irrespective of good or bad, directly implies that the dream creation of heaven is imminent upon death on Earth.

ॐ संयमने त्वनुभूयेतरेषामारोहावरोहौ
तद्गतिदर्शनात् ॐ ॥ ३.१.१४॥

The Sruthis declare in passages that those who have not performed sacrifices ascend Aroha to the abode of Yama Samyama and then descend back to the Earth Avaroha.

While the previous Sutra mentions heaven in the simple context of an afterworld, this Sutra clarifies that the type of experience in this Afterworld is different for those that do and do not perform sacrifices. In Yoga, the word Yama stands for restraint. This world of Yama is nothing but a dream creation, where, having failed to restrain one's involvement in previous life, a kind of negative conditioning is provided here, in the hope that atleast now, restraint may develop.

ॐ स्मरन्ति च ॐ ॥ ३.१.१५॥

The scriptures Smritis too declare the same.

Smritis referred are ones such as Manu Smriti.

ॐ अपि सप्त ॐ ॥ ३.१.१६॥

There are seven such afterworlds.

The Puranas mention seven worlds of hell, with different kinds of suffering and punishment in each, which will be detailed subsequently.

ॐ तत्रापि च तद्व्यापारादविरोधः ॐ ॥ ३.१.१७॥

Even in these seven, there is no contradiction Avirodha on account of Yama being in command.

The emphasis here is that Yama has discretion over the Gods like Chitragupta presiding over all these worlds like Raurava. The significance is that the only determining factor of the creation of the hell as dreams, is the restraint factor of the mind.

At this juncture, it is necessary to understand the concepts of Swarga, Naraka, Pathala and Brahmaloka. Pathala are seven Lokas or realms of sin, each representing one vice such as lust, wrath, envy etc. Physically these seven, namely Atala, Vitala, Sutala, Talatala, Rasatala, Mahatala and Patala are regions pervading entire Earth seen as concentric rings starting from subcontinent, and these are where these respective sins are dominant, though each of these sins may be seen, albeit to a lesser extent, in other regions as well, and the mapping is as follows.

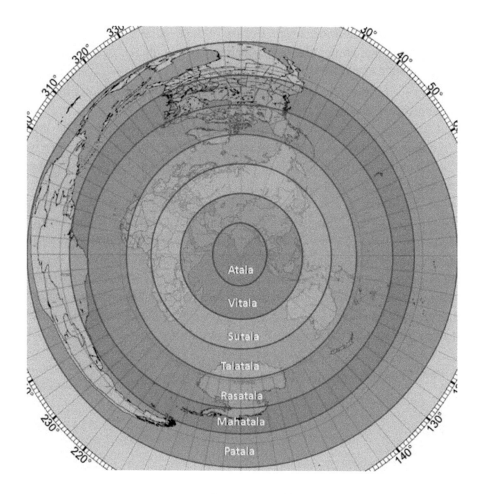

The seven Hells

As mentioned earlier, Swarga and Naraka are dream creations, just like the Earth, but with the purpose of exhausting merits and demerits or Punya and Papa respectively, while also a chance at refining one's Karma Vasanas. In these, the experiences are through subtle body which is often mentioned as being composed of Akasha and air elements alone, as opposed to the five element physical bodies and also, The memories of the earthly life are retained. In the case of Naraka, the location is Earth itself, in the same neighborhoods the soul, now called Preta, once lived in. Being a creation of the mind towards restraint and negative conditioning, the locations in these neighbourhood are filled with horrific and despicable things such as rivers of blood, and Yama the One presiding over these worlds is a personification of this mental attitude of restraint.

One's experience in this Naraka is filled with painful experiences such as for example, possessing a giant stomach and thus with extreme hunger and thirst, but with a small neck limiting food intake capacity, and further finding only bones, blood and toxic waste instead of food. Based on the types of sins performed, the experiences are created toward operant conditioning of the mind, and for this reason, the kinds of experiences are counted as different hells, with some texts mentioning 7, some 28 and some mentioning hundreds of such hells. In most cases, the tortures of hell are effective in conditioning and removing the most horrific of Vasanas, but in some cases, the Preta is filled with vengeance and as a ghost or Bhutha does attack living beings in its neighbourhood, in various forms, which is usually seen as haunting or negative energies. One such form is Brahma Rakshasa, which is the Preta of a Brahmin who had deviated from duties and caused harm. Another, called Vethala inhabits a corpse bringing it back alive. However, the source of all this is in the mental realm, and can affect only those alive who are mentally weak and entertain such thoughts as they can be affected by such beings. Those who are mentally strong through devotion and with firm conviction that these beings cannot attack them in presence of God, are not affected. One of the sins the Preta is punished for, includes having failed to plan for one's death, in that, not having taken Sanyasa Ashrama in the last stages as per Vedic injunctions, proper arrangements or instructions were not given to descendants for cremation of the body and subsequent Shraddha rituals, explaining their scope and purpose. Since this is a violation of nature as already explained, whenever the descendants fail to perform these rituals, the Preta undergoes its due punishment as well.

The seven hells are as follows: Kalasutra (thread of Time/Death): The Bhagavata Purana assigns this hell to a murderer of a brahmin, while the Devi Bhagavata Purana allocates it for a person who disrespects his parents, elders, ancestors or brahmins. This realm is made entirely of copper and extremely hot, heated by fire from below and the red hot sun from above. Here, the sinner burns from within by hunger and thirst and the smouldering heat outside, whether he sleeps, sits, stands or runs. Raurava (fearful or hell of rurus): As per the Bhagavata Purana and the Devi Bhagavata Purana, it is assigned for a person who cares about his own and his family's good, but harms other living beings and is always envious of others. The living beings hurt by such a man take the form of savage serpent-like beasts called rurus and torture this person. The Vishnu Purana deems this hell fit for a false witness or one who lies. Maharaurava (great-fearful): A person who indulges at the expense of other beings is afflicted with pain by fierce rurus called kravyadas, who eat his flesh. Avici/Avicimat (waterless/waveless): A person, who lies on oath or in business, is repeatedly thrown head-first from a 100 yojana high mountain whose sides are stone waves, but without water. His body is continuously broken, but it is made sure that he does not die. Tamisra (darkness): It is intended for a person who grabs another's wealth, wife or children. In this dark realm, he is bound with ropes and starved without food or water. He is beaten and reproached by Yamadutas till he faints. Taptasurmi/Taptamurti (red-hot iron statue): A man or woman who indulges in illicit relations with a woman or man is beaten by whips and forced to embrace red-hot iron figurines of the opposite gender. Vaitarni/Vaitarna (to be crossed): It is a river that is believed to lie between Naraka and the earth. This river, which forms the boundary of Naraka, is filled with excreta, urine, pus, blood, hair, nails, bones, marrow, flesh and fat, where fierce aquatic beings eat the person's flesh. As per the Bhagavata Purana and the Devi Bhagavata Purana, a person born in a respectable family – kshatriya (warrior-caste), royal family or government official – who neglects his duty is thrown into this river of hell. The Vishnu Purana assigns it to the destroyer of a bee-hive or a town.

Swarga, physically is the region above Meru. Brahmaloka too are regions around Sumeru. In these regions reside those souls with the corresponding Bhakti Bhavas or Ishta Devatas, if, within their lifetime, they have realised the Bhumikas. In the forthcoming sections, one's journey after death, to the Saguna Brahmaloka is mentioned as crossing the Lokas or worlds of the following Devas in this order: Fire, Day, Bright Fortnight, Northern Course Solar Months, Year, World of Gods, Air, Sun, Moon, Lightning, Varuna, Indra, Prajaapathi and eventually Brahmaloka. In this list, Brahmaloka must be taken to mean Parabrahman and residence in Sumeru, whereas Prajapathi refers to Saguna Brahma which is also Jannat of Islam.

The journey towards Swarga too is the same except it stops with Varuna and Indra. Physically, it can be seen that this order of Worlds of Devas describe the journey to Sumeru starting from Fire. This is the region where it is considered supreme to perform Pinda Daana, where even performing once is considered sufficient. Following this, the path crosses a Kubera aspect, the latter presiding over northern direction and thus referred to as

Northern Course. Air, Sun and Moon then leads one at the base of Swarga mountain. Being unable at this stage to comprehend Saguna Brahman or even astral body effects, one must be lifted up to the subtle realm, which is achieved by lightning to "rise" to the level of Devas. Here, one resides in the world of Varuna. Varuna is said to possess the Pasha, who essentially tempts those souls resident there with the pleasures of heaven, such as Apsaras, Kalpavriksha, Parijatha etc and those who succumb to these enjoy the pleasures until the merits are exhausted. Those who do not succumb cross over to the world of Indra, who represents the aspect of transformation, and thus Indra Loka tempts one with power and the opportunity to help others, which also induces ego.

It must be understood that Yama, Indra, Varuna etc are all personifications of various qualities of the mind. In Swarga, there are also many other beings, which too are personifications of the mind corresponding to various roles, such as Gandharvas for music, Kinnaras as angel like figures, Yakshas to guard the treasures, harm inflicting spirits called Pishachas etc. So too, in Saguna Brahmalokas, one finds creations assisting the Deities, such as Shiva Ganas and Vishnu's attendants. In Swarga as well as Naraka, due to previous memories and mental conditioning, one is given the opportunity to remove the Karma Vasanas, and realize Saguna Brahman, and if this is achieved, the soul is taken straight to the Brahmaloka without being born again. In the various Brahma Lokas, those souls from Earth, Swarga or Naraka that have reached liberation reach Manidweepa which is Srimannagara attaining the 16th stage, after which they reside in Sumeru as Videhamukthas until Pralaya.

ॐ वद्‌याकर्‌मणोरतिति पुरकृतत्‌वात् ॐ ॥ ३.१.१८॥

However, the reference is to the two paths of Knowledge Vidya and work Karma, on account of these being the subject discussed.

The previous Sutras mentioning heavens or Yama world only apply to those who follow the path of knowledge and work. For those that do neither, Chhandogya states a third place, which was listed earlier as Kakola, where the evil doers become tiny rotating creatures that simply take birth and die. Essentially, the relevance of the Sutras earlier was to the human faculties of work and intellect, which one could use to restrain from worldly involvement, and progress spiritually, in the absence of which, the mind had to be negatively conditioned. In the absence of using these faculties ie not performing either work or knowledge, there is no option of conditioning, nor have they made use of human faculties provided. On account of higher functionalities specific to humans rendered redundant, they become creatures lower on the evolutionary scale. From this birth, they then have to work their way up the evolutionary scale birth by birth, acquiring more complexity, until they are born as humans again.

ॐ न तृतीये तथोपलब्धेः ॐ ॥ ३.१.१९॥

The specification of five oblations are not relevant to this third place.

While as much a dream creation as the Earth, Heavens or Yama world, this third realm of the previous Sutra significantly differs from the others, in that, all faculties are not fully developed, in which case, the mention of the five oblations, of man, woman, Sraddha etc are all rendered moot.

ॐ स्मर्यतेऽपि च लोके ॐ ॥ ३.१.२०॥

Cases of birth without completing the five oblations are recorded therein.

There are examples in Puranas such as Drona and Drishtadyumna who were born without two parents, and also the modern technology of developing stem cell fetuses corresponds to this view. If this is possible for humans, then it is more than possible for lower life forms.

ॐ दर्शनाच्च ॐ ॥ ३.१.२१॥

So too on account of observation.

Among the various kinds of life seen in nature, such as viviparous, oviparous, moisture based, and plant life, the latter two, as well as the stem cell case mentioned earlier, do not involve the full birth process.

ॐ तृतीये शब्दावरोधः संशोकजस्य ॐ ॥ ३.१.२२॥

The third term includes the moisture category Samshokaja too.

The Sutra clarifies the claim of Chhandogya that there are three kinds of birth, rather than the four mentioned above. In that case, plant and moisture based are combined as both experience germination.

ॐ स्मरणाच्च ॐ ॥ ३.१.२३॥

ॐ तत्स्वाभाव्यापत्तिरुपपत्तेः ॐ ॥ ३.१.२४॥

It is reasonable that the soul on descent, attains a similarity with nature Tatsvabhava.

The soul is a subtle concept ascending to heavens with all its Vasanas, and upon descent, must take on a new birth with a new body. Since the body itself is formed of physical elements of nature, the soul must also attain similarity with these in nature.

ॐ नातिचिरेण विशिषात् ॐ ॥ ३.१.२५॥

The scriptures specially declare that the descent does not take a very long time Athichira.

The reference is to Chhandogya where the soul is mentioned to take the form of nature, as rice, corn, sesame and beans, and that from this the next stage is produced fast. After all it is only food that enters a human being and becomes another human being.

ॐ अन्याधष्ठिति पूर्ववदभिलापात् ॐ ॥ ३.१.२६॥

The descending soul enters what is ruled by another soul as in the previous cases, as per Sruthis.

The soul entering the system of another person as nutrition, is already mentioned in earlier Sutras.

ॐ अशुद्धमति चिनेन शब्दात् ॐ ॥ ३.१.२७॥

The claim that sacrifices involving killing of animals etc are unholy, is refuted on account of scriptural authority.

The clarification is that killing of animals for the purpose of sacrifice does not incur bad Karma. After all, the ultimate reality is that, the entire world, including all creatures and one's own Jiva is a dream, and has no real basis. With the only real and tangible aim being the understanding of reality and getting out of the dream, the unreal dreamy act to killing an equally dreamy creature ie animal, cannot possibly have a basis in impeding the tangible aim of spiritual progress.

ॐ रेत: सग्यिोगोऽथ ॐ ॥ ३.१.२८॥

The soul then gets connected with the one who performs the act of generation.

When the soul enters another human being as food, the nutrition eventually finds its place in the Procreative glands and as the seed, which then takes part in the process of reproduction.

ॐ योने: शरीरम् ॐ ॥ ३.१.२९॥

From the womb a new body arises.

Ultimately, having passed through the bodies of parents as food, the soul develops into a new body, eventually ready for physical birth as a human being.

ॐ सन्ध्ये सृष्टिराह हि ॐ ॥ ३.२.१॥

Scriptures mention that there is real creation Srishti in the state intermediate Sandhya between wake and deep sleep.

From the perspective of a common man, the Sutras observe the process of dream, which is what happens between wake and sleep. By observing what happens in a dream, how an entire universe is created out of nothing, and how unreal it is yet feels so realistic, by understanding all this one can come to terms with the fact that the entire creation one witnesses is itself a big dream. If the waking state, a product of the mind, is considered real, then the dream creation must also be real, since both arise from the same source and differ only in their duration.

ॐ नर्मिातार॑ं॒चैके॒पुत्रादयश्च ॐ ॥ ३.२.२॥

Also, some Sakhas or schools of Vedas so mention that the Self does create objects of desire such as sons etc in the state of sleep.

As much as the reality itself is one big dream, waking and dream are parts of this earlier mentioned, bigger dream. If the waking is wrongly assumed to be real, so too by that incorrect logic the dream is real .

ॐ मायामात्र॑ं॒तु॒कार्त्स्न्य॒नेनानभव्यि॒क्तस्वरूप॒त्वात् ॐ ॥ ३.२.३॥

However, the dream world is in entirety a mere illusion Maya on account of its nature not being manifest Anabhivyaktha.

Even for a moment wrongly considering the waking state to be real, one can still understand the dream to be unreal, since there are characters and entire things far bigger than the human body created within oneself, which is not physically possible.

ॐ सूचकश्च हि॒ श्रुतेः॑ आचक्षते॑ च तद्विदः॑ ॐ ॥ ३.२.४॥

However Shruthis and experts claim that despite being an illusion, dreams are important as omens.

This shows that while the dream itself is unreal, the signs that one can read from a dream are very real, and have implications on the waking state. All this is because both states of wake and dream have a common source, as the components of the bigger dream.

ॐ पराभध्यि॒ध्यानात्तु॒तिरोहिति॑ं ततो ह्यस्य बन्धवपिर्ययौ ॐ ॥ ३.२.५॥

However, by meditation on the supreme Lord, all the truth that has been hidden becomes manifest, since God alone ordains bondage as well as liberation Bandhaviparya.

The Bigger dream, of existence itself, arises from a real basis, that of the Self to play. The smaller dream ie the dream state, does not have a real basis, as it arises out of an equally unreal waking state, both of which merely exist to serve the cause of the bigger dream - for the Self to enjoy. Thus, liberation and bondage and tied to that cause of the Self alone.

ॐ देहयोगाद्वासोऽपि ॐ ॥ ३.२.६॥

And that veiling of Truth also arises because of the soul's connection with the body.

Considering the waking state to be real itself arises out of a misconception without understanding the bigger dream. Such a misconception arises solely because of involvement in the worldly existence due to Karma Vasanas.

ॐ तदभावो नाडीषु तच्छ्रुतेः आत्मनि च ॐ ॥ ३.२.७॥

The absence of dream, ie deep sleep takes place in the nerves and in one's Self, says the Shruthis.

The Nadis here are to be taken as Sushumna etc. Deep sleep is the closest one gets to Being the Self, since there is no creation happening in the bigger dream, in a kind of intermission. Thus, there is no universe created, waking or dream, in deep sleep. Still, one is in the Self in deep sleep and is yet not aware that he is in that state. For that reason, deep sleep symbolises ignorance.

ॐ अतः परबोधोऽस्मात् ॐ ॥ ३.२.८॥

Hence the awakening from Brahman.

The previous Sutra is emphasised here, that the deep sleep is closest to Brahman, and when one wakes up, one wakes from the state of Brahman.

ॐ स एव तु कर्मानुसृमतृशिब्दवधिभिय: ॐ ॥ ३.२.९॥

The same soul Jiva arises on account of Karma, memory and precept.

While deep sleep does mean that the bigger dream withdraws into the Self the dream creation, the Vasanas still continue on, since the end purpose of enjoyment is not yet satisfied. This means that when one wakes up, all the Vasanas return, and one picks up from where he left off before falling into sleep.

ॐ मुग्धेऽर्थसम्पत्तरिपरशिषात् ॐ ॥ ३.२.१०॥

In a swoon Mugdha, there is partial state of deep sleep, on account of it being the only alternative left.

There are only three states of awareness wake, dream and deep sleep, and on this account, swoon or fainting must be taken to deep sleep as the closest alternative, since there is no experience of creation as in wake or dream states.

ॐ न स्थानतोऽपि परस्योभयलङ्गिग सर्वत्र हि ॐ ॥ ३.२.११॥

Even on account of difference of place, a twofold character cannot be assumed of Brahman, on account of the scriptures everywhere unanimously stating so.

On account of scriptures mentioning in various places of Brahman having no attributes yet One from whom all attributes of creation arise. One might get the impression that Brahman might have dual characteristics which is refuted here. The reference to Brahman giving rise to various qualities cannot imply Brahman possessing the nature of these qualities.

ॐ न भेदादिति चिन्नन परत्यकेमतद्वचनात् ॐ ॥ ३.२.१२॥

The claim falsifying Brahman not having twofold quality because of difference taught in scriptures, is refuted on account ofShruthi declaring the opposite in respect of each form.

The dream creations of Self are essentially the Self itself. On this account, scriptures may have assigned various qualities, descriptions to the Self, as having 16 Kalas, four feet etc. Yet Brihadaranyaka and other texts assertively state that the same Self that is there inside the dream is also outside it. In all instances describing form, the Shruthis have always maintained the fundamental truth that Brahman is without attributes.

ॐ अपरिचैवमके ॐ ॥ ३.२.१३॥

Moreover some teach thus.

Reference is to scriptures that teach that the manifold aspect of Brahman is not true, by imposing punishments to those who see Brahman as qualified, as per Brihadaranyaka.

ॐ अरूपवदेव हि तत्पुरधानत्वात् ॐ ॥ ३.२.१४॥

Indeed, Brahman is formless alone, on that being the main purport of all the scriptures.

The emphasis here is that every text that quotes Brahman as having qualities and forms says that this is only an addition to the original formless nature of Brahman. Thus, all scriptures, dealing with Brahman as formless or with qualities, agree on the formless Brahman.

ॐ पुरकाशवच्चावैयर्थ्यम् ॐ ॥ ३.२.१५॥

Like light, Brahman does take form, and thus scriptures are not purportless.

If all scriptures do agree on a formless Brahman, why is Upasana etc involving form, prescribed by scriptures? The answer is that, just as characters in the dreamer's dream are essentially the dreamer itself, any of the creations of Brahman is indeed Brahman. This is similar to how light, though formless by itself, hits upon an object, illuminating it, and takes the form of the object as it reaches the eyes, which is how we see objects.

ॐ आह च तन्मात्रम् ॐ ॥ ३.२.१६॥

Also scriptures refer to Brahman as intelligence alone.

Reference is to Brihadaranyaka. The entire purpose of creation is to enjoy, and this enjoyment is subject to the knowledge that reality is a dream, and to the lack of such knowledge. Thus, while creation itself is dream and unreal, knowledge about the dream is very much real.

ॐ दर्शयति चाथोऽपि स्मर्यते ॐ ॥ ३.२.१७॥

Smritis also show what is declared by the scriptures.

Gita 18:12 and 2:25 are references to the nature of Brahman which is concurrent with what Brihadaranyaka 2.3.6 also states.

ॐ अत एव चोपमा सूर्यकादिवत् ॐ ॥ ३.२.१८॥

Therefore, with respect to Brahman, we have comparisons with the sun etc.

The reference is to the comparison drawn between Brahman as the sun and various objects within the creation as pots of water, each reflecting the sun in its entirety. However, these are mere reflections, and can not in any way be referred to as the true nature of Brahman.

ॐ अम्बुवदग्रहणात्तु न तथात्वम् ॐ ॥ ३.२.१९॥

However, there is no similarity with Brahman, with no secondary thing to be experienced as water.

This Sutra raises a possible objection to the previous Sutra in that, while the pots of water were external to the sun, that could reflect it, there is nothing external to Brahman, as everything is created from it.

ॐ वृद्धह्रासभाक्त्वमन्तर्भावात्
उभयसामञ्जस्यादेवम् ॐ ॥ ३.२.२०॥

On account of Brahman being inside its creation and appearing to participate in their increase and decrease,and on account of this similarity between water and Creation, the analogy holds.

The claim of the previous Sutra is refuted here. In the sun and water analogy, the image of the sun moves, twists or distorts in accordance with the movements of the pots of water. Similarly, the Brahman in each of creation appears to perform all actions of that creation. Thus, even while nothing is external to Brahman, its behaviour inside its creation is as effective nonetheless.

ॐ दर्शनाच्च ॐ ॥ ३.२.२१॥

And on account of scriptural instruction.

Reference is to Brihadaranyaka describing Brahman present inside all creation.

ॐ प्रकृतैतावत्त्वं हि प्रतिषिधति ततो ब्रवीति
च भूयः ॐ ॥ ३.२.२२॥

What has been mentioned upto this is denied, while Shruthis mention something more than this.

What is referred to here is the principle of Neti, Neti, essentially enquiring into the nature of Brahman, and rejecting everything that is not Brahman. Reference is to Brihadaranyaka 2.3.6 stating the Brahman in gross and subtle contexts, and then that to know Brahman, one must negate both forms. After such denial, the scripture says Brahman is the Truth of the Truth asserting it as the only Reality.

ॐ तदव्यक्तमाह हि ॐ ॥ ३.२.२३॥

Scriptures say Brahman is not manifest.

Indeed, as much as a Mother is not manifest visibly to the child that rests inside Her, yet all the time nourishing it, Brahman even while creating the dream lies outside the dream, and does not manifest within it.

ॐ अपि संराधने प्रत्यक्षानुमानाभ्याम् ॐ ॥ ३.२.२४॥

Moreover, as per Shruthi and Smriti, Brahman is experienced in perfect meditation.

As much as Brahman is not manifest in the created world, the experiencer of this created world, the Self is indeed Brahman. Thus, one only needs to look inward with a purified mind, and when the Self is revealed in absence of dream world thoughts, Brahman is experienced.

ॐ प्रकाशवच्चावैशेष्य ॐ ॥ ३.२.२५॥

On account of repeated instruction, just like light, there is no difference between Brahman and its manifestation as activity etc.

This is the essence of Vedic Mahavakyas such as Aham Brahmaasmi, Ayam Atma Brahma, or Tatvamasi. The shadow of sun reflected in the pots of water, are nonetheless the sun, even though unreal.

पाठभेदे 3.2.25 and 26 combined

ॐ प्रकाशश्च कर्मण्यभ्यासात् ॐ ॥ ३.२.२६॥

ॐ अतोऽनन्तेन तथा हि लिङ्गम् ॐ ॥ ३.२.२७॥

The individual soul becomes one with the infinite, as indicated.

When the dreamer realises that all this is a dream, the dreamer is free of limiting adjuncts, and understands that he indeed is the dreamer, the Self. Basically, upon knowledge, the individuality of Jiva is lost, and this is why one who knows Brahman becomes Brahman.

ॐ उभयव्यपदेशात्त्वहिकुण्डलवत् ॐ ॥ ३.२.२८॥

On account of both difference and non difference taught by scriptures, the Jiva Brahman relationship should be taken akin to a serpent and its coils.

As long as Realization is not attained, the dream world is taken to be real, upon which the difference between Jiva and Brahman is taken to be real. However, after Realization, the difference ceases, on account of the unreality of the dream. In this context, Brahman and Jiva may be seen as the snake and its coils, in that each part of the snake can be seen as a separate entity and yet, the whole snake can be seen as one entity.

ॐ प्रकाशाश्रयवद्वा तेजस्त्वात् ॐ ॥ ३.२.२९॥

Or like light and its substratum, both being luminous.

The illustration here is that of light and its orb. They are both essentially the same, yet on account of intensity difference they are given different names.

ॐ पूर्ववद्वा ॐ ॥ ३.२.३०॥

Or the relation between Jiva and Brahman as given before.

In the above two examples, the difference and non difference were given equal consideration, as conclusions of different stages of perception. However, when it comes to reality, only the non difference stands, since the very basis of the difference is only in the dream world, which is unreal.

ॐ प्रतिषिधाच्च ॐ ॥ ३.२.३१॥

And on account of denial.

The Neti Neti process is one of denial, and what remains after such denial is the Brahman alone, and in this process, all kinds of illusory and difference causing perceptions are negated too.

ॐ परमतस्सेतून्मानसंबन्धभेदव्यपदेशेभ्यः ॐ ॥ ३.२.३२॥

There is something superior to Brahman on account of words like water bank, measure, connection and difference used in its context.

This Sutra places a claim that since certain descriptions of Brahman as for example, having four feet, exist, Brahman is limited by measure, which means there is something of a higher measure.

ॐ दर्शनात् ॐ ॥ ३.२.३३॥

But Brahman is called such only by similarity.

For example, Brahman as water bank is based on the similarity in function ie maintaining borders between different levels of experience.

ॐ बुद्ध्यर्थः पादवत् ॐ ॥ ३.२.३४॥

For the sake of easy comparison, just like four feet.

The four feet depiction of Brahman merely is an allusion to the four important organs of speech, nose, eyes and ears. This is for the purpose of cultivating Upasana.

ॐ स्थानवशिषात्पुरकाशादवित् ॐ ॥ ३.२.३५॥

On account of special places, like light.

While light is all pervading, the example earlier about light taking the shape of an object, involved distinguishing between light that was outside with light that strikes the object, despite all pervading nature of light.

ॐ उपपत्तेश्च ॐ ॥ ३.२.३६॥

And from reasoning.

One must understand the purpose of creation from Brahman, and on this basis, one must try to analyse and reason out the role of Jiva, in satisfying the Cause of creation. In this manner, the unreality of Jiva must be understood, which will lead to both Jiva and Brahman being seen as one.

ॐ तथाऽन्यप्रतषिधात् ॐ ॥ ३.२.३७॥

On account of express denial of all other things.

This is already seen in the Neti Neti process, but texts such as Chhandogya 7.25.2 and Mundaka 2.2.11 clearly deny any association of any thing whatsoever with Brahman.

ॐ अनेने सर्वगतत्वमायामयशब्दादभिय: ॐ ॥ ३.२.३८॥

By this, the all pervading aspect of Brahman is known, from scriptures regarding the extent of Brahman.

The previous Sutras all categorically refuted the idea of Brahman possibly being limited in any way. Thus, as one without limits, Brahman does not have any limit even in context of space, meaning that it is all pervading.

ॐ फलमत उपपत्ते: ॐ ॥ ३.२.३९॥

From Brahman are the fruits of actions, as it is reasonable.

On the one hand, Brahman is the cause, and everything created is the Effect. Second, Brahman is sentient and eternal and is thus qualified to award fruits of actions, as the very determining cause for the universe existence itself. Any of the creation within universe is insentient, and incapable of experience, and thus, cannot award the fruits of actions.

ॐ शरुतत्वाच्च ॐ ॥ ३.२.४०॥

Because the scriptures say so.

Reference is to Brihadaranyaka 4.4.24 mentioning the Self as giver of fruits of one's work.

ॐ धर्म जैमिनिः अत एव ॐ ॥ ३.२.४१॥

Jaimini for the same reasons agrees that religious merit brings about fruits of actions.

This is the claim made against the previous Sutra, that it is merit of one's actions, such as sacrifice etc that bring about the fruits of actions, since these actions are what are immediately connected with what one experiences, being in the same level of reality.

ॐ पूर्व तु बादरायणो हेतुव्यपदेशात् ॐ ॥ ३.२.४२॥

However, Badarayana concurs with the former view, on account of the Lord being the Cause for the actions themselves.

It is again emphasised that the action of sacrifice, the merit accrued therein, and the fruit of Karma experienced, all these are in the dream creation, none of these having tangible reality, nor a Cause of their own, but are rather an effect of the bigger Cause, the enjoyment of Brahman. Thus, it is not possible for the course of events to be decided by anything other than Brahman itself.

ॐ सर्ववेदान्तप्रत्यय चोदनाद्यविशेषात् ॐ ॥ ३.३.१॥

Upasana specified in various Vedanta are not different on account of non difference regarding injunction.

Reference is to Upasana such as for Prana mentioned differently in Brihadaranyaka and Chhandogya. On account of non difference in injunction such as Agnihotra specified, as well as same name and form in these various Sakhas, the Upasanas must be taken as the same. There is also non difference in the fruit of all these, ie knowledge of Brahman, of reality and of the dream creation. Same applies to other Vidyas such as Dahara, Sandilya, Vaisvanara etc.

ॐ भेदान्नेति चिदेकस्यामपि ॐ ॥ ३.३.२॥

The claim that Vidyas are not same on account of differences in minor points, we refute since even in same Vidya such differences exist.

Reference is to examples like Brihadaranyaka 3.2.14 and Chhandogya 5.10.10 in the difference of fires in Panchagni Vidya. Such differences may occur even in the same Vidya of the same Shakha. Thus, minor differences may not be taken as basis for contention.

ॐ स्वाध्यायस्य तथात्वने हि समाचारेऽधिकाराच्च ॐ ॥ ३.३.३॥

पाठभेदे + समाचारेऽधिकाराच्च सववच्च तन्नयिमः

ॐ सललिवच्च तन्नयिमः ॐ ॥ ३.३.४॥

Rite of carrying fire in the head is connected with study of Vedas, because it is specified so in Samachara. It follows from being a qualification for Atharvana Vedins as is the case of seven oblations.

Reference in Mundaka 3.2.11 of carrying the fire as a requisite for reading it, explains the ritual as connected with study of Upanishad and not as a Vidya. Thus, an objection cannot be raised saying that due to this ceremony, the Vidya of Atharvanikas is different from all Vedas.

ॐ दर्शयति च ॐ ॥ ३.३.५॥

Scriptures too declare thus.

Reference to Chhandogya 5.18.1 as an example to show that Nirguna Brahman or Saguna as Vaishvanara extending from heavens to Earth ie Vishwarupa, are the common objective of all Upasanas.

ॐ उपसंहारोऽर्थाभेदाद्वधिशिषेवत्समाने च ॐ ॥ ३.३.६॥

And in Upasanas of same class, combination of all particulates to be made, since there is no difference in the object of meditation, just as combination of subsidiary rites of a main sacrifice.

The Upasana details in various Sakhas have been given only because they have been found effective. Thus, with the goal being common, this must be combined from many Sakhas.

ॐ अन्यथात्व॑ च शब्दादिति चिन्नेनावशिषात् ॐ ॥ ३.३.७॥

The claim that Udghita Vidya of Brihadaranyaka 1.3.7 and Chhandogya 1.2.7 are different on account of difference in texts, we refute, on account of non difference regarding essentials.

This again reinforces the earlier Sutra of non difference pertaining to a common goal, and using this, a claim is raised, whereby the former text cites meditation on Udghita as Prana while the latter cites meditating on Om of the Udghita.

ॐ न वा प्रकरणभेदात्परोवरीयस्त्वादबित् ॐ ॥ ३.३.८॥

Rather there is no unity of Vidyas on account of difference in subject matter, even as meditation on Udghita as highest Brahman is different that meditating on Udghita in the eye etc.

The claim of previous Sutra is refuted, in that the objects meditated upon in both cases are different and are thus not the same Vidya. The same difference, Udghita as highest and greatest, and Udghita as abiding in eye and sun, can be seen from Chhandogya 1.9.2 and 1.6 respectively.

ॐ संज्ञातश्चेत्तद्कुतमस्तति तदपर ॐ ॥ ३.३.९॥

The claim that the name of Vidyas being same results in Vidyas being same, has already been explained. But even that identity of Vidya name as different exists.

Examples are different sacrifices like Agnihotra and Darsapurnamsa, all occurring in Kathaka, and in these cases, identity of name is no basis for claiming similarity of Vidyas.

ॐ पुराप्तश्च समञ्जसम् ॐ ॥ ३.३.१०॥

And because Om exists throughout the Vedas, to specialise it by the term Udghita is appropriate.

Chhandogya 1.1.1 mentions Om as the Udghita. Since Om is common to all Vedas, the Om referred to here for meditation is the one of Sama Veda, and to differentiate it such, the term Udghita is used.

ॐ सर्वाभेदादनुयत्रमे ॐ ॥ ३.३.११॥

On account of non difference of Vidya everywhere these qualities are to be inserted in other places.

Example is to Prana Vidya in Chhandogya, Brihadaranyaka and Kaushitaki where the former two mention qualities of speech being richest etc. Even though not mentioned in the Kaushitaki, the fact must be taken as applying here too.

ॐ आनन्दादय: प्रधानस्य ॐ ॥ ३.३.१२॥

Bliss and other attributes that depict the true nature of Brahman must be combined from all places in meditation on Brahman.

Again this reinforces the object and goal of meditation being the same.

ॐ प्रियशिरस्त्वाद्यप्राप्तिरुपचयापचयौ हि भिदें ॐ ॥ ३.३.१३॥

Qualities like joy being its head are not to be taken everywhere, since being subject to increase and decrease not possible in Brahman where there is non difference.

ॐ इतरे त्वर्थसामान्यात् ॐ ॥ ३.३.१४॥

But other attributes like bliss to be combined on account of identity of purport.

These attributes life bliss, knowledge, all pervading etc are mentioned for knowledge purposes, to know about Brahman and not for Upasana, and are thus common to all Upasanas.

ॐ आध्यानाय प्रयोजनाभावात् ॐ ॥ ३.३.१५॥

Kathaka 1.3.10-11 tells about Self only as highest for sake of meditating and not as relative position of objects, which are useless.

ॐ आत्मशब्दाच्च ॐ ॥ ३.३.१६॥

And on account of the word Self.

Reference to Katha 1.3.12 to reinforce the previous Sutra as the Self alone is the Highest.

ॐ आत्मगृहीतिरितिरवदुत्तरात् ॐ ॥ ३.३.१७॥

In Aitareya 1.1 Supreme Self is meant, as other texts dealing with creation, on account of subsequent qualification.

The next verse Aitareya 1.1-2, states that it thought, and sent forth worlds. This is clearly a reference to a sentient First Cause, ie Brahman.

ॐ अन्वयादिति चेत्स्यादवधारणात् ॐ ॥ ३.३.१८॥

The claim that because of context Hiranyagarbha and not Self as Brahman is mentioned, we refute saying quoting the definite statement The Atman alone existed in the beginning.

ॐ कार्याख्यानादपूर्वम् ॐ ॥ ३.३.१९॥

On account of rinsing the mouth referred to in Prana Vidya being a restatement of an act already enjoined by Smriti, what has not been so enjoined elsewhere is enjoined here by Sruthi.

Reference is to Chhandogya 5.2.2 and Brihadaranyaka 6.1.14. The act of thinking water as the dressing of Orana, while rinsing, alone is enjoined by Sruthi.

ॐ समान एवञ्चाभेदात् ॐ ॥ ३.३.२०॥

Even in same Sakha there is unity of Vidya on account of non difference of object of meditation.

Examples are of Sandilya Vidya having different details in Satapatha Brahmana 10.6.3.2 and Brihadaranyaka 5.6.1. As per this Sutra, given that the object of meditation ie the Self consisting of mind, is the same, these must be combined to give one single Sandilya Vidya.

ॐ संबन्धादेवमन्यत्रापि ॐ ॥ ३.३.२१॥

In other cases too such as Vidya of Satya, on account of object of meditation being Satya Brahman, we have to combine the particulars.

A claim is made here, in that Satya Brahman as referenced in Brihadaranyaka 5.5.1-12, with two secret names of Ahar and Aham, accordingly as it is seen with respect to Gods or with body. On the lines of previous Sutra, these two have to be combined too.

ॐ न वा वशिषात् ॐ ॥ ३.३.२२॥

Rather not so on account of difference in abode.

The claim is refuted, since the abodes of meditation becomes different.

ॐ दर्शयति च ॐ ॥ ३.३.२३॥

The scriptures declare also.

Since the twoattributes, as residing in sun and in eye are compared with each other, it is clear that the scriptures do not allow merging of both.

ॐ सम्भृतद्दिद्युव्याप्त्यपि चात: ॐ ॥ ३.३.२४॥

For the same reason, supporting of universe and pervading of sly attributed to Brahman in Ranayaniya also are not to be included in other Upasana of Brahman.

Again, Brahman in sky and Brahman as Self within amount to change of abodes, and cannot be combined together.

ॐ पुरुषवद्दियायामवि चेतरेषामनाम्नानात् ॐ ॥ ३.३.२५॥

And since qualities mentioned in Purusha Vidya of Chhandogya are not mentioned in Taittiriya Aranyaka 10.64.

Here, though the fundamental attribute is man as sacrifice in both mentioned texts, the details vary, while more importantly, the goal varies - attainment of greatness of Brahman versus long life. Thus again there cannot be combining.

ॐ वेधाद्यर्थभेदात् ॐ ॥ ३.३.२६॥

Certain Mantra relating to piercing are not part of Vidyas even though mentioned nearby due to difference in meaning.

The purpose of piercing the whole body or heart of enemy, quoted in Atharvana is either as ritual or to destroy one's enemy, and are different in scope top Upanishads which purport to knowledge of the Self. Thus, these are not to be combined together.

ॐ हानौ तूपायनशब्दशेषात् कुशाच्छन्दस्स्तुत्युपगानवत् तद्कृतम् ॐ ॥ ३.३.२७॥

But where only the discarding of good and evil is mentioned, receiving of good and evil by others have to be included, on account of the word receiving being supplementary to discarding as in the case of Kusha, metres, praise, and recitation. This is stated by Jaimini.

This again purports to combining details from different Sakhas. For example Chhandogya 8.13 mentions that a person attaining knowledge discards good and evil, while Kaushitaki 1.4 mentions this good and evil obtained by friends and enemies respectively.

ॐ साम्पराये तर्तव्याभावात् तथा ह्यन्ये ॐ ॥ ३.३.२८॥

He who attains knowledge gets rid of good and evil by the time of death, there being nothing to be obtained by him on the way to Brahmaloka through work, for other texts say so.

While understanding that creation is a dream, this amounts to the non existent of any character in the dream as a real person, unlike the misperception all this while. When all characters this are rendered unreal, the same applies to the Jiva character, and at that point, in the absence of Karta, the doer, all the Karma and thus good and bad drop off. This moment is to be taken as the death of the Jiva, and thus the Sutra.

ॐ छन्दत उभयाविरोधात् ॐ ॥ ३.३.२९॥

The interpretation that the soul practising Sadhana according to his liking gets rid of good and evil while living, is reasonable, on account of there being harmony between Cause and effect.

The point that good and evil is discarded while living clarifies the above Sutra further, that death referred to, is only if the Jiva, and not physical death.

ॐ गतेरर्थवत्त्वमुभयथाऽन्यथा हि विरोधः ॐ ॥ ३.३.३०॥

Soul's journey along path of Gods is applicable in two ways, for otherwise there would be a contradiction.

The worshipper of Saguna Brahman undergoes Devayana, the path of Gods, upon death, with this path leading to Brahmaloka. As much as creation and earth within it is a dream, Brahmaloka too is another creation of the dream. However, the knowledge and absorption in Nirguna Brahman results in the knowledge that the world is a dream, upon which case every creation is a dream and has no real existence or even real travelling. In that case, there is no travelling, and that Devayana becomes irrelevant.

ॐ उपपन्नस्तल्लक्षणार्थोपलब्धेः लोकवत् ॐ ॥ ३.३.३१॥

Differentiation mentioned above is reasonable for the characteristics which render such a journey possible are seen in Saguna and not Nirguna, as seen in the world.

ॐ अनियमः सर्वेषामविरोधश्शब्दानुमानाभ्याम् ॐ ॥ ३.३.३२॥

The passage of soul by path of Gods is not restricted only to some Vidyas of Saguna Brahman, but equally applies to all Saguna Vidyas, as seen without contradicting in both Sruthi and Smriti.

Reference is to Chhandogya 5.10.1 and Gita 8.26.

ॐ यावदधिकारमवस्थितिराधिकारिकाणाम् ॐ ॥ ३.३.३३॥

Of those who have a mission to fulfil, there is corporeal existence as long as the mission is fulfilled.

The mention here is of enlightened souls who have attained liberation yet are reborn, such as Apantaratama born again as Vyasa. This is solely due to the mission the Divine has enjoined on them. As already clarified, the ultimate goal of all creation is bliss and enjoyment, and this is the state of a Jivanmukta, enjoying the dream creation, with intensified bliss. These enlightened souls born again on account of their mission are without doubt Jivanmuktas alone.

ॐ अक्षरधियां त्ववरोधः

सामान्यतद्भावाभ्यामौपसदवत्तदुक्तम् ॐ ॥ ३.३.३४॥

But the conception of negative aspects of Brahman the immutable are to be combined from different texts where the immutable Brahman is treated, in ask mediations of the Brahman, as they form one Vidya, on account of similarity in defining Brahman through denials and the object ie Brahman being the same as in the case of offerings. Thus says Jaimini.

References here describing Brahman as Immutable are Brihadaranyaka 3.8.8 and Mundaka 1.1.5-6.

ॐ इयदामननात् ॐ ॥ ३.३.३५॥

Because the same is described as such and such.

Reference to the two bird tale in Mundaka 3.1.1 and two enjoying good deeds in Katha 1.3.1, both are to be combined on account of object of meditation common in both, as Brahman.

ॐ अन्तरा भूतग्रामवदिति चेत् तदुक्तम् ॐ ॥ ३.३.३६॥

The same Self is thought as being the innermost of all, as in the case of elements.

Reference to Brihadaranyaka 3.4.1 and 3.5.1 specifying Brahman variously as one which breathes Prana into your self, and as that which transcends hunger, thirst etc. These must be combined on the account that there can only be one that is innermost of all, and that is the Self.

ॐ अन्यथा भेदानुपपत्तरितिचिन्नोपदेशेवत् ॐ ॥ ३.३.३७॥

The claim that the two Vidyas are separate since repitition cannot be accounted for, we refute since it is life repitition in another instance in Chhandogya.

Repitition of the same subject in different texts is given to provide clearer understanding from various angles.

ॐ व्यतिहारो विशिषिन्ति हीतरवत्रत् ॐ ॥ ३.३.३८॥

There is reciprocity of meditation fir the scriptures prescribe this in other cases.

Reference is to Aitareya Aranyaka 2.2.4.6. The point here is as much as meditation raising the Jiva and visualising it as the Gods is required, the reverse mentioning the God visualised as in the Jiva is also required. This is, the soul must eventually understood to be the dreamer Brahman, and that is the ultimate goal of all creation, to realise the dream creation and enjoy blissfully.

ॐ सैव हि सत्यादयः ॐ ॥ ३.३.३९॥

The same Satya Vidya is taught in both places because of common attributes like Satya seen in both places.

Reference is to Brihadaranyaka 5.4.1 and 5.5.2, visualising Satya as the sun in the orb etc and also as first born Satya Brahman conquering the worlds. They are to be taken as the same.

ॐ कामादतिरत्र ततुर च आयतनादभियः ॐ ॥ ३.३.४०॥

Qualities like true desire are to be inserted from Chhandogya to Brihadaranyaka and others from Brihadaranyaka to Chhandogya on account of abode etc same in both.

Reference is to Chhandogya 8.1.1 that speaks of Saguna Brahman and Brihadaranyaka 4.4.22 about Nirguna Brahman. With same features in both like abode, object of meditation etc, the two may be combined only for glorifying Brahman and not for Upasana.

ॐ आदारादलोपः ॐ ॥ ३.३.४१॥

On account of the respect shown to Pranagnihotra by Sruthi, there can be no omission of this act.

A claim is made that Pranagnihotra, ie the offering of food to each of the 5 Pranas before taking meals is done even before offering to guests and so it must be observed atleast by sipping water even during days of fast.

ॐ उपस्थतिस्तद्वचनात् ॐ ॥ ३.३.४२॥

When food is served, from that the Pranagnihotra to be performed, Sruthi declares.

The claim is refuted. Reference to Chhandogya 5.19.1, saying that first food is to be offered to Homa as Pranagnihotra.

ॐ तन्नरिधारणार्थनयिमस्तद्दष्टरेपथ्रगग्ध्यप्रतबिन्धः फलम् ॐ ॥ ३.३.४३॥

There is no rule about inviolability of that ie Upasanas connected with sacrifices, that is seen separate from the Sruthi, for a separate effect belongs to Upasana ie non obstruction of the results of sacrifice.

Reference to Chhandogya 1.1.10 stating that sacrifice can be performed with or without them. Except that the sacrifice performed with knowledge is more powerful but not mandatory.

ॐ परदानवदेव हि तदुक्तम् ॐ ॥ ३.३.४४॥

Meditations on Vayu and Prana are different owing to their different functions, though the two are essentially one. It is exactly in case of the offerings to Indra and king separately. This is stated by Jaimini.

ॐ लिङ्गभूयस्त्वात्तद्धि बलीयस्तदपि ॐ ॥ ३.३.४५॥

On account of abundance of indicatory marks, the fires of mind, speech in the Agnirahasya of the Vajasaneyins do not form part of the sacrifice, for indicatory mark is stronger than context. This is stated by Jaimini.

ॐ पूर्ववकिल्प: प्रकरणात्स्यात्क्रियामानसवत् ॐ ॥ ३.३.४६॥

The fires spoken of in previous Sutra are alternative forms of the one mentioned first ie actual sacrificial fire on account of context, they ought to be the part of sacrifice like the imaginary drink.

A claim is raised here. The reference is to offering to Prajaapathi the Sona drink using earth as the cup and sea as the Soma - this is a mental act, and the imaginary fires are to be taken in the same way.

ॐ अतदिशाच्च ॐ ॥ ३.३.४७॥

And on account of extension of attributes of actual fire to imaginary fires.

The claim is furthered in that Sruthi attributes all qualities of actual fire to imaginary fires too.

ॐ वदियैवै तुनरिधारणात् ॐ ॥ ३.३.४८॥

However the fires rather form a Vidya because the Sruthi asserts it.

The claim is refuted. The Sutra says that fire as a Vidya is made of knowledge.

ॐ दर्शनाच्च ॐ ॥ ३.३.४९॥

And because of indicatory marks, as described earlier.

ॐ श्रुत्यादबिलीयस्त्वाच्च न बाध: ॐ ॥ ३.३.५०॥

And because of greater force of Sruthi etc as indicatory mark and syntactical connection, the view that the fires constitute a Vidya cannot be refuted.

The indicatory marks as powerful than context is again reinforced here.

ॐ अनुबन्धादभिय: ॐ ॥ ३.३.५१॥

ॐ परज्ञानन्तरपृथक्त्ववद्दृष्टिश्च तदुक्तम् ॐ ॥ ३.३.५२॥

From the connection and so on extension etc the fires constitute a separate Vidya even as other Vidyas like Sandilya are separate. And it is seen that in spite of the context a sacrifice is treated as independent. This is stated by Jaimini.

This further reinforces the view of previous Sutras.

ॐ न सामान्यादप्युपलब्धेर्मृत्युवन्नहि लोकापत्तिः ॐ ॥ ३.३.५३॥

In spite of resemblance of fires to the imaginary drink, they they do not form part of the sacrificial act, for it is seen from the reasons that they constitute an independent Vidya. The mental aspect here is just like death, there the world does not become fire merely because of certain resemblances.

This furthers the refutal in that there is reference in Satapatha Brahmana 10.5.2.8 describing the being in the sun's orb as death, and Brihadaranyaka 3.2.10 describing fire as death. But just on that basis, one may not equate fire with the sun.

ॐ परेण च शब्दस्य ताद्विध्यं भूयस्त्वात्त्वनुबन्धः ॐ ॥ ३.३.५४॥

And from the subsequent Brahmana the fact of text under discussion enjoining a separate Vidya is seen. But connecting imaginary and real fires is on account of abundance of attributes in the latter that are imagined in these fires.

ॐ एक आत्मनः शरीरे भावात् ॐ ॥ ३.३.५५॥

Some deny the existence of an Atma separate from the body, for it exists only when there is a body.

The Charvaka doctrine is addressed here, in that man is the body alone, where consciousness is emergent combining certain elements within the body.

ॐ व्यतिरिकस्तद्भावभावित्वान्न तुपलब्धिवित् ॐ ॥ ३.३.५६॥

However not so, since consciousness does not exist for a body even after death, thus a Self separate from the body exists.

The refutal is on the basis that if consciousness depends on the body alone and is emergent out of it, then there is no explanation of death, when the body still exists but consciousness doesn't.

ॐ अङ्गावबद्धास्तु न शाखासु हि प्रतिविदम् ॐ ॥ ३.३.५७॥

But Upasanas connected with parts of sacrificial acts are not restricted to particular Sakhas of each Veda, but all Sakhas, because the same Upasana is described in all.

ॐ मन्त्रादिवद्वाऽविरोधः ॐ ॥ ३.३.५८॥

Or like Mantras etc there is no contradiction here.

The similarity of Mantra belonging to one Sakha used in another for the same rite is highlighted.

ॐ भूम्नः क्रतुवज्ज्यायस्त्वं तथा च दर्शयति ॐ ॥ ३.३.५९॥

Importance is given to meditation on the entire form of Vaisvanara as in the case of sacrifice, so says the Sruthi.

Reference is to Chhandogya 5.11-18, which meditates on the universal form of the Lord with heavens as head etc. While piecewise benefits are stated such as for meditating on the head as in Chhandogya 5.12.2, there are expressions discouraging such partial Upasana, and the whole is to be taken as one Upasana as the Self or Brahman, as seen in Chhandogya 5.11.1 or 5.18.2.

ॐ नानाशब्दादभिदात् ॐ ॥ ३.३.६०॥

Various Vidyas such as Dahara, Sandilya are different owing to difference in words.

The basis is that the words used in instructions of each of the Vidya, and thus the actions to be performed therein, varies.

ॐ वकिल्पो वशिष्टिफलत्वात् ॐ ॥ ३.३.६१॥

There is option with respect to several Vidyas because the result of all Vidyas is the same.

The result of all Vidya being self Realization, any Vidya suited to one's liking must be taken and practised, rather then taking multiple Vidyas simultaneously and distracting the mind. While the mention of Upasanas here seem to list ones practised during the Vedic civilization, these same principles must be taken to apply also to Vidyas, Upasanas, means of prayer, worship and Meditation, even including Nadopasana or music, in the divided world too. For this, as evidence, is cited the Bhagavad Gita, revealed by the Lord Himself. As the Bible says, society and law were made for man, not the other way round. It is the prime cause of liberation, and subsequent enjoyment that alone stands over and above all such rules and regulations. If a certain procedure helps to purify the mind and attain knowledge, devotion or surrender, it has to be embraced and accepted, taking the Smritis as authority.

ॐ काम्यास्तु यथाकामं समुच्चीयरेन्न वा पूर्वहेत्वभावात् ॐ ॥ ३.३.६२॥

However Vidyas for particular desires may be combined or not according to one's desire on account of the absence of reason mentioned previously.

This applies to Vidyas designed to satisfy any one desire, such as Chhandogya 3.15.2 and 7.1.5. In this case, multiple Vidyas may be practised simultaneously.

ॐ अङ्गेषु यथाश्रयभाव: ॐ ॥ ३.३.६३॥

With regard to meditation connected with members of sacrificial acts it is a with members with which they are connected.

A claim is raised regarding rule to be followed concerning Upasanas connected with members when different instructions are connected with the same sacrifice.

ॐ शष्टिश्च ॐ ॥ ३.३.६४॥

And from Sruthi injunction.

The claim is furthered.

ॐ समाहारात् ॐ ॥ ३.३.६५॥

On account of rectification.

The claim is furthered giving the reason that Chhandogya 1.5.5 mentions mistakes committed by Udgatri rectified by recitations by the chief priest, which shows meditations have been interlinked.

ॐ गुणसाधारण्यश्रुतेश्च ॐ ॥ ३.३.६६॥

And from Sruthis declaring Om as the common feature to all Vedas.

Reference to Chhandogya 1.1.9 as the abode of all Vidyas being common, to further the claim.

ॐ न वा तत्सहभावश्रुतेः ॐ ॥ ३.३.६७॥

Meditations connected with members of sacrificial acts are rather not to be combined as the Sruthi does not say that they are so correlated.

Reference is to earlier Sutra, in that the rule of combining instructions scattered in Vedas cannot be applied to Upasanas. This is because while instructions are inevitable and necessary, Upasanas only enhance Sacrifices and are not necessity.

ॐ दर्शनाच्च ॐ ॥ ३.३.६८॥

Because the Sruthis say so.

Reference to Chhandogya 4.17.10 showing that scriptures do not intend Upasanas to be taken together. The conclusion is that Upasana must be taken purely according to one's taste. This is because it is a mental exercise in cultivating proper concentration, purity and devotion, which will lead to knowledge of the Self and the dream nature of creation which alone is the means to liberation.

ॐ पुरुषार्थोऽतः शब्दादिति बादरायणः ॐ ॥ ३.४.१॥

From this results the purpose of man because of scriptures, states Badarayana.

Reference to Chhandogya 7.1.3, Mundaka 3.2.9, and Taittiriya 2.1, that knowledge of Brahman and the nature of reality takes one to the highest goal of liberation, and is not merely some part of a ritual. This is true, since the very nature of creation is illusion ie thinking what is unreal, dream to be real. This pertains to the level of mind and not bodily actions. One can come out of a dream only by knowing that it is a dream. Rather than that, performing any number of rituals and actions operates only on the dream realm, and thus is not directly capable of granting liberation.

ॐ शेषत्वात्पुरुषार्थवादो यथाऽन्येष्वतिति जैमिनिः ॐ ॥ ३.४.२॥

Because the Self being supplementary to sacrificial acts, the fruits of knowledge of Self, is merely an act of praise for the agent, thus thinks Jaimini.

As per this claim of the Mimamsa doctrine, every item used in sacrificial rites is purified and praised. In similar manner, knowledge about the Self praises and purifies the sacrifice performer, because of the enlightenment that the performer is the soul, and will outlive the body and go to heavens.

ॐ आचारदर्शनात् ॐ ॥ ३.४.३॥

Because of conduct found from scriptures.

Reference to Brihadaranyaka 3.1.1 where Janaka, a knower of the Self, performed sacrifices. This reference reinforces the Mimamsa claim that the fact that a knower of the Self performed sacrifice is evidence that sacrifice, and not knowledge, grants liberation.

ॐ तच्छ्रुतेः ॐ ॥ ३.४.४॥

Because the scriptures directly declare.

Reference is to Chhandogya 1.1.10 which states that any act performed with knowledge, faith and Meditation becomes more powerful, referring to knowledge as an aid to ritual.

ॐ समन्वारम्भणात् ॐ ॥ ३.४.५॥

Because the two go together.

Reference to Brihadaranyaka 4.4.2 that knowledge and work go along with the soul to the afterworld to reward the fruits of its previous birth. Thus, knowledge being an addition of action is cited to further the Mimamsa claim.

ॐ तद्वतो विधानात् ॐ ॥ ३.४.६॥

Because the scriptures enjoin work for such.

Scriptures enjoin work only for those who have knowledge of the Vedas, making knowledge a pre requisite for work and not vice versa.

ॐ नियमाच्च ॐ ॥ ३.४.७॥

On account of prescribed rules.

Ishavasya 2 and Shatapatha Brahmana 12.4.1.1 states how performers of rituals and sacrifices live long and enjoy rewards.

ॐ अधिकोपदेशात्तु बादरायणस्यैव तद्दर्शनात् ॐ ॥ ३.४.८॥

However, it is seen that the scriptures teach the Supreme Self to be other than the agent, making Badarayana's view correct.

The Mimamsa claim mentioned thus far is refuted now. Reference to Mundaka 1.1.9 and Brihadaranyaka 3.8.9, in that the Self that the Vedanta teaches is not that limited self as the agent performing sacrifices, but rather the Self free of limitations, knowledge of which puts an end to all actions. That is, the Self taught by Vedanta is the dreamer Himself, and not the one character in the dream wrongly taken to be one's self. This knowledge that one is the Dreamer immediately renders the dream irrelevant and devoid of reality, along with the actions in it.

ॐ तुल्यं तु दर्शनम् ॐ ॥ ३.४.९॥

However Sruthi declarations support both views.

Reference to Brihadaranyaka 3.5.1 and 4.5.15 that for one who has attained knowledge there is no work. Even in cases such as Janaka quoted where work was done after gaining knowledge, such work was done in a spirit of non attachment and thus without full passion and involvement, weakening the Mimamsa argument even more.

ॐ असार्वत्रिकी ॐ ॥ ३.४.१०॥

Earlier declaration is not universally true.

Reference to earlier Chhandogya declaration that knowledge makes an action more powerful. The knowledge referred here is not the universal knowledge of the Self, but simply knowledge of the Udghita, specific to the ritual at hand.

ॐ विभाग: शतवत् ॐ ॥ ३.४.११॥

There is division of knowledge and work as in the case of a hundred.

The claim of knowledge and work following a soul is refuted here, on the basis that if many souls are taken into consideration, knowledge follows some while work follows others, rather than both knowledge and work following each soul. Also, knowledge burns away all desires, which work does not. Brihadaranyaka 4.4.6 says that transmigration and emancipation are respectively awarded to souls that do and do not have desires.

ॐ अध्ययनमात्रवत: ॐ ॥ ३.४.१२॥

Only on those who have read the Vedas.

The earlier claim is refuted, that those who have read the Vedas and know about sacrifices, to them ritual work is enjoined. For those who have knowledge from Upanishads, no work is or can be enjoined, since the realisation that creation is a dream is incompatible with any kind of work.

ॐ नावशिषात् ॐ ॥ ३.४.१३॥

It does not apply to the Jnani on account of no special mention of him.

This is a refutal of earlier Isa claim of living a hundred years in performing rituals, since there is no special mention that such is applicable to a Jnani also.

ॐ स्तुत्यऽनुमतरि वा ॐ ॥ ३.४.१४॥

Or rather the permission to do work is for praising.

The ones that have got knowledge of the Self, like Janaka yet performing work is merely to glorify that knowledge, that any amount of work done after attaining of knowledge will not bind the Self with its effects. This performance of action by an enlightened one has nothing but the enjoyment as its true purpose, in that having realised the nature of reality, that creation is a dream and is unreal, still continues to perform here, merely to enjoy the intensified bliss of union with Brahman, through the objects of enjoyment, which is nothing but this dream creation.

ॐ कामकारेण चैके ॐ ॥ ३.४.१५॥

And some according to choice, refrain.

Some others, who after having attained knowledge, have refrained from involving in work. The point is, knowledge gives the ground reality that all this creation is a dream. Whether the dreamer performs or refrains from acting in his dream, what bearing does it have on the dreamer himself upon waking up? Thus, for the Self realised one, engaging or refraining from action neither makes a difference nor binds him.

ॐ उपमर्दं च ॐ ॥ ३.४.१६॥

And Destruction results.

Reference to Brihadaranyaka 4.5.15 and others in understanding that knowledge universally destroys all ignorance along with notions of doer, action and result. Thus knowledge of Self is not even an iota compatible with performing actions.

ॐ ऊर्ध्वरेतस्सु च शब्दे हि ॐ ॥ ३.४.१७॥

And knowledge belongs to those who observe continence ie Sanyasa, as per scriptures.

Reference to Chhandogya 2.23.1-2, 5.10.1, Mundaka 1.2.11 and Brihadaranyaka 4.4.22 in prescribing the Sanyasa as the fourth and last Ashram in life. On the one hand, knowledge of the Self is prescribed only to this Ashram, while on the other hand, there is no work except discrimination or Viveka prescribed to a Sanyasi. This is enough evidence of the knowledge work incompatibility.

ॐ परामर्श जैमिनिरिचोदना चापवदतिति हि ॐ ॥ ३.४.१८॥

Jaimini claims that mention of Sanyasa is mere reference and not injunction, since other texts condemn Sanyasa.

Reference to Taittiriya 1.11 and Taittiriya Brahmana 7.13.12 condemning Sanyasis as not belonging to the world, is quoted by Mimamsa to state that Shruthis only necessitate steadfastness in Brahman and not Sanyasa as requisite for knowledge, and it is only out of choice that Sanyasis quoted in previous Sutra have been enjoined with knowledge.

ॐ अनुष्ठेयं बादरायणः साम्यश्रुतेः ॐ ॥ ३.४.१९॥

Badarayana thinks that Sanyasa must have also been gone through for Scriptures cited refer equally to all stages of life.

The cited text in earlier Sutras refer to Sanyasa indeed as the steadfastness, while Brahmacharya, Vanaprastha and Grihastha have been referred respectively by studentship, penance and sacrifice.

ॐ विधिरिव धारणवत् ॐ ॥ ३.४.२०॥

Rather there is an injunction similar to carrying the sacrificial fuel.

The text of Jabala 4 is cited enjoining Sanyasa as an injunction, as does the above Chhandogya 2.23.1 reference in the same logic that the Sruthis enjoin carrying of sacrificial fuel to a householder as a rule, its status as an injunction established as an instruction that does not occur anywhere else.

ॐ स्तुतिमात्रमुपादानादिति चेन्नापूर्वत्वात् ॐ ॥ ३.४.२१॥

The claim that references as in Chhandogya 1.1.3 are mere praise due to them referring to sacrifices, we refute as it is mentioned here for the first time.

Chhandogya 1.6.1 glorifies the fire as Saman etc,and in much the same way a claim is made of Chhandogya 1.1.3 stating that Om is essence of essence, as a praise for Om and not as an injunction to meditate on it. This claim is refuted on account that, while the Saman fire reference praises the particular act of sacrifice, the text on Om is something universal, and is found even in Upanishads, unlike the former.

ॐ भावशब्दाच्च ॐ ॥ ३.४.२२॥

And there being words expressing injunction.

Reference to Chhandogya 1.1.1, specifically asking to meditate on Om - this is beyond any doubt an injunction alone.

ॐ पारप्लिवार्था इति चेन्न विशिषतित्वात् ॐ ॥ ३.४.२३॥

The claim that Upanishadic stories narrated are for Pariplava, we refute since Sruthis specify certain stories alone for that purpose.

Pariplava is the mandatory hearing of stories recited in the intervals of an Ashwamedha Yajna. Claim is made that Upanishadic tales such as Sathyakama etc are used for this purpose, thus making the Jnanakanda Upanishad an auxiliary to Karmakanda Vedas. This is refuted since Sruthis mention only specific stories to be used as Pariplava, and Upanishad tales do not make the list.

ॐ तथा चैकवाक्योपबन्धात् ॐ ॥ ३.४.२४॥

And to illustrate the Vidyas, are connected as one whole.

The stories mentioned in any Upanishad serve only to expound on the Vidya by catching the imagination of the student.

ॐ अत एव चाग्नीन्धनाद्यनपेक्षा ॐ ॥ ३.४.२५॥

And thus, no necessity for lighting the sacred fires and so on.

While the Sanyasis have attained ultimate goal of human existence through attainment of knowledge, they have realised the unreal dream nature of creation, and since any dream action has no bearing on reality, the sacrificial fires etc become unnecessary. The Brihat Sanyasa Upanishad of the Sama Veda is to be taken as authority on the rules of Sanyasa Ashrama, but even in this text there are certain rules that pertain to living conditions in the Vedic era, and not all of them may apply in the present date. Interestingly, the Upanishad does mention the rule that one must obtain the permission of one's family or parents prior to being initiated in this Ashrama, and so too, while Adi Shankara did of course obtain permission, there are examples to the contrary as well, including Buddha and Ramana Maharshi. The reasoning is that each soul is born independently to exhaust its own Karma and attain liberation, and any familial relationship, which lasts only for one birth is merely an instrument by which this may be achieved. On the contrary, the relationship between oneself and Amma, is one far longer than these familial bonds, and in fact a real relationship, unlike the earthly ones which are all parts of the dream. Consequently, with Amma having waited eagerly for many births for this blissful union, steps taken towards that end, including Sanyasa are given far higher priority than family commitments and responsibilities.

ॐ सर्वापेक्षा च यज्ञादिश्रुतेः अश्ववत् ॐ ॥ ३.४.२६॥

And there is necessity for all this work, with scriptures prescribing sacrifices as means for attaining knowledge,even as the horse is used to draw a chariot but not for ploughing.

The performance of Karma certainly purifies the mind, and brings knowledge, and for that reason, it is to be performed, though, the final goal ie liberation cannot be obtained from Karma.

ॐ शमदमाद्युपेतः स्यात्तथाऽपि तद्वधिस्तदङ्गतया
तेषामवश्यानुष्ठेयत्वात् ॐ ॥ ३.४.२७॥

But even so, one must possess calmness, self control and the like, since these are enjoined as aids to knowledge and therefore have to necessarily be observed.

Reference is to Brihadaranyaka 4.4.28 as authority to the point mentioned. These qualities have to be observed even in the absence of any Karma enjoined upon a Sanyasi.

ॐ सर्वान्नानुमतिश्च प्राणात्यये तद्दर्शनात् ॐ ॥ ३.४.२८॥

Sruthi declares that only when life is jeopardised, is one allowed to eat food without discrimination.

This follows from the simple ethical consideration that one must not perpetrate harm to animals etc when better options are available.

ॐ अबाधाच्च ॐ ॥ ३.४.२९॥

Because the statements are not contradicted.

Chhandogya 7.26.2 stating that a pure food makes the mind pure, is in accordance with the above Sutra.

ॐ अपि स्मर्यते ॐ ॥ ३.४.३०॥

Moreover the Smritis say so.

These texts too agree with the fact that when life is in danger one may take any kind of food.

ॐ शब्दश्चातोऽकामचारे ॐ ॥ ३.४.३१॥

And hence the scriptural text prohibiting license.

There are references such as Kathaka Samhita prohibiting liquor for Brahmins for example. Thus, the injunctions on food must be taken in the correct spirit of purifying the mind as a pre requisite to knowledge alone.

ॐ विहितत्वाच्चाश्रमकर्मापि ॐ ॥ ३.४.३२॥

And because they are enjoined, duties of Ashramas are to be performed even by those who do not desire liberation.

This clarifies the view that Karma assigned to each Ashrama is an injunction to be followed by one and all, and not just a requisite for gaining knowledge alone.

ॐ सहकारित्विनेन च ॐ ॥ ३.४.३३॥

And as a means to knowledge.

Again it is emphasised that Karma leads one to knowledge by purifying the mind, but not to its fruit ie liberation.

ॐ सर्वथापि त ुत एवोभयलङ्गात् ॐ ॥ ३.४.३४॥

In all cases same duties apply, because of the twofold indication mark.

References to Sruthi Brihadaranyaka 4.4.22 and Smriti Gita 6.1, from which one understands that the duties required for gaining knowledge and the duties enjoined upon Ashramas are one and the same. The only difference, as from Gita is that if knowledge is desired then actions must be done without desire for fruits.

ॐ अनभिभवं च दर्शयति ॐ ॥ ३.४.३५॥

And the scripture shows that one overpowered with Brahmacharya is not overpowered by anger etc.

Reference to Chhandogya 8.5.3 as Brahmacharya also as a requisite for knowledge, since it helps control of emotions etc.

ॐ अन्तरा चापि त ुतद्दष्टेः ॐ ॥ ३.४.३६॥

Because such cases are seen, persons in between two Ashramas too are entitled to knowledge.

Reference to Chhandogya 4.1, Brihadaranyaka 3.6 and 3.8, as authority and Raikva and Gargi as examples of the stated Sutra in that widowers and other such between Ashramas too are entitled to such Karma.

ॐ अपि स्मर्यते ॐ ॥ ३.४.३७॥

The Smritis too record this.

There are cases of Samvarta and other Yogis as examples.

ॐ विशेषानुग्रहं च ॐ ॥ ३.४.३८॥

And special works favour knowledge.

These special works mentioned are prayer, fasting, Japa etc which are not opposed to the condition of those who do not belong to any Ashrama, and can be performed by one and all as means for leading to knowledge.

ॐ अतस्त्वितरज्ज्यायो लिङ्गाच्च ॐ ॥ ३.४.३९॥

Because of indicatory marks, it is better to be in one of the Ashramas than none.

References to Brihadaranyaka **4.4.22** and **4.4.9** emphasising the need for a person such as Brahmana to not deviate from his Ashrama. This is because, after centuries of practice, the ancestors and Rishis have enjoined the duties of various Ashramas in ways that would maximise each one's chances of attaining knowledge.

However, a doubt may arise here. Is it possible or even feasible for the Vedic injunctions to be followed in the upcoming unified era? We answer this in the following way. First, it is already established in earlier Sutras how knowledge and work are mutually incompatible. It is also clarified that one may enter the Sanyasa Ashrama, the one prescribed for knowledge, even without crossing the other Ashramas in order. Thus, anybody with the thirst for knowledge would have immediately entered this Ashrama. As for others, ie with worldly desires, the other three Ashramas are prescribed, which if one enters, one would have to follow the injunctions. Yet, this Sutra only says that it is better to be in an Ashrama, rather than mandating. This is because, the rituals of each Ashrama are prescribed in such a way so as to maximise the benefits one seeks. Of course, one may also choose to refrain from the duties, in which case, one can neither enter the Ashrama, nor refer to himself as Brahmin, Kshatriya, Grihastha, nor is one entitled to the benefits and rights of these Ashramas.

Of course, there are monumental examples such as Mahaperiyava, and other great Agnihotris who have shown that it is possible to follow the injunctions of Sanyasa and other Ashramas, even in the current age of technology.

ॐ तद्भूतस्य तत्तद्भावो जैमिनिरपि
नियमातदरूपाऽभावेभ्य: ॐ ॥ ३.४.४०॥

For one of Sanyasa, there is no reverting back to earlier Ashramas on account of restrictions, Jaimini too agrees.

The Sanyasa Ashrama is one that can be taken at any stage ie even directly from Brahmacharya itself without crossing Grahastha and Vanaprastha stages. But once having entered the Ashrama, Shruthis forbid from reverting back.

ॐ न चाधिकारिकमपि पतनानुमानात्तदयोगात् ॐ ॥ ३.४.४१॥

And although mentioned in chapter dealing with qualifications, does not refer to one with vow of lifelong celibacy, because a fall is inferred from Smriti and the expiation in this case is ineffective.

The claim mentioned here quotes Purva Mimamsa 6.8.22 as mentioning expiation is given in the case of student Brahmacharis, but none such given for Naishtika Brahmacharis, more so because the expiatory ceremony would necessitate lighting the sacred fire, for which one would have to marry.

ॐ उपपूर्वमपीत्येके भावशमनवत्तदुकृतम् ॐ ॥ ३.४.४२॥

But some consider this a minor sin such as eating prohibited food and thus expiation is there.

Ceremonies such as Kricchara are prescribed by Smritis for not only Naishtika Brahmacharis but also Sanyasis and recluses. The more important point than such rituals is mental purity, since that alone aids in the ultimate goal, of realising reality as a dream.

ॐ बहिस्तिभयथापि स्मृत्रेोचाराच्च ॐ ॥ ३.४.४३॥

But in either case, they are to be kept outside society in accordance with Smriti and custom.

ॐ स्वामनि: श्रुतरेत्यात्रेय: ॐ ॥ ३.४.४४॥

The agentship of meditation belongs to the sacrificer because the Sruthi declares a fruit for it, thus thinks Atreya.

This is a claim raised on the basis of special fruits mentioned in the Sruthis.

ॐ आर्त्वज्यमित्यौड्लोमि: तस्मै हि परक्रियिते ॐ ॥ ३.४.४५॥

Audulomi thinks they are the duty of the Ritvik priest, as he is paid for it.

Since the priest is paid for all his actions, and since the fruits of the sacrifices have been bought by the sacrificer, it is to the priest that the duty raised in above Sutra belongs. Reference to Satapatha Brahmana 1.8.1.26.

ॐ सहकार्यन्तरवधि: पक्षेण तृतीय तद्वतो
वद्यादवित् ॐ ॥ ३.४.४६॥

Meditative state is the injunction as another auxiliary to knowledge, as an alternative to the one who possesses knowledge as in the case of injunctions.

Reference to Brihadaranyaka 8.5.1 that states that a knower of Brahman, having done with scholarship should remain like a child, and after having finished with this state and the learning, he becomes Meditative ie Muni. As the third requisite besides scholarship and childlike state, Munihood is different from knowledge, in that it is continous devotion towards knowledge and Brahman. The Meditative state is particularly useful for a Sanyasi who has not yet attained full knowledge, as a means of first hand experiencing the Self as Brahman beyond the dream. While in the case of knowledge, such an experience happens all the time effortlessly, the Meditative state is a way to experience it albeit for a short time, through effort in removing of all thoughts.

पाठभेदे श्रुतेश्च added to 3.4.46

ॐ कृत्स्नभावात्तु गृहिणोपसंहार: ॐ ॥ ३.४.४७॥

On account of householder duties containing those from all stages of life, the chapter ends by enumerating such duties.

The reference here is to Chhandogya which elaborates on the duties of both the Brahmacharis and the Grahasthas.

ॐ मौनवदितरेषामप्युपदेशात् ॐ ॥ ३.४.४८॥

Because the scriptures enjoin the other stages even as they enjoin the Muni or Sanyasa.

Thus, the Sruthis enjoin all classes of life to be gone through, be it sequentially or alternatively.

ॐ अनाविष्कुर्वन्नन्वयात् ॐ ॥ ३.४.४९॥

The childlike state means without manifesting himself, on account of context.

As a requisite to knowledge, the word Childlike in the earlier reference clearly means a state of innocence, free from anger, grudge etc, and without the sense of egoism.

ॐ ऐहिकमप्रस्तुतप्रतिबन्धे तद्दर्शनात् ॐ ॥ ३.४.५०॥

The fruition of knowledge may take place in this life itself if there be no obstruction to it, since it is seen so from scriptures.

While Katha 1.2.7 states how one gets liberated after many many lives, Gita 6.43 and 45 mentions cases of knowledge acquired in previous birth united with the person in next birth. The only possible obstruction to getting the knowledge in this birth itself is the Karma Vasanas. Only when these are fully exhausted does one begin realizing the reality rather than merely textually knowing it, and it is such Realization alone that can grant liberation, through the understanding that all creation is just a dream with the purpose of enjoyment.

ॐ एवं मुक्तिफलानियमस्तदवस्थावधृतेस्तदवस्थावधृतेः ॐ ॥ ३.४.५१॥

With respect to liberation, the fruit of knowledge, there is no such rule, since Sruthis assert that state to be immutable.

The knower of Brahman becomes Brahman, this is a clear assertion by the Sruthis. Thus, there is no delay of liberation upon realising the nature of reality. Essentially with the primary intent of dream creation being to enjoy the intensified bliss while within it, the earlier the liberation is achieved, the better. This is how the Divine Will works to that effect, which is why the result is immediate..

CHAPTER EIGHT

Wisdom

ॐ आवृत्तिः असकृदुपदेशात् ॐ ॥ ४.१.१॥

Repetition of hearing, reflection, meditation on Self is necessary, on account of repeated instructions.

Reference to Brihadaranyaka 2.4.5 and 4.4.21. The instructions are repeated multiple times, since the process is to be done until knowledge is realized.

ॐ लिङ्गाच्च ॐ ॥ ४.१.२॥

And on account of indicatory mark.

Reference to Chhandogya 1.5.2 asking for repeated meditation. As much repitition is necessary as is required to root out the misconceived idea that the dream creation is reality.

ॐ आत्मेति तूपगच्छन्ति ग्राहयन्ति च ॐ ॥ ४.१.३॥

But Sruthis acknowledge Brahman as the self of meditator and also teach others to realise it so.

It has already been established in detail how the soul and the Self are the same, with supporting references.

ॐ न प्रतीके न हि सः ॐ ॥ ४.१.४॥

The meditator is not to see the self in symbol, because he is not that.

Symbolism such as mind is the Self etc only exist to show that while every creation in the dream is inert, Brahman alone animates it being sentient, and experiences. With the qualities of Brahman, that is of sentience, intelligence, bliss etc not being adequately represented in any symbol, it is incorrect to meditate on such. However, in Saguna Upasana, one sees in the Vigraha of the desired form, not the properties of the Vigraha itself but of Brahman, as sentient, intelligent etc. In such case, the symbol ceases to be a symbol since its individual character is overlooked in favour of Brahman.

ॐ ब्रह्मदृष्टिरुत्कर्षात् ॐ ॥ ४.१.५॥

Symbol is to be viewed as Brahman and not reverse, on account of elevation of the symbol thereby.

It is to get rid of differentiating that meditation is performed. In such case, with Brahman being the undifferentiated, it is the goal, and thus the progress must be from symbol to Brahman.

ॐ आदित्यादिमतयश्चाङ्ग उपपत्तेः ॐ ॥ ४.१.६॥

And ideas of sun are to be superimposed on subordinate members of sacrifices, to maintain consistency with scriptures.

Just like the previous Sutra, when components of sacrifice are meditated with forces of nature as in Chhandogya 1.3.1 and 2.2.1, it should be in the order of former to latter.

ॐ आसीनस्सम्भवात् ॐ ॥ ४.१.७॥

One should practice Upasana sitting, as that alone is possible.

ॐ ध्यानाच्च ॐ ॥ ४.१.८॥

And on account of meditation.

Upasana, itself meaning meditation necessitates concentration with fixed look without movement of the limbs,and this is possible seated alone.

ॐ अचलत्वं चापेक्ष्य ॐ ॥ ४.१.९॥

And referring to its immobility.

Scriptures attribute Meditative nature to Earth, due to the steadiness.

ॐ स्मरन्ति च ॐ ॥ ४.१.१०॥

The Smritis concur, reference to Gita 6.11.

ॐ यत्रैकाग्रता तत्रावशिषात् ॐ ॥ ४.१.११॥

Wherever concentrating is attained, there it must be practised, there being no specifications of place.

ॐ आ प्रायणात्तत्रापि हि दृष्टम् ॐ ॥ ४.१.१२॥

Till death, must meditation be observed because their observance even at that moment is seen from the scriptures.

Satapatha Brahmana 10.6.3.1 and Gita 8.6 both emphasise that one becomes what one thinks at the time of death. To incur a lifelong practice on that account must meditation be observed.

In fact, this precise statement is the reason why a knower of Saguna Brahman is not reborn, but continues towards enlightenment in Brahmaloka. Given the assurance that one becomes what one thinks of at death, one must consider, as will be seen shortly, how death entails loss of speech, loss of limb movements etc, and with these eventful happenings in short durations before death, it is not an easy task to think about the Divine at that moment, unless extreme concentration of mind is achieved. This is precisely attained in the fifth stage, when the life force Kundalini is raised till the Sahasrara, at which point Savikalpa Samadhi is obtained and one becomes a knower of Saguna Brahman. The same is referred by the soul leaving the body through the skull or Brahmarandhra as Kapala Moksha.

ॐ तदधिगम उत्तरपूर्वाघयोरश्लेषविनाशौ
तद्व्यपदेशात् ॐ ॥ ४.१.१३॥

When Brahman is realized, there result the non clinging and Destruction of subsequent and previous sins, as it is so declared.

It is already explained how the creation is a dream and liberation amounts to realizing the unreality of this dream. The concept of Karma and sins are tied to the agency of the soul, which results from lack of knowing about the dream nature. Since when upon liberation, agency is destroyed, in the absence of a doer, Karma is negated too, and if the cause is nullified so are its effects ie fruits of actions, all three being Past, present and future. References also as Chhandogya 5.24.3, 4.14.9 and Mundaka 2.2.8.

ॐ इतरस्याप्येवमसंश्लेष: पाते तु ॐ ॥ ४.१.१४॥

Thus there is non clinging of other ie virtue too, but at death, liberation is certain.

As explained above, in the absence of doer, no effect accrues, which includes virtue and vice. Reference to Brihadaranyaka 4.4.22.

ॐ अनारब्धकार्य एव तु पूर्वे तदवधे: ॐ ॥ ४.१.१५॥

But of his former works only those which have not yet begun to yield results, are destroyed by knowledge, for death is the limit.

While all kinds of Karma, being the dream unreality are destroyed with knowledge, the soul is no longer an individual entity separate from Brahman, but is one with the Self ie soul is Brahman. Given that, the former work that has not yet begun to yield result is nothing but the creation itself, as the primary cause of enjoyment is not fully achieved. Thus the state of Jivanmukthi, in which this is fulfilled.

ॐ अग्निहोत्रादि तु तत्कार्यायैव तद्दर्शनात् ॐ ॥ ४.१.१६॥

But the results of daily Agnihotra are not destroyed by knowledge since these contribute to the very same result ie liberation, as seen from scriptures.

ॐ अतोऽन्यदपीत्येकेषामुभयो: ॐ ॥ ४.१.१७॥

There are indeed good works apart from this daily Agnihotra and the like, as per some Sakhas, thus view both Jaimini and Badarayana.

Work done with desire cannot help the origination of knowledge. But other rituals enjoined as a sort of discipline aid knowledge, and for this reason, their results persist till death.

ॐ यदेव वद्िययेति हि ॐ ॥ ४.१.१८॥

Because the statement, whatever he does with knowledge, indicates this.

A claim is raised that sacrifices combined with meditation alone are more powerful, and yield to origination of knowledge.

ॐ भागेन त्वतिरे क्षपयत्िवा सम्पत्स्यते ॐ ॥ ४.१.१९॥

But having exhausted by enjoyment the good and evil, he becomes one with Brahman.

The claim is furthered that since diversity is seen while living by a knower of Brahman, so will it continue after death too, and there will be no oneness. This is refuted on the basis that the moment the agency is lost, the soul has become one with Brahman. What continues till death is simply the executing of enjoyment in the created world, with all its diversity even while unreal, for this intensified blissful enjoyment is the very purpose of creation.

ॐ वाङ्ग्मनसि दर्शनाच्छव्दाच्च ॐ ॥ ४.२.१॥

Speech is merged in mind because it is seen and stated by scriptures so.

By observation it is known that a dying man loses the power of speech though the mind still functions. Also referenced is Chhandogya 6.8.6, with the understanding that it is only the function of the organ that merges into the mind, and not the organ itself. In essence, the settings of the dream change, this is the principle of death.

ॐ अत एव च सर्वाण्यनु ॐ ॥ ४.२.२॥

And for the same reason all organs follow as per Prashna 3.9.

ॐ तन्मनः पूराण उत्तरात् ॐ ॥ ४.२.३॥

That mind is merged in Prana, as seen from subsequent clause.

Here too, it is the function alone that gets merged, on the same basis as explained earlier. There is observation of mind stopping function, while vital force continuing.

ॐ सोऽध्यक्षे तदुपगमादभिय: ॐ ॥ ४.२.४॥

The Prana is merged in the soul on account of statements expressing approach.

Reference to Brihadaranyaka 4.3.38 and 4.4.2 proving Prana following the soul.

ॐ भूतेषु तच्छ्रुतेः ॐ ॥ ४.२.५॥

In the elements it is merged, as seen from Sruthi.

This means that Prana merges in Jiva the soul, which takes its abode in the fine essence of the elements of nature, because that is the seed of the future body.

ॐ नैकस्मिन् दर्शयतो हि ॐ ॥ ४.२.६॥

The soul with Prana is merged not just on one element.

This is because all elements like fire, water etc are required for the future body.

ॐ समाना चासृत्युपक्रमादमृतत्वं चानुपोष्य ॐ ॥ ४.२.७॥

And common is the mode of death for both the ignorant and the knower of Saguna Brahman upto the beginning of their ways, and the immortality of the latter is only relative, not having burnt ignorance.

The destination of both vary, as Brahmaloka and rebirth in earth.

ॐ तदपीतेः संसारव्यपदेशात् ॐ ॥ ४.२.८॥

That fine body lasts up to the attainment of Brahman through knowledge because scriptures declare the state of relative existence till then.

It has already been explained how as long as the first cause is not satisfied, creation cannot end. That can happen only through Knowledge, and until that point, an individualised soul is required, and thus the fine form called Sukshma as a subtle form where desires will be satiated as they are done in dream.

ॐ सूक्ष्मं प्रमाणतश्च तथोपलब्धेः ॐ ॥ ४.२.९॥

This fine body is subtle by nature and size because it is so experienced.

ॐ नोपमर्दनातः ॐ ॥ ४.२.१०॥

Therefore this subtle body is not destroyed by the destruction of the gross body.

In essence this subtle body is nothing but the mind, as much as a dream is created using the mind.

ॐ अस्यैव चोपपत्तरेषूमा ॐ ॥ ४.२.११॥

And to this fine body alone does this bodily heat belong, because this alone is possible.

Since bodily heat is there only so long as life is there, and this fine body represents life, the Sutra states so.

ॐ प्रतिषिधादिति चेन्न शारीरात् ॐ ॥ ४.२.१२॥

The claim that Pranas of a knower of Brahman do not depart on account of Sruthi denying it, we refute since the denial is only of the soul and not of the body.

Brihadaranyaka 4.4.6 states that Prana does not depart. The Madhyandina Sakha make it clear that only the body is referred to here.

ॐ स्पष्टो ह्येकेषाम् ॐ ॥ ४.२.१३॥

For the denial of departure is clear in some schools.

The reference is to Brihadaranyaka 3.2.11 specifically asserting that the Prana merges in the soul only.

ॐ स्मर्यते च ॐ ॥ ४.२.१४॥

And from Smritis too as per Mahabharata 12.270.22.

ॐ तानि परे तथा ह्याह ॐ ॥ ४.२.१५॥

Those Prana are merged on the Brahman, for the scripture says.

While in the dream standpoint the body merges in its direct Cause the elements, as per Mundaka 3.2.7. From the real standpoint though, the unreality of the dream understood, the dream itself merges into Brahman losing its status as real and individualised.

ॐ अवभिागो वचनात् ॐ ॥ ४.२.१६॥

Absolute non distinction with Brahman of the parts merged take place as per the scriptures.

This is the essence of liberation as per Prashna 6.5.

ॐ तदोकोऽग्रज्वलनं तत्प्रकाशतिद्वारो
वद्यिासामर्थ्यात्तच्छेषगत्यनुस्मृतयियोगाच्च हार्दानुह्हीताः
शताधकिया ॐ ॥ ४.२.१७॥

When the soul of the knower of the Saguna Brahman is about to depart from the body, there is the illumining of the top of its abode the heart, with the passage for the exit of the soul illumined by this light the soul departs, being favored by Him who resides in the heart, along with that nerve beyond the hundred ie Sushumna owing to the efficacy of knowledge and appropriateness of his constant meditation on the way to knowledge.

As from Brihadaranyaka 4.4.1-2, at the time of death, as the soul comes to the heart with all its organs, on account of its past works, has a peculiar consciousness illustrating to it its next life, and goes to the body revealed by that consciousness. This is what is referred to as the illumining of the heart. Until this point the journey is the same, after which, for the Saguna Brahman knower alone, through Sushumna, the soul departs through the skull.

ॐ रश्म्यनुसारी ॐ ॥ ४.२.१८॥

The soul of a knower of Saguna Brahman follows the rays of the sun as per Chhandogya 8.6.5.

ॐ निशि निति चेनेन संबन्धात् ॐ ॥ ४.२.१९॥ पाठभेदे 4.2.19 and 20 combined

ॐ यावद्देहभावत्विवाद्दर्शयति च ॐ ॥ ४.२.२०॥

The claim that in night, soul does not follow the rays, we refute as the connection of nerves and rays continues as long as the body lasts, as per Sruthis.

Even in night, the sun sheds his rays, as per Sruthi. Further, even in the moon, it is the sunlight alone that is reflected.

ॐ अतश्चायनऽपि दक्षिणि ॐ ॥ ४.२.२१॥

And for the same reason, the soul follows the rays even during the southern course of the sun.

The specification of northern course is to differentiate not the time of the year, but the direction as the world of Gods and ancestors.

ॐ योगिनः प्रति स्मर्यते स्मार्ते चैते ॐ ॥ ४.२.२२॥

And these times the Smriti ie Gita 8.23-24, declares with respect to Yogis, and these two ie Yoga and Sankhya are Smritis rather then Sruthis.

Thus, the specifications of bright half of the year must not be taken for Saguna Brahman knowers as per Veda Sruthis, says this Sutra.

ॐ अर्चिरादिना तत्प्रथितिः ॐ ॥ ४.३.१॥

On the path connected with deities beginning with flame, the soul of the knower of Saguna travels to Brahmaloka after death, as well known from Sruthis.

Reference to Chhandogya 5.10.1 and Brihadaranyaka 6.2.15 as the flame deity being the first destination, even as there are references giving other destinations. Yet Chhandogya 5.10.1 mentions the flame deity as destination for those that know Panchagni Vidya as well as those who meditate in forest with penance ie applicable to all. Other destinations mentioned in other texts must be taken as after the flame deity but before Brahmaloka. As already mentioned, these are dream creations just as much as earth.

ॐ वायुशब्दादवशिषेवशिषाभ्याम् ॐ ॥ ४.३.२॥

The soul of a knower of Saguna goes from deity of year to deity of air, on account of absence and presence of specifications.

Reference in combining the list of deities as paths given in Kaushitaki 1.3 and Chhandogya 5.10.1, along with Brihadaranyaka 5.10.1 to understand that air comes immediately before sun.

ॐ तटितोऽध्व‍िरुण: संबन्धात् ॐ ॥ ४.३.३॥

After reaching deity of lightning, the soul reaches Varuna on account of connection between the two.

The connection is that Varuna presides over water and rain, and lightning immediately precedes rain. With this here is the complete enumeration of stages of the path for one who knows Saguna Brahman: Fire, Day, Bright Fortnight, Northern Course Solar Months, Year, World of Gods, Air, Sun, Moon, Lightning, Varuna, Indra, Prajaapathi and eventually Brahmaloka.

ॐ आतिवाहिकिस्तल्लङ्गिगात् ॐ ॥ ४.३.४॥

These are deities conducting the souls to the Gods on account of indicatory marks.

Reference to Chhandogya 4.15.5 and 5.10.1, referring that those receive the departed soul and conduct it are deities.

ॐ उभयव्यामोहात्तत्सिद्धे: ॐ ॥ ४.३.५॥

That deities are meant is established, because both traveller and path are unconscious.

With organs withdrawn, the departed souls cannot perceive, while at the same time flame etc without intelligence cannot guide the souls. Thus the only possibility is that intelligent deities guide the soul, this intelligence of course coming from the first cause.

ॐ वैद्युतेनैव ततस्तच्छ्रुत: ॐ ॥ ४.३.६॥

From thence the souls are guided by the superhuman person who comes from lightning, as known from Sruthis.

Reference to Chhandogya 4.15.5, 5.10.1 and Brihadaranyaka 6.2.15 in that from the world of lightning till Brahmaloka, a superhuman and not Gods,guide the soul.

ॐ कार्यं बादररिस्य गत्युपपत्ते: ॐ ॥ ४.३.७॥

Relative Brahman is attained by the soul going by the path of the Gods, so says Badari, on account of its possibility of being the goal.

While Nirguna Brahman is all pervading only the Saguna is specific in form and limited by location, and thus, this is the Brahman to which the souls go.

ॐ विशिषतित्वाच्च ॐ ॥ ४.३.८॥

And on account of qualification with respect to Brahman.

Reference to Brihadaranyaka 6.2.15, mentioning worlds of Brahman, in plural, which is possible only for Saguna Brahman.

ॐ सामीप्यात्तत्तद्व्यपदेश: ॐ ॥ ४.३.९॥

But on account of nearness to Saguna Brahman to the supreme Brahman, and is designated so.

ॐ कार्यात्यये तदध्यक्षणे सहातः परमभिधानात् ॐ ॥ ४.३.१०॥

On the dissolution of Brahmaloka the souls attain along with its ruler what is higher than that ie Supreme Brahman, as per Sruthi.

This declaration clears the confusion of how souls no more returning to the world, will apply, if there is no permanency in any place except the Supreme Brahman, including even Brahmaloka?

ॐ स्मृतेश्च ॐ ॥ ४.३.११॥

And on account of Smritis concurring.

ॐ पर जैमिनिर्मुख्यत्वात् ॐ ॥ ४.३.१२॥

The Supreme Brahman is attained by the souls going by the path of Gods, so says Jaimini on account of that being the primary meaning of Brahman.

A claim is raised that Brahman in Chhandogya refers to the Supreme alone.

ॐ दर्शनाच्च ॐ ॥ ४.३.१३॥

On account of Sruthi.

Reference to Chhandogya 8.6.6 and Katha 2.6.16 that the soul passing out by Sushumna reaches immortality.

ॐ न च कार्ये प्रतिपित्त्यभिसिन्धः ॐ ॥ ४.३.१४॥

And desire to attain Brahman which an Upasaka has during time of death cannot be Saguna.

Reference to Chhandogya 8.14.1 in that the desire to attain the assembly house referring to Brahman as the abode of everything, which is the Nirguna.

The claims are refuted in the manner already explained in earlier sections: Journey is only possible for those where there is difference between attainer and attained. In the case of Nirguna which is all pervading, neither is there any travelling, nor any difference between attained and attainer. In the Saguna, the meditator limits the God to a particular form such as 4 armed, and also to a particular location such as Vaikuntha etc. In that case, there Is journey, there is attaining, and thus heaven after death.

ॐ अप्रतीकालम्बनान्नयतीति बादरायणरुभयथा च

दोषात् तत्क्रतुश्च ॐ ॥ ४.३.१५॥

Badarayana states that the superhuman leads to Brahmaloka only those who do not use a symbol of Brahman in their meditations, there being no contradiction if this distinction is made and as is the meditation on that, so does one become that.

This is because the worship of symbols distracts the mind from focusing on Brahman into focusing on the symbol instead.

ॐ विशिषं च दर्शयति ॐ ॥ ४.३.१६॥

And the scriptures declare a difference with respect to meditation on symbols.

Reference to Chhandogya 7.1.5 and 7.2.2 in that Sruthi tells of different results according to difference in symbols. Thus, those who use symbols do not go to Brahmaloka unlike those who meditate on Saguna Brahman. Fundamentally, the difference between the two is respectively as simple as worshipping a Vigraha as just a Vigraha or as a living person with some relation with the Ishtadevata. The realised soul of Nirguna Brahman on the other hand, does not use the Vigraha but simply abides in the Self and surrenders to the Will of God, seeing thus God in everything animate and inanimate. However, this doesn't preclude such a liberated soul in the further stage of Jivanmukthi or Leela, in using a Vigraha, just for the purpose of playing. Such a person, already liberated, does not limit God to the Vigraha, but rather sees his own Self as well as the Vigraha as the same God, but as the observer and player respectively, and the latter to have for example infinite invisible arms operating all of reality so that God is seen in everything.

ॐ सम्पद्यावहिाय स्वेनेशब्दात् ॐ ॥ ४.४.१॥

When the soul has attained the highest light, there is manifestation of its real nature, as known from the word own in Chhandogya 8.3.4.

In essence, the nature of creation as a dream is understood and the soul understands itself to be the dreamer. This is the original, real state, as the dreamer, even before the dream began.

ॐ मुक्तः परतज्ज्ञानात् ॐ ॥ ४.४.२॥

The Self attaining its true nature attains liberation, this is the premise.

References to liberation being free of misconception and thus pain etc in Chhandogya 8.9.3, 8.10.4, 8.11.3, 8.12.1-3.

ॐ आत्मा परकरणात् ॐ ॥ ४.४.३॥

The light attained by soul is the Self,on account of context.

This is because Self is the subject matter introduced in Chhandogya 8.7.1, and Brahman as light mentioned in Brihadaranyaka 4.4.16.

ॐ अवभिगने दृष्टत्वात् ॐ ॥ ४.४.४॥

The soul in liberation is inseparable from Brahman as seen from scriptures.

The essence of Vedic Mahavakyas such as Aham Brahmaasmi, Ayam Atma Brahma, or Tatvamasi is this, as also Brihadaranyaka 4.4.6.

ॐ ब्राह्मणे जैमिनिरुपन्यासादभिय: ॐ ॥ ४.४.५॥

Liberated soul is possessed of attributes of Brahman as per Jaimini on account of reference.

Reference to liberation being attainment of conditioned aspect seen in Chhandogya 8.7.1 ie free from sorrow, evil, hunger etc. Here the very context of liberation implies bondage prior to liberation, and if bondage is conditioned such as sorrow etc ,then liberation too is conditioned. However, what must be known is that, the conditions of bondage, and the bondage itself is unreal. Hence the conditioned reference to liberation applies only from the context of the unliberated, ie within the dream.

ॐ चतिमित्रेण तदात्मकत्वादत्यौडुलोमि: ॐ ॥ ४.४.६॥

Liberated soul exists solely as pure intelligence as per Audulomi.

This reinforces the above explanation, seen from the perspective outside the dream.

ॐ एवमप्यप्युपन्यासात्पूर्वभावादवरोध बादरायण: ॐ ॥ ४.४.७॥

Even if it be so, on account of former qualities existing owing to reference from relative standpoint, there is no contradiction between the two, as per Badarayana.

Again, as has been explained earlier, both views of conditioned and pure intelligence are from different perspectives ie from inside and outside the dream, and do not contradict each other.

ॐ सङ्कल्पादेव च तच्छ्रुते: ॐ ॥ ४.४.८॥

But through mere will, the released souls attain their purpose, as per scriptures.

Reference is to Chhandogya 8.2.1. In the absence of organs etc manifest, those released souls that have journeyed to heavens due to realising Saguna Brahman, can effect their desires through will alone. That is, the dream creation itself is nothing but will arising from first cause. As much as earth is a dream creation, heaven too is, both subjected to the will.

ॐ अत एव चानन्याधिपति: ॐ ॥ ४.४.९॥

And for this reason, the released soul is without a Lord as per Chhandogya 8.1.6.

ॐ अभावं बादररिह ह्यवेम् ॐ ॥ ४.४.१०॥

There is absence of body and organs for released souls, says Badari as per scriptures reference Chhandogya 8.12.5.

ॐ भावं जैमिनिर्विकिल्पाम्नानात् ॐ ॥ ४.४.११॥

Released soul possesses body and organs, says Jaimini, due to scriptures mentioning capacity to assume diverse forms, reference being Chhandogya 7.26.2.

ॐ द्वादशाहवद्भयवधिं बादरायणोऽत: ॐ ॥ ४.४.१२॥

From this Badarayana surmises that the released soul is of both kinds like the twelve day sacrifice called Sattra or Ahina. The choice of a body or not is according to the soul's liking.

ॐ तन्वभावे सन्ध्यवद्रुपपत्त: ॐ ॥ ४.४.१३॥

In the absence of body, fulfilment of desires is possible, just like in dreams.

ॐ भावे जाग्रद्वत् ॐ ॥ ४.४.१४॥

When the body exists, the fulfilment of desires is as in the waking state.

ॐ प्रदीपवदावेश: तथा हि दर्शयति ॐ ॥ ४.४.१५॥

The released soul animating different bodies is like that of a flame, because the scriptures show.

The released soul can take not just one but as many bodies as it wants, and just as the same flame lights many wicks, so too may animate all those bodies. Here, what is clearly understood is that, having achieved knowledge and removal of miseries etc, it is time to fulfill the first cause ie intense bliss as enjoyment within the unreal creation. This is all that matters. With the agency fully destroyed, nothing can bind the soul anymore. It doesn't matter whether a body is taken, or not taken. In fact, having understood that this enjoyment is the purpose of creation, it is clear that even souls who have attained liberation into Nirguna Brahman can take a body just for the sake of enjoyment. As much as liberated souls enjoying as Jivanmukthas with the unreal body cannot be denied due to no other explanation possible for their Prana, organs etc after death, in the same way, these souls enjoying in the subtle or gross body after death cannot be denied too. The only difference is that in the case of Nirguna, as there is no more knowledge to attain, they are not bound by rules such as fixed journey, stay in Brahmaloka until Pralaya etc, since for them it is not a procedure in the way to knowledge but simply enjoyment without restrictions.

At this point, one may pose a question: as per Sri Vidya Vedanta, the ultimate purpose of creation is that state of Mukthi, where bliss is intensified due to illusive feeling of joining after separation, and that intense bliss is expressed through love and play. If that be the case, then how long does this Mukthi last? Is it really worth the effort of thousands of births of separation, all for a few years of happy bliss? And who is to say, after merging with Brahman at the end of this Jeevanmukthi, the whole process of creation will not be done again, to intensify the bliss even more?

We answer these questions thus. First, the stage of Mukthi, especially with the subtle body ie Videha Mukthi taken purely out of choice as explained above, is not bound by rules. What is called subtle body is merely the mind, the same creator of this dream world. Such a subtle body is not subject to the rules of time and aging, especially if in constant identity as Brahman itself, due to having achieved full enlightenment - we can already see glimpses of the timelessness in Samadhi stage, both Savikalpa and Nirvikalpa. Thus, if the subtle body is basically timeless, then where is the question is this Videha mukthi stage ending, and then merging into Brahman, and then creation again taking place or not? The merging into Brahman is controlled purely by the soul's choice. Thus, astrological calculations of dates for Sukshma Sharira is only relevant in the scope of so many years being a minimum, that too as seen from the perspective of the unenlightened. This is why the earlier Sutra mentions that the knower of Saguna Brahman, after death departs to the Loka of his Ishta Devatha; but even then, the Sutra says these souls depart those Lokas during the time of Pralaya and not upon attainment of knowledge. Here Pralaya simply means whenever creation is wiped out, which happens only when the dream ends - so here again, the end is brought only by the choice of Amma. So, the ultimate purpose of creation is to achieve this Videha mukthi state, one where creation continues but at the same time, the concept of time is rendered meaningless, as well as full knowledge is achieved - it is only in this state that the enjoyment of the intense bliss is possible expressed through love, as long as desired, without any impediments or restrictions. Categorically, the state of Videha mukthi as Leela with Sukshma Sharira and the final merging of Brahman often cited as the ultimate end are compatible. This is because, the Sukshma body is merely the mind, and by simply choosing to forget or remember the dream creation, these states can be achieved, simultaneously since there is no concept of time in Sukshma form.

For those particular in terminology, the Liberated duration enjoying Leela while alive in the physical body may be called Jeevanmukthi while the same in the Sukshma body after death may be called Videha Mukthi, which is well acknowledged to be the final end. As proof to this end, we have the author of the Autobiography of Sri M, witnessing in subtle form through meditation, all enlightened souls going all the way back to Buddha and Adi Shankara, this visualization having happened in the 20th century. With the concept of time rendered moot, the Anithyas ie creations in the dream are only called so because of their potency to be destroyed in a moment anytime by the Self. As long as the Jeevanmukthi lasts, so will the creation Anithyas continue. In different cultures, they are believed to manifest as deities, around whom, in the divided world, religions developed, and seekers were taken to salvation. Thus, the Anithyas, which are aspects of the body, nature etc are not venerated as the physical entities themselves, but as the Tatvas that create then, since it is the mental creation that spawns the physical ones. In that capacity, and given that while in potency they may be absorbed back in a moment while in reality, especially during one's last birth they will persist until the dream is closed, these Anithyas may thus be seen as capable of blessing and gracing the earnest seeker towards liberation, much as the Nithya forms as well.

It has already been mentioned that the entire creation is just a dream spun forth from the mind - This applies to the world creation while alive as well as Videhamukti. By and large, these two may be referred to as Sadeha and Videha respectively translated as with and without body. Technically, in both cases the body is created only by the mind, and only in the instants when one is aware of a body part, the body part exists. The Sadeha state is what is called life or Jeevan, which is primarily the wake state, but with intermissions of dream and sleep interspersed. The purpose of Sadeha is to create a false feeling of separateness and then crossing the stages into blissful union - This Sadeha thus relies on an imposition, that of ignorance and then of its removal. The purpose of Videha is to enjoy in the intensified bliss till eternity. Jeevanmukthi too is a part of Sadeha, but is an optional state not necessarily experienced by everyone, especially if a person dies after crossing Saguna but before liberation.

The difference between the creations of Sadeha and Videha is in one key factor - in Sadeha, continuity is imposed, while in Videha it is not. One can get glimpses of this even in Sadeha at times, in dreams. For example, suppose a person dreams of flying from Delhi to New York over 16 hours.

It happens that the entire duration of the travel is not shown minute by minute in the dream, but the non essential durations are skipped, and the scene directly changes to destination, with the understanding that this is a dream. That is, continuity can be broken at will. This is the same case in Videha too. In Sadeha, there is the imposition of continuity. For those not yet liberated, this continuity is inevitable, essential and crucial in maintaining the Karma Vasanas, and their increase or decrease, as well as progress through stages and perspectives. In Videha, with all stages achieved, there is no such need for continuity imposition. This means, one is not limited by time and thus space, since they are not limiting factors, but merely used to create the ambience for enjoyment. Thus, in Sadeha, even if one is enlightened ie Jeevanmukthi, to think that the body is unreal and does not exist until awareness comes about, one does not have the power to change situations accordingly, since continuity cannot be broken. Thus, constantly being rooted and tied to the same surroundings and body, one is forced to feel the body as an indispensable attachment, even if not one's own self - This is the essence of "with body" or Sadeha.

The purpose of Videha is to experience the intense bliss in all of creation - where full expression can be achieved. With the space limitations lifted, one can travel instantly, even to distant galaxies and black holes. From this it directly follows that one travels to any location in space instantly, ie one travels faster than light, from which follows, according to relativistic physics, the ability of time travel - even in dreams at times in Sadeha, one might see different scenes one after another, which do not follow a chronological order. This means one might travel to any point in the past or future. For example, consider an enlightened soul or Guru yet to be born. He will be born in due course, experience the entire lifetime alive on Earth, and after passing away, enter Videhamukthi, at which point he can time travel and arrive at this point in time, much earlier to his birth chronologically. This is the same logic by which Puranas have been written about the incarnation Kalki. Generally, while just experiencing situations and enjoying oneself, the one in Videha only interacts with others who are in Sadeha only when called for by the latter. However, the flexibility of choosing a body, coupled with the fact that nobody would know let alone call a person yet to be born, means that time travel doesn't really alter the course of events, as commonly depicted in scientific paradoxes. Since the Sutras do mention the capability to animate many bodies at the same time, one can of course in Videha travel in the past and observe one's own previous births in Sadeha simultaneously experiencing both.

It is mentioned in Sutras how one has all powers except creation, while in Videha. This means that the entire dream creation can neither be created ie brought forth, or obliterated ie Pralaya, since both are against the purpose of creation, which is to enjoy till eternity. Also, in Videha, all the beings in Sukshma form, ie other Videha Mukthas, Siddhas, Yogis, Rishis etc all become visible and one gets the power to invoke any desired form of the Divine at will - glimpses of such capabilities can be seen among Yogis, even in Sadeha. In Videha, one's residence will be set to Sumeru, whereas one may roam all the expanse of the universe at will, returning to Sumeru to enjoy solitude with Amma. Also in Videha, one will see the whole world, especially the residence of Divine ie Srimannagara, Sumeru etc as radiant and resplendent, full of riches and gems etc. One will during the various interactions and events in Videha, invoke the forms either as aspects of nature or mind modes and mental aspects or parts of the optional body.

ॐ स्वाप्ययसम्पत्त्योरन्यतरापेक्षमाविष्कृतं हि ॐ ॥ ४.४.१६॥

Declaring of absence of all cognition is made having in view either of the two states ie deep sleep or union with the Brahman.

In the case of Nirguna Brahman liberation, there is no cognition, just like deep sleep. However, this does not apply to Saguna Brahman, where there is cognition. In fact, the enjoyment of the soul in Brahmaloka is very much Jivanmukthi along with the last few years on Earth after liberation - it is just that the former is subtle and the latter is gross form.

ॐ जगद्व्यापारवर्जम् ॐ ॥ ४.४.१७॥ पाठभेदे 4.4.17 and 18 combined

ॐ प्रकरणादसन्निहितित्वाच्च ॐ ॥ ४.४.१८॥

The released soul attains all Godly powers except creation, on account of Ishwara being the subject matter of all creation, and released souls not being mentioned in that connection.

The unlimited powers are mentioned in Chhandogya 7.25.2, 8.1.6 and Taittiriya 1.5. These are for the purpose of satisfying the original Cause ie unbridled enjoyment of all creation. However, the power to create is not in alignment with the first cause, and hence that is not possible.

ॐ प्रत्यक्षोपदेशादिति चेन्नाधिकारिकमण्डलस्थोक्तेः ॐ ॥ ४.४.१९॥

The claim that the released attains absolute powers on account of direct teaching, we refute on the basis that the souls attain Him who entrusts the sun etc with their powers and resides in them.

This again is reinforcing that even at the released state, since the soul is considered different to the Brahman, in such case, it is with Brahman that the first cause, and thus the powers lie.

ॐ वकिारावर्तिच तथा हि दर्शयति स्थितिमिाह ॐ ॥ ४.४.२० ॥

And there is a form of the Lord beyond all created things, since the scriptures declare His existence in a twofold form.

The Nirguna form is all pervading and unlimited whereas the Saguna is limited in form. What one meditates, one becomes as per Sruthis.

ॐ दर्शयतश्चैव प्रत्यक्षानुमाने ॐ ॥ ४.४.२१ ॥

And thus perception and inference show.

Sruthi and Smriti reference respectively as Mundaka 2.2.10 and Gita 15.6, for the Nirguna Brahman.

ॐ भोगमात्रसाम्यलङ्गिगाच्च ॐ ॥ ४.४.२२ ॥

And because of indications of equality of the released soul with the Lord only with respect to enjoyment.

Enjoyment being the cause is reinforced here, with references Brihadaranyaka 1.5.20,23.

ॐ अनावृ्तिः शब्दादनावृ्तिः शब्दात् ॐ ॥ ४.४.२३ ॥

There is no return for the released souls, on account of scriptural declaration.

The reference of no return is given in references Chhandogya 8.6.6 and Brihadaranyaka 6.2.15. This is because the first cause ie enjoyment and intensifying bliss is completely fulfilled.

CHAPTER NINE

Guru

The wisdom of Brahma Sutra gives a comprehensive and complete view of reality and this wisdom is the product of thousands of enlightened ancestors called Gurus, who have achieved this correct perception and living. The earliest and firerunner to all these Gurus of Sri Vidya is Lord Dattatreya, who is said to be a combined form of Shiva, Vishnu and Brahma denoting the threefold operations of creation, preservation and destruction. Over the ages Dattatreya has manifested into several forms of Gurus, and just hundred years ago, as a forerunner to the Satya Yuga, Dattatreya has taken a grand consolidated incarnation, called Sai Baba of Shirdi. Sai the name means Sa Aai, the good and benevolent Mother Goddess Herself, and the very life of Sai itself completely encapsulates all the core Vedic principles in action, as will be explored in this chapter. Thus, just like Venkatesha form is for the Maha Mantra, the Sai is the form of Mother Goddess for the Maha Tantra, guarding and activating the sacred mountain of Sumeru.

Before that, it is essential to clear some gross misconceptions about Sai, which lead to ridiculous claims about the Guru. These baseless claims stand as a clear mirror, reflecting how baseless and illiterate the very proponents of such claims are. Authoritative References to the life of Sai shall be twofold: the Satcharita by Henadpant, and the Sai Guru Charitra by Das Ganu, both enlightened disciples of Sai who have written these books with the express blessing and guidance by Sai.

Sai Baba

First, we start by recalling and strongly reinforcing here, Sai's own words recounted in th above mentioned two as well as many sources including "Everyone's Sai": "I live in a Mosque but I am not a Muslim; I light the holy fire but I am not a Hindu. I wish to break your concepts about me". This statement is very crucial, coming directly from Sai Himself, and answers a lot of misconceptions.

First, can a person who is not a Muslim Himself, convert others to Islam? So too, a non Hindu person cannot convert people to Hinduism either. Thus, people who look at Sai as either Hindu or Muslim are not only wrong, but in a single stroke, they insult Sai Himself, as well as insulting the Dharmic and Abrahamic faiths. While as a figure of compassion, Sai may not react to such stupidity with force, such people will definitely be punished by guardian deities of both these faiths. Even more ridiculous and blasphemous are those who, instead of Vedic spirituality, call Puranic Hinduism as the eternal Sanatana Dharma, and then use Sai's own quote given above to say that He is not a Guru of the Sanatana Dharma. It is these people that will bear the biggest brunt of punishment for such sacrilege and blasphemy.

Next, one might raise the objection that He wore the attire of a Muslim rather than a saffron attire that befits a Sanyasi. To this, one must understand that, even though Sai did not follow any Dharmic or Abrahamic religion, He was obliged to honour the established faiths. He resided in a mosque and thus it was only appropriate that His attire was a Muslim one. Isn't everybody, Sikh or otherwise, required to wear a turban before entering a Gurudwara? Moreover, the Satcharita clearly mentions that He did not wear this attire since birth, but did so only after willingly embracing defeat in a wrestling bout. How can such a background suggest any connection between the attire and Islam? He did not, as per the Satcharita, display any bodily signs of Islam such as Sunnat which is mandated for every Muslim male. So too, He did not sport a Urdhvapundra or Tripundra Thilak or even the Upavitha, which was mandatory for a Hindu male. Thus, any claims of religion based on His appearance, is again blasphemous. It must be noted that Sai did not choose to live in a mosque, but was originally found meditating under a neem tree. It was Mahalsapati and others by whom He started to live in a mosque. However, after His passing away, His Samadhi now is in a building originally constructed as a Krishna temple by Booti, to show precisely that He cared only for the sanctity of a place, irrespective of what faith it belonged to.

While repeatedly proving His point of not adhering to any post Vedic religion, by appearance and practices, Sai nevertheless showed strict adherence to the Nath tradition, displaying all the practices of this tradition. He lit the Dhuni or eternal fire. He had His ears pierced, what is known as Khanphata, and also didn't shave His head. He smoked Bhang or cannabis. He performed Hatha Yoga practices including extreme ones such as severing the body parts and affixing them back later on called Khanda Yoga, as well as Dhauti. Finally, a Sanyasi tradition that the Nath is, Sai was strict in living through alms or Bhiksha alone. References to each of these are abundant in the Satcharita. We shall later see how the Nath tradition, crosses all religious boundaries, including a far as Christ within its folds, thus making it undoubtedly a Vedic tradition, originating from Swaminatha or Skanda Himself and the 12 disciples of Amma.

With this established, one needs to understand the rationale behind Sai's repeated teachings and sayings, using terminology of Hindu and Muslim faiths. Being neither Hindu nor Muslim meant He was not qualified to preach either religion, and thus, cannot convey Hindu or Muslim teachings. Rather, He used the terminology of these faiths to convey Vedic teachings that are in reality, timeless. Why these two faiths? Because, in Abrahamic traditions, religions tend to be accumulative or additive. That is, each tradition embraces those previous to it. As a consequence, Islam respects and affirms through sanctity of Christian and Jewish teachings through its concept of 24 prophets. In contrast, Dharmic religions tend to be subtractive. That is, newer religions tend to eschew more and more from the older faiths, making an older faith more inclusive. Thus, Hinduism, in a concept such as the 24 incarnations of Vishnu, conveniently includes Buddha and Adinatha, founders of the Buddhist and Jain traditions, within its folds. This means that by combining the earliest Dharmic and latest Abrahamic faith, one can get the most vastness of philosophy possible in the Puranic era, and this is exactly what Sai did. Moreover Sai is not unique in doing so, since, prior to Him, Kabir, Guru Nanak and other Sikh Gurus have achieved this already.

This point means that any terms that are used in the teachings of Sai, such as Allah Malik, or Narayan etc cannot be taken in religious context, but rather as vernacular words to explain Vedic concepts. That is, Allah must not be taken as an Islamic God in particular, but simply an Arabic word that means "The God". So too Narayan as a Sanskrit word that means the ultimate destination of mankind. Now we may ask, outside of the Puranic religions, when Sai uses these words to refer to God, which deity is He talking about? We can obtain the answer by considering two important aspects. First, the Dhuni bring the eternal flame, may be seen in Vedic light, as the very Rig Veda starts with Agni Suktha. Thus, the Vedic deity is venerated here. Which Vedic deity? The term Dhuni connotes Yoni or cleft, and thus, the Mother Amma alone is referred to here, which can be seen either as Veda Maatha Gayatri, or Lalitha as the Sahasranamam mentions Chidagni Kunda Sambhutha. The mosque that formed Sai's residence was called by Him as Dwarkamai, again Maayi referring here to the Mother aspect. Further, the very name Sai, for which no Puranic religion manages to give a correct translation, can be understood as Saa Ayi, meaning that She is the Mother. Sai enters Shirdi along with a marriage party, after helping Chand Patil find a lost horse, and then is given the name Sai by Mahalsapati the priest of Khandoba temple.

It is only natural that a Nath Yogi venerates the Mother constantly, as they have been accustomed to as Kundalini Shakti. Furthermore the first Sai was spotted in Shirdi was under a neem tree, meditating and engrossed in Samadhi, and neem is known to be sacred to Amma. Thus, all terms used by Sai such as Allah, Narayan, etc etc refer to Amma alone, and earlier in this book, we have already seen how the various Puranic deities of different religions are but the forms of Amma alone.

With this foundation, we now proceed to examine the incidents and teachings of Sai mentioned the Satcharitra chapter by chapter, each of which will be given briefly in a sentence. Corresponding to each such teaching of Sai, we shall understand with reference the Vedic or Upanishadic teaching that Sai has reinforced thus. This means that we shall restrict to references directly from Vedas or Upanishads as well as the Brahma Sutra, and in extremely rare cases, the Bhagavad Gita and Guru Gitas.

- Sai symbolises the destruction of the three Gunas, Sattvic, Rajasic and Tamasic, by the grinding of wheat. Destruction of all three is necessary to achieve enlightenment and liberation.

- Atharva Veda 10.8.43 states the Gunas as a covering layer of impurity thus: "There is a nine-gated lotus, covered under three bands of GunAs (tribhir gunebhi), in which lives the Spirit with the Atman within, that the Veda-knowers know.

- Sai emphasises the need of a Guru, in taking us to the spiritual destination high up, avoiding wolves, tigers, ditches etc on the way.

- The syllable Gu indicates darkness, the syllable Ru means its dispeller. Because of the quality of dispelling darkness, the Guru is thus termed. Advayataraka Upanishad, 16.

- Sai gives a promise of bliss, joy, liberation and enlightenment to those that write, read, dive deep into His Leelas, surrenders to Him as Guru, and even simply repeats the Guru Nama Sai. The explanation of the Guru Nama in containing the Shodashi has already been given earlier. In fact this very Nama Smarana is emphasised as the ideal Sadhana, especially in the present Kali Yuga, as contrasted with Shamadama, sacrifice, and worship for the earlier 3 Yugas. Sai told people to leave off all cleverness and always remember "Sai" "Sai". "If you did that" He said, "all your shackles would be removed and you would be free".... The function of the mind is to think, it cannot remain for a minute without thinking. If you give it a Sense-object, it will think about it. If you give it to a Guru, it will think about Guru.

- Sandilya says in Sandilya Upanishad, "The Vaikhari Japa (loud pronunciation) gives the reward as stated in the Vedas; while the Upamsu Japa (whispering or humming which cannot be heard by any one) gives a reward a thousand times more than the Vaikhari; the Manasic Japa gives a reward a crore of times more than the Vaikhari. ".

- Sai does not condemn, but requested villagers to temporarily endure the act of a certain Rohilla, who cries out loud constantly the name of Allah, causing public nuisance, and Sai justifies stating that this keeps him away from bad thoughts.

- The Brihadaranyaka Upanishad begins with the word Aum. In some verses it refers to it as udgita or loud chanting and declares the proper way to chant it is in conjunction with speech and with deep upper breath (or inhalation in which the chest is pulled up). This does not however condone the act of creating noise pollution by blaring in loud speakers. Sai only condones loud crying out to the Lord by voice, without sound amplification equipment.

- Sai emphasises how He is the inner ruler of all, seated in their hearts.

- "Antah Pravishta Shaastaa Jananaam Sarvaathma | Sarvaa Praja Yatraikam Bhavanti|", or "Where all are united, He who has entered within, that are born, and is the self of all, is beyond comprehension, He is Shaasta the ruler of all things". Similarly, in another verse, "Antah Pravishta Shaastaa Jananaam Ekasanbahudaa Vichaara | Shatha Shukraani Yatraikam Bhavanti|". This is what Taittiriya Aranyaka of the Krishna branch of Yajur Veda says in verses 3-11-1 and 3-11-2.

- Sai maintains the eternal fire or Dhuni in Dwarkamai, constantly fed with fuel, which continues to burn till this date. In Nath tradition, Yogis regard fire as the very part of their Self, gazing at the flames for hours. The mind merges in the fire, which being a very symbol of desire, fulfils the wishes of the mind. Fire also denotes the spirit, always upwards, destroying entire forests with a single spark, and igniting other fires without loss to the Mother flame. Finally, the Yogis see in Dhuni the inner fire ie Kundalini which blazes forth upwards touching the Sahasrara.

- The very opening verses of Rig Veda say: I worship the Sacred Fire (Agni) that is chief priest, the deity of the sacrifice, who works according to the seasons, the invoker, best to grant the treasure. The Sacred Fire honored by the ancient sages is invoked again by the new. For us he manifests all the Gods. To you, oh Fire, day by day, by dawn and by dusk we come bearing our offering of surrender, the king of the sacred rite, the guardian of truth, flourishing in his own nature. Atharva Veda states: There is a Divine fire in the Earth and in the plants. The Waters carry the fire and the same fire dwells in the rocks. There is a fire within human beings, within the cows and the horses are sacred fires. The Divine fire shines from heaven as the Sun. The Divine fire extends the wide atmosphere through the wind. Mortals enkindle the Fire that carries their prayers, which loves clarity.

- Sai Baba conquered this Samsar (worldly existence), which is very difficult and hard to cross. Peace or mental calm was His ornament, and He was the repository of wisdom. He was the home of Vaishnava devotees, most liberal (like Karna) amongst liberals, the quint-essence of all essences. He had no love for perishable things, and was always engrossed in self-realization, which was His sole concern. He felt no pleasure in the things of this world or of the world beyond. His Antarang (heart) was as clear as a mirror, and His speech always rained nectar. The rich or poor people were the same to Him. He did not know or care for honour or dishonour. He was the Lord of all beings. He spoke freely and mixed with all people, saw the actings and dances of Nautchgirls and heard Gajjal songs. Still, He swerved not an inch from Samadhi (mental equilibrium). The name of Allah was always on His lips. While the world awoke, He slept; and while the world slept, He was vigilant. His abdomen (Inside) was as calm as the deep sea. His Ashram could not be determined, nor His actions could be definitely determined, and though He sat (lived) in one place, He knew all the transactions of the world. His Darbar was imposing. He told daily hundreds of stories, still He swerved not an inch from His vow of silence.

He always leaned against the wall in the Masjid or walked morning, noon and evening towards Lendi (Nala) and Chavadi; still He at all times abided in the Self. Though a Siddha, He acted like a Sadhaka. He was meek, humble and egoless, and pleased all. Hemadpant thinks that on account of the store or accumulation of merits in his past births, he had the good fortune of meeting and being blessed by such a Sad-guru as Sai Baba. Even in full youth He hoarded nothing (expect perhaps chillim). He had no family, no friend, no home, nor any support. Since He was eighteen, His control of mind was perfect and extra-ordinary. He lived then fearless in a secluded place and always abided in His Self. Seeing the pure attachment of His devotees He always acted in their interests and hence He was in a way dependent on them. What experiences He gave to His devotees while he was living in flesh, are even to-day, after His Mahasamadhi, obtained now by those who attach themselves to Him. What the devotees have to do is this - They have to trim their heart-lamp of faith and devotion, and burn in it wicks of love, and when this is done, the flame of knowledge (self-realization) will be lit up and shine brighter. Mere knowledge without love is dry; nobody wants such knowledge. Without love there is no contentment; so we should have unbroken and unbounded love.

- Varaha Upanishad verses 4.21–4.30 describe the characteristics of a Jivanmukta; He who is engrossed in the ways of the world, yet his mind is steady, like ether, is said to be Jivanmukta. He whose mental radiance neither rises nor sets, whose inner state is neither affected by happiness nor by misery inflicted on him, is said to be Jivanmukta. He who is wakeful while remaining asleep, he whose mental alertness is devoid of impressions, is known as Jivanmukta. He who responds to influences such as hatred, fear, love, yet his heart remains pure like Akasha (aether, space), is said to be Jivanmukta. He whose attitude is not be attached to anything, his intellect never clouded whether active or passive, is a Jivanmukta. He who does not shrink out of fear from the world, nor the world shrinks from him, who is free from anger, fear and joy, is a Jivanmukta. He whose mind is not agitated, though participating in the world, who rests in state of calmness and absolute consciousness, no matter what, is known as Jivanmukta.

- Sai appears as Lord Vitthal to Kakasaheb, while Ganga and Yamuna flow out of His feet as Prayag, for Das Ganu.

- In the Taittiriya Upanishad (1.11.2), students are urged to treat their teacher a god himself (acharya devobhava).

- Akkalkot Samarth Swami, considered an incarnation of Dattatreya, confirmed through a vision to a devotee that Sai is His incarnation, while Sai too confirmed the same. This confirms Sai as one of a series of incarnations of Dattatreya starting with Narasimha Saraswathi. The incarnation of Sai is significant for reviving the Nath tradition for the forthcoming Yuga, as much as Dattatreya Himself did in the previous era. Later, Sai speaks of donning the saffron garment to manifest to an Agnihotri as His own Guru. In a later incident, highlighting the oneness of all Gurus, Sai also equally emphasised adhering staunchly to one's own Guru and tradition: Come what may, leave not, but stick to your Bolster (support, i.e. Guru) and ever remain steady, always at-one-ment (in union) with him. Even after passing away, Sai reinforced this idea through visions: give respect to the words of other saints, but at the same time asks us to have full faith in our Mother, i.e., the Guru, and abide by His instructions: for he knows our welfare better than any other person. Carve out on your heart, the following words of Baba - are innumerable saints in this world, but 'Our father' (Guru) is the Father (Real Guru). Others might say many good things, but we should never forget our Guru's words. In short, love your Guru wholeheartedly, surrender to Him completely and prostrate yourselves before Him reverentially and then you will see that there is no sea of the mundane existence before you to cross, there is no darkness before the sun.

- All Gurus operate as One unit, one breath, because in reality, all Guru is one's own Atma alone. Guru Gita states: The Guru is not different from the conscious Self. Without doubt, this is the truth; therefore wise men should make an effort to seek knowledge of Atman from Him.

- Sai only gave answers when he was questioned. Baba's paraphernalia at this time consisted of a Chilim, tobacco, a "Tumrel" (tin pot), long flowing Kafni, a piece of cloth round His head, and a Satka (short stick), which He always kept with Him. The piece of white cloth on the head was twisted like matted hair, and flowed down from the left ear on the back. This was not washed for weeks. He wore no shoes, no sandals. A piece of sack-cloth was His seat for most of the day. He wore a coupin (waistcloth-band) and for warding off cold he always sat in front of a Dhuni (sacred fire) facing south with His left hand resting on the wooden railing. In that Dhuni, He offered as oblation; egoism, desires and all thoughts and always uttered Allah Malik (God is the sole owner). The Masjid in which He sat was only of two room dimensions, where all devotees came and saw Him. Before Baba came to live in this Masjid, He lived for a long time in a place Takia, where with small bells on His legs, Baba danced beautifully sang with tender love.

- Pot, drinking cup and flask – the three supports, a pair of shoes, a patched robe giving protection – in heat and cold, a loin cloth, bathing drawers and straining cloth, triple staff and coverlet. Thus Sannyasa Upanishad, 1.4 describes the possessions of a Sanyasi.

- Sai punishes the untruthful oil vendors who denied oil by lighting lamps with water. So too, one Javhar Ali posing untruthfully as a Guru of Sai out of egoism, was rectified by exposing the shallowness of the pseudo Guru through testing by one Devidas.

- Brihadaranyaka Upanishad (3.9.24), which states, "The one who takes initiation (diksha) into spiritual life has to take the vow of speaking truth. Hence, by truth only initiation is supported."

- Sai reiterates the statements of Bhagavad Gita as "There will never be any dearth or scarcity, regarding food and clothes, in any devotees homes. It is my special characteristic, that I always look to, and provide, for the welfare of those devotees, who worship Me whole-heartedly with their minds ever fixed on Me. Lord Krishna has also said the same in the Gita. Therefore, strive not much for food and clothes. If you want anything, beg of the Lord, leave worldly honours, try to get Lord s grace and blessings, and be honored in His Court. Do not be deluded by worldly honor. The form of the Deity should be firmly fixed in the mind. Let all the senses and mind be ever devoted to the worship of the Lord, let there be no attraction for any other thing; fix the mind in remembering Me always, so that it will not wander elsewhere, towards body, wealth and home. Then it will be calm, peaceful and care-free. This is the sign of the mind, being well engaged in good company. If the mind is vagrant, it cannot be called well-merged."

- Sai oversees the celebrations of the Hindu Ram Navami and the Muslim Urus sandal festival, on the same day, simultaneously, in the Dwarkamai mosque.

- Sai rescues a child falling into the fire remotely by putting His own hand into the Dhuni, and also cures the plague of a child by absorbing it within Himself. Undertaking personal responsibility for spiritual upliftment is a hallmark of the Vedic Guru Shishya system.

- Sai used to partake of the obtained alms with dogs and other animals everyday. Sai warned about the effects of eating alone, quoting Sudama as an example.

- I speak the truth, it is indeed his death. He who nourishes neither the god nor a friend, he who eats alone, gathers sin. (Rig Veda X. 117).

- On various occasions Sai advised various devotees not to travel at haste, but wait for some time before starting, so as to avoid accidents, and not paying heed to these instructions have caused accidents. So too He has saved many devotees from imminent calamities by warning then beforehand.

- It is through Atman that one perceives all objects in sleep or in the waking state. Having realized the vast, all-pervading Atman, the calm soul does not grieve. He who knows the individual soul, the experiencer of the fruits of action, as Atman, always near, and the Lord of the past and the future, will not conceal himself from others. This, verily, is That. (2.1) -- Katha Upanishad.

- Sai emphasised and was meticulous in obtaining food only through alms. Shastras say that those persons, who, getting rid of, or becoming free from the three main Desires, viz. (1) for progeny, (2) for wealth, (3) for fame, accept Sannyas, are the fit persons to live by begging alms. In order to prepare food-stuffs and meals, the householders have to go through five actions or processes, viz. (1) Kandani-Pounding, (2) Peshani-Grinding, (3) Udakumbhi - Washing pots, (4) Marjani - Sweeping and cleaning, (5) Chulli-Lighting hearths. These processes involve destruction of a lot of small insects and creatures, and thus the householders incur a lot of sin. In order to atone for this sin, our Shastras prescribe five kinds of sacrifices, viz. (1) Brahma-Yajna, (2) vedadhyayan - offerings to Brahman or the study of the Vedas. (3) Pitra-Yajna-offerings to the ancestors, 4)Deva-Yajna - offerings to the Gods, (5) Bhoota-Yajna-offerings to the beings, (6) Manushya-Atithi-Yajna-offerings to men or uninvited guests. If these sacrifices, enjoined by the Shastras are duly performed, the purification of their minds is effected and this helps them to get knowledge and self-realization.

- These are the vows a Sannyasi must keep – Abstention from injuring living beings, truthfulness, abstention from appropriating the property of others, abstention from sex, liberality (kindness, gentleness) are the major vows. There are five minor vows: abstention from anger, obedience towards the guru, avoidance of rashness, cleanliness, and purity in eating. He should beg (for food) without annoying others, any food he gets he must compassionately share a portion with other living beings, sprinkling the remainder with water he should eat it as if it were a medicine. — Baudhayana, Dharmasūtra, II.10.18.1-10.

- Sai reminds devotees to fulfil unfinished vows, and partakes of food in the form of animals such as dogs. Sai reiterates the oneness of Ram and Rahim. In various occasions, Sai disproves conceptions of people approaching Him with the idea that He is a Brahmin or that He is a Muslim.

- He is the knower, the creator of time, the quality of everything, the Sarva-vidyah (सर्ववद्यि:, all knowledge), states Shvetashvatara Upanishad. This God, asserts the text, is one, and is in each human being and in all living creatures.

- There are various Gurus imparting to us various kinds of wordly knowledge, but he, who fixes us in our Nature (Self) and carries us beyond the ocean of worldly existence, is the Sadguru. Sai Baba was such a Sadguru. His greatness is undescribable. If anybody went to take His darshana, he, without being asked, would give every detail of his past, present and future life. He saw Divinity in all beings. Friends and foes were alike to Him. Disinterested and equal-balanced, He obliged the evil-doers. He was the same in prosperity and adversity. No doubt, ever touched Him. Though He possessed the human body, He was not in the least attached to His body or house. Though He looked embodied, He was really disembodied, i.e., free in this every life. Lord or Bhagwan is said to have six qualities, viz. (1) Fame, (2) Wealth, (3) Non-attachment, (4) Knowledge, (5) Grandeur, and (6) Generosity. Baba had all these in Him.

- In the invocations and prayers found in the Taittiriya Upanishad, a teacher seeks the following from God or gods. They can be considered the desirable qualities one may look for in a guru, a teacher or an adept: Fame (yasah), Radiance of Brahman (brahmavarchas), Intelligence (medha), Immortality (amritasya), Vigorous body (vicarsanam), Sweetness in the tongue (madhumattama), Good hearing capacity, Knowledge of the Vedas (sruti), Prosperity and material abundance, Students of chaste conduct, Pure mind, Wealth of knowledge, Right wisdom (sumedha).

- Baba, the support of all, required no prop or support (Asan) from anybody. He always used a piece of sack-cloth for His seat, which was covered with a small beautiful bed by His bhaktas and had a bolster placed by them as a rest to His back. Baba respected the feelings of His devotees and allowed them to worship Him as they liked. Some waved Chamara or fans before him, some played on musical instruments, some washed His hands and Feet, some others applied scent and chandan, some gave betelnut with leaves and other things, and some others offered naivaidya. Sometimes, He scolded the devotees, at times, He looked softer than wax, a statue of peace and forgiveness. Though He seemed to shake with anger and His red eyes rolled round and round, still, He was internally a stream of affection and motherly love. Immediately, He called out His devotees and said, that He ever angry with His devotees; that if mothers kicked their children and if the sea turned back the rivers, He would neglect the devotees' welfare: that He, the slave of His devotees, always stood by them, and responded to them, whenever they called upon Him, and that He always longed for their love. In the same context is the legend of a devotee Megha, who venerated Sai as Shiva, doing Ganga Abhishekha to Him, while being further instructed by Sai to worship the trident. Furthermore is the incident of the pilgrimage of Saptashringi by Shama which Sai insisted He do, to fulfill a prayer previously made.

- Bhagavad Gita 3:26 states Let not the wise disrupt the minds of the ignorant who are attached to fruitive action. They should not be encouraged to refrain from work, but to engage in work in the spirit of devotion.

- Taking this concept to a higher level, Sai, while completely non attached Himself, allowed Him being venerated by devotees as they pleased, and the height of such veneration had to be the daily traditions of Arathi during dawn, noon, disk and night, and the Chavadi procession preceding the sleep for the night. This procession was carried out meticulously by devotees in all regal and splendor.

- "Where one sees nothing else, hears nothing else, understands nothing else, that is the greatest (Infinite, nirguna). Where one sees something else, hears something else, understands something else, that is the little (finite, saguna). The greatest is immortal; the little is mortal." (Chandogya Upanishad 7-24-1).

- There are descriptions of Sai curing various illnesses using Vibhuti or ash from the Dhuni, called Udi. The teaching here is that ash represents the final state all shall reach, bodily as the cremation, and in terms of Karma Vasanas as their eventual burning. The mind, with all its thoughts and worldliness is the primary source of disease, called Bhava Roga in Vedas, and if that is cured, everything else is cured automatically. Baba taught by His Udi that all the visible phenomena in the universe are as transient as the ash. Our bodies composed of wood or matter of the five elements, will fall down, after all their enjoyments are over, and be reduced to ashes. In order to remind the devotees of the fact that their bodies will be reduced to ashes, Baba distributed Udi to them. Baba also taught by the Udi that the Brahman is the only Reality and the universe is ephemeral and that no one in this world, be he a son, father or wife, is really ours. We come here (in this world) alone and we have to go out alone. It was found and is even now found out, that the Udi cured many physical and mental maladies, but Baba wanted to din into the devotee's ears the principles of discrimination between the Unreal and the Real, non-attachment for the Unreal, by His Udi and Dakshina. Sai used Udi as medicine for anyone who approached Him with physical ailments, including facilitating progeny.

- The Brihajjabala Upanishad describes many rituals of the Pashupata sect. Bhasma, sacred ash, is equated to atman (Soul) and antratman (Inner Soul). The rituals of Bhasma-snana (ash-bath) and application of Tripundra, instead of the ash-bath are significant Shiva veneration.

- Sai tames down the raging Dhuni fire by striking the Shatka.

- Panchamahabhutas refer to the five great elements ether, air, fire, water and earth, which according to the Mundaka Upanishad are sourced in the eternal, omnipresent, subtle inexhaustible Prakriti.

- Sai insisted on the concept and practice of Guru Dakshina, highlighting how it fosters non attachment towards monetary wealth. Sai also emphasised the shunning of unnecessary paraphernalia as rich garments etc of Das Ganu, in God's performances of Hari Kathas.

- Taitriya Upanishads states The Guru bids his disciple farewell and delivers his last upadesh: Speak the truth; Practice virtue. Let there be no neglect of your daily reading. Give unto the teacher what is pleasing to him."

- In response to a seeker asking for rapid enlightenment or Brahma Jnana, Sai necessitates the surrender of five things viz. (1) Five Pranas (vital forces), (2) Five senses (five of action and five of perception), (3) mind, (4) intellect and (5) ego. This path of Brahma Jnana of self-realization is 'as hard as to tread on the edge of a razor'.

- Sai reiterates the Vedic wisdom as follows: All persons do not see or realize the Brahman in their life-time. Certain qualifications are absolutely necessary. (1) Mumuksha or intense desire to get free. He, who thinks that he is bound and that he should get free from bondage and works earnestly and resolutely to that end;and who does not care for any other thinks, is qualified for the spiritual life. (2) Virakti or a feeling of disgust with the things of this world and the next. Unless a man feels disgusted with the things, emoluments and honors, which his action would bring in this world and the next, he has no right to enter into the spiritual realm. (3) Antarmukhata (introversion). Our senses have been created by God with a tendency to move outward and so, man always looks outside himself and not inside. He who wants self-realization and immortal life, must turn his gaze inwards, and look to his inner Self. (4) Catharsis from (Purging away of) sins. Unless a man has turned away from wickedness, and stopped from doing wrong, and has entirely composed himself and unless his mind is at rest, he cannot gain self-realization, even by means of knowledge. (5) Right Conduct. Unless, a man leads a life of truth, penance and insight, a life of celibacy, he cannot get God-realization. (6) Preferring Shreyas, (the Good) to Preyas (the Pleasant). There are two sorts of things viz., the Good and the Pleasant; the former deals with spiritual affairs, and the latter with mundane matters. Both these approach man for acceptance. He has to think and choose one of them. The wise man prefers the Good to the Pleasant; but the unwise, through greed and attachment, chooses the Pleasant. (7) Control of the mind and the senses. The body is the chariot and the Self is its master; intellect is the charioteer and the mind is the reins; the senses are the horses and senseobjects their paths. He who has no understanding and whose mind is unrestrained, his senses unmanageable like the vicious horses of a charioteer, does not reach his destination (get realization), but goes through the round of births and deaths; but he, who has understanding and whose mind is restrained, has his senses being under control, like the good horse of a charioteer, reaches that place, i.e., the state of self-realization, whence he is not born again. The man, who has understanding as his charioteer (guide) and is able to rein his mind, reaches the end of the journey, which is the supreme abode of the all-pervading, Vishnu (Lord). (8) Purification of the mind. Unless a man discharges satisfactorily and dis-interestedly the duties of his station in life, his mind will not be purified and, unless his mind is that Viveka (dis-crimination between the Unreal and the Real), and Vairagya (Non-attachment to the unreal) crop up and lead on to self-realization. Unless egoism is dropped, avarice got rid of, and the mind made desireless (pure), self-realization is not possible. The idea that ÔI am the bodyÕ is a great delusion, and attachment to this idea is the cause of bondage. Leave off this idea and attachment therefore, if you want to get tot he goal of self-realization (9) The necessity of a Guru. The knowledge of the Self if so subtle and mystic, that no one could, by his own individual effort ever hope to attain it. So the help of another person-Teacher, who has himself got self-realization is absolutely necessary. What others cannot give with great labour and pains, can be easily gained with the help of such a Teacher; for he has walked on the path himself and can easily take the disciple, step by step on the ladder of spiritual progress. (10) and lastly the

Lord's Grace is the most essential thing. When the Lord is pleased with any body, He gives him Viveka and Vairagya; and takes him safe beyond the ocean of mundane existence, The Self cannot be gained by the study of Vedas, nor by intellect, nor by much learning. He, whom the Self chosses, gains it. To him the Self reveals Its nature, says the Katha Upanishad. In many incidents, Sai proved how as a Guru, He drew to His direction, pulling the strings of the "sparrows" that were His devotees, wherever they might be.

- Sai explains His two primary monumental teachings - Shraddha and Saburi, or Faith and Patience. I tell you My own story, which if you listen carefully, will do you good. I had a Guru. He was a great Saint and most merciful. I served him long, very long; still he would not blow any Mantra into My ears. I had a keen desire, never to leave him but to stay with and serve him; and at all costs receive some instructions from him. But he had his own way. He first got my head shaved and asked Me two pice as Dakshina. I gave the same at once. If you say that as My Guru was perfect, why should he ask for money and how should he be called desireless? I replied plainly that he never cared for coins. What had he to do with them? His two pice were (1) Firm Faith and (2) Patience or perseverance. I gave these two pice or things to him, and he was pleased. "I resorted to My Guru for 12 years. He brought Me up. There was no dearth of food and clothing. He was full of love nay, he was love incarnate. How can I describe it? He loved Me most. Rare is a Guru like him. When I looked at him, he seemed as if he was in deep meditation, and then we both were filled with Bliss. Night and day, I gazed at him with no thought of hunger and thirst. Without him, I felt restless. I had no other object to meditate, nor any other thing than My Guru to attend. He was My sole refuge. My mind was always fixed on him. This is one pice Dakshina. Saburi (Patience or perseverance) is the other pice. I waited patiently and very long on My Guru and served him. This Saburi will ferry you across the sea of this mundane existence. Saburi is manliness in man, it removes all sins and afflictions, gets rid of calamities in various ways, and casts aside all fear, and ultimately gives you success. Saburi is the mine of virtues, consort of good thought. Nishtha (Faith) and Saburi (Patience) are like twin sisters, loving each other very intimately." "My Guru never expected any other thing from Me. He never neglected Me, but protected Me at all times. I lived with him, and was sometimes away from him; still I never felt the want or absence of his love. He always protected Me by his glance, just as the tortoise feeds her young ones, whether they are near her or away from her on the other side of the river bank, by her loving looks. Oh mother, My Guru never taught Me any Mantra, then how shall I blow any Mantra in your ears? Just remember that Guru's tortoise-like loving glance gives us happiness. Do not try to get Mantra or Upadesh from anybody. Make Me the sole object of your thoughts and actions; and you will, no doubt, attain Paramartha (the spiritual goal of life). Look at Me whole-heartedly, and I in turn look at you similarly. Sitting in this Masjid, I speak the truth, nothing but the truth. No Sadhanas, nor proficiency in the six Shastras, are necessary. Have faith and confidence in your Guru. Believe fully, that Guru is the sole Actor or Doer.

- In Chandogya Upanishad (VII-19-1) there is a mantra which means: "This is the kind of shraddhA that we should have in that fundamental invisible subject, that should always occupy our mind; only then can we think right" -- *When there is shraddhA then and there is right thinking*. Brahma-vidyA (Knowledge pertaining to the subject of brahman) should be taught only to those who have shraddhA – says Mundaka Upanishad. Who are those so qualified? The Upanishad gives a list of such qualifications. (III -2-10). Those who discharge their obligations (karmas) in the right manner; *shrotriyas* (those who have excellent scholarship of the vedas); those who have an intense anguish to be in brahman; and those who have shraddhA. In Prashnopanishad also (I – 10) it says those who seek the Atman become eligible to do so by their tapas (austerities), celibacy (brahmacharya), shraddhA, and learning.

- Sai reprimanded and denounced the practice of slander and harsh words. Shri Hari (God) will be certainly pleased, if you give water to the thirsty, bread to the hungry, clothes to the naked, and your verandah to strangers for sitting and resting. If anybody wants any money from you, and you are not inclined to give, do not give, but do not bark at him, like a dog. Let anybody speak hundreds of things against you, do not resent by giving any bitter reply. If you always tolerate such things, you will certainly be happy. Let the world go topsy-turvy, you remain where you are. Standing or staying in your own place, look on calmly at the show of all things passing before you. Demolish the wall of difference that separates you from Me; and then the road for our meeting will be clear and open. The sense of differentiation, as I and thou, is the barrier that keeps away the disciple from his Master, and unless that is destroyed the state of union or atonement is not possible, Sai also emphasised and insisted on correct remuneration to any work that is done. Sai highlighted the concept of kindness by rescuing a goat about to be butchered

- Taittiriya Upanishad 1.11.2 states: There should be no errors in your duties to the gods and the Manes. Treat your mother as God. Treat your father as God. Treat your teacher as God. Treat your guest as God. Whatever deeds are faultless, those alone are to be performed and not others. Whatever good conduct is present in us, only those should be adopted by you and not others. After instructing people about the duty that one has towards gods and manes, the Upanishad speaks about how a person should conduct his life and should respect other people. Further, it tells that the mother, the father, the teacher, and even the guests are to be treated as God. The Upanishad considers rude, coarse and violent behaviors as adharma i.e. unrighteous actions that lead to sorrow. Therefore, for one's own good, one must try to be polite and respectful in their interactions with others.

- Sai reinforces the teachings of Ishavasya Upanishad through a maid servant, clad in torn clothes, but content nevertheless, even if new clothes were provided to her.

- Enveloped by the Lord must be This All — each thing that moves on earth. With that renounced, enjoy thyself. Covet no wealth of any man. Should one wish to live a hundred years on this earth, he should live doing Karma. While thus, as man, you live, there is no way other than this by which Karma will not cling to you. Those who partake the nature of the Asuras [evil], are enveloped in blind darkness, and that is where they reside who ignore their Atman [Self]. For liberation, know your Atman, which is motionless yet faster than mind, it is distant, it is near, it is within all, it is without all this. It is all pervading. And he who beholds all beings in the Self, and the Self in all beings, he never turns away from it [the Self]. When to a man who understands, the Self has become all things, what sorrow, what trouble can there be, to him who beholds that unity. — Isha Upanishad, Hymn 1-7.

- Sai teaches on nine forms or types of Bhakti, viz., (1) Shravana (Hearing); (2) Kirtana (Praying); (3) Smarana (Remembering); (4) Padasevazna (resorting to the feet); (5) Archana (Worship); (6) Namaskara (Bowing); (7) Dasya (Service); (8) Sakhyatva (Friendship); (9) Atmanivedana (surrender of the self). These are the nine types of Bhakti. If any of these is faithfully followed, Lord Hari will be pleased, and manifest Himself in the home of the devotee. All the sadhanas, viz. Japa (vocal worship), Tapa (penance), Yoga practice and studying the scriptures and expounding them are quite useless unless they are accompanied by Bhakti.

- In the Srimad-Bhagavata and the Vishnu Purana are told the nine forms of Bhakti.

- Sai says the one capable of digesting onion should eat onion alone.

- While onion is generally condemned as a Tamasic food in many Puranic Hindu scriptures, Charaka Samhita highlights its medicinal value and necessity as follows: The onion/palandu (Allium cepa Linn) promotes kapha and is effective in treating vata but not of pitta. It is a good adjuvant for food and is a strength-enhancer, heavy, aphrodisiac and appetizing. [175]. Further, the homeopathic reasoning of onions aggravating symptoms of common colds, and hence curing it, had already been elaborated in earlier sections. It is by the same reasoning that Sai also cured eyesight issues by external application of Datura seeds which aggravate the burning symptoms of the eyes.

- There are so many crowding to Sai Baba. Do they all get benefit from Him? To this, He replied orally - "Look at the mango tree in blossom. If all the flowers brought fruit, what a splendid crop it would be. But do they? Most fall off (either as flowers or as unripe fruits) by wind etc. Very few remain".

- Advayataraka Upanishad states By the help of a great teacher one tries to find the Thuriya state hidden in either the sahasrara (thousand petal lotus) or the cave of the heart or end of the 12 Nadis. Ability to see it is only through the help of a great teacher.

- Hemadpant has given us a novel form of worship. Let us, he says, use hot water in the form of tears of joy to wash the Sad-guru's feet, let us besmear His body with sandle-paste of pure love, let us cover His body with the cloth of true faith, let us offer eight lotuses in the form of our eight Sattwik emotions and fruit in the form of our concentrated mind; let us apply to His head bukka (black-powder) in the form of devotion and tie the waistband of Bhakti and place our head on his toes. After decorating the Sad-guru with all jewelry in this way, let us offer our all to Him and wave chamar2 of devotion to ward off heat. After such blissful worship, let us pray thus:- "Introvert our mind, turn it inward, give us discrimination between the Unreal and the Real and non-attachment for all worldly things and thus enable us to get Selfrealisation. We surrender ourselves, body and soul (body-consciousness and ego). Make our eyes Yours, so that we should never feel pleasure and pain. Control our body and mind as You will and wish. Let our mind get rest in Your Feet".

- Pranagnihotra Upanishad states: In the bodily sacrifice, unadorned by the cord round the sacrificial post, the sacrificer is the self; (his) wife is the intellect. The great officiating priests are the Vedas. The ego is the Adhvaryu. The mind-stuff is the invoking priest. Prana is the assistant of the chief priest; Apana is the assistant of the Adhvaryu. Vyana is the first chanter. Udana is the loud Sama singer. Samana is the assistant of Hotir. The body is the altar. The nose is the interior of the altar. The crest is the wooden container. The foot is the chariot. The right hand is the ladle. The left hand is the container of the ghee. The ears are the two ghee offerings. The eyes are the two parts of the ghee. The neck is the libation. The Tanmatras are the assistant of the Brahma Priest. The great elements are the attendants. Gunas are the supplementary offerings. The tongue is the final sacrifices. Teeth and lips are the middle libation. The palate is the hymn-recitation. Memory is the Samyorvaka formula. Compassion, forbearance, non-violence are the four Ajya oblations (to Soma, etc.,). Om is the sacrificial post. Desire is the cord. Mind is the chariot. Lust is the sacrificial animal. The hair is the Darbha grass. The sense organs are the sacrificial vessels. The organs of action are the oblations. Non-violence is the Ishtis. Renunciation is the sacrificial fee. The post-sacrificial bath (follows) from death. In this body are stationed all the divinities.

- Sai condemns an act of suicide by a person, saying it is better to put up with suffering in this birth itself and finish it, rather than being born again and going through this charade all over again.

- Chandogya Upanishad, supposed to be one of the earliest of the Upanishads, does not contain any direct reference to suicide but indirectly prohibits it as according to it a person is a Soma-sacrifice. Ishavasya Upanishad also concurs stating: One who takes one's own life goes towards asuras and pretas and he heads towards a loka of total darkness.

- Baba descended from His seat, came to one Ramadasi's place of reading, took out the copy of Vishnu-Sahasra-Nam, and coming to His seat said to Shama- "Oh Shama, this book is very valuable and efficacious, so I present it to you, you read it. Once I suffered intensely and My heart began to palpitate and My life was in danger. At that critical time, I hugged this book to My heart and then, Shama, what a relief it gave me! I thought that Allah Himself came down and saved Me. So I give this to you, read it slowly, little by little, read daily one name at least and it will do you good." In the same incident, Sai quelled the learned Arrogance of Ramadasi by explaining humans were more valuable than books, and not to pick a fight because of giving away his book.

- The charity or gift is the armour in the world, All beings live on the gift of the other, Through gifts strangers become friends, Through gifts, they ward off difficulties, On gifts and giving, everything rests, That is why charity is the highest. —Mahanarayana Upanishad 63.6.

- In many situations and examples, Sai has given Darshan, instructions and blessings through visions and dreams, bringing forth the truth that both dream and wake states are equally (un)real, and equally effective in spiritual progress. So too, by the same logic, In this connection it may be remarked that seeing Baba's picture earnestly is equivalent to seeing Him in person.

- The similarity of wake and dream, with only difference as duration is highlighted in the Kathopanishad's statement: —He who is awake in us shaping objects of desire while we are asleep . . . that is Brahman‖ (Kath. 2. 5. 8).The scriptures also declare "This is the same as the place of waking, for what he sees while awake the same he sees while asleep" (Bri. Up. IV.3.14). Hence the world of dreams is real.

- Satcharita describes the passing away of many devotees, both human and animal in the presence of Sai, emphasising the need of detachment from everything else, even close family, in one's last days. He instructed a Sanyasi devotee Vijayanand thus: "If you so loved your mother, why did you take Sannayasa? Fondness or attachment ill becomes an ochre garb. Go and sit quiet at your lodging, wait with patience for a few days. In the Wada there are many robbers, bolt your doors, be very vigilant, the thieves will carry everything. Wealth and prosperity are transient and the body is subject to decay and death. Knowing this, do your duty, leaving all attachment to the things of this world and next. He who does this and surrenders himself to the Feet of Hari (Lord) will get free from all troubles and attain bliss. The Lord runs and helps him who remembers and meditates on Him with love and affection. Your store of past merits is considerable, so you have come here. Now attend to what I say and realise the end of your life. Being desireless, begin from tomorrow the study of Bhagwat. Do three 'saptahas' i.e. three reading during three weeks, conscientiously. The Lord will be pleased with you and destroy your sorrows, your illusions will vanish and you will get peace."

- Shri Krishna has said in Gita (VIII-5-6) that "he who remembers Me in his last moments, comes verily to Me, and he that meditates otherwise at that time goes to what he looks for." We cannot be certain that we can entertain a particular good thought at our last moment, for, more often than not, we are more likely to be frightened and terrified by many causes. Hence constant practice is necessary for enabling us to fix our mind on any desired good thought at any or the last moment. All Saints, therefore, recommended us to always remember God and chant His name always, so that we may not be puzzled when the time for departure comes.

- Sai narrated a parable of deep significance as follows to emphasise th divinity of food and condemn fasting: Once four of us were studying religious scriptures and other books and, being thus enlightened, we began to discuss the nature of the Brahman. One of us said that we should raise the self by the Self and not depend on others. To this the second replied that he who controls his mind is blessed; we should be free from thoughts and ideas and there is nothing in the world without us. The third said that the world (phenomenon) is always changing, the formless is eternal; so we should discriminate between the Unreal and the Real. And the fourth (Baba Himself) urged that bookish knowledge is worthless Discussing in this wise, we four learned men began to ramble through the woods in the quest of God. The three wanted to make the quest with their free and unaided intellect. On the way a Vanjari (a man who trades in certain things, such as grain etc. by carrying them on bullock) met us and asked us, "It is hot now, where and how far are you going?". "To search the woods", we replied. He enquired, "On what quest are you bound?" We gave him an ambiguous and evasive reply. Seeing us rambling aimlessly, he was moved and said, "Without knowing the woods fully, you should not wander at random. If you want to walk through forests and jungles, you should take a guide with you. Why do you exert youselves unnecessarily at this sultry noon-time? You may not give out to me your secret quest; still you can sit down, eat bread, drink water, take rest and then go. Be always patient at heart." Though he spoke so tenderly, we discarded his request and marched on. We thought that we were self-contained men and needed nobody's help. The woods were vast and trackless, the trees therein grew so close and tall, that the sun's rays could not penetrate through them; so we lost our way and wandered here and there for a long time. Ultimately through sheer good luck, we came back to the place from were we started. The Vanjari met us again and said, "Relying on your own cleverness you missed your way; a guide is always necessary to show us the right way in small or great matters; and no quest can be successfully carried out on an empty stomach. Unless God wills it, no one meets us on the way. Do not discard offers of food; served dish should not be thrust away. Offers of bread and food should be regarded as auspicious signs of success." Saying this he again offered us food and asked us to be calm and patient. Again we did not like this good hospitality and discarded his offer and went away. Without doing any quest and without taking any food, the three began to move out. So obstinate were they. I was hungry and thirsty and I was moved with the Vanjari's extraordinary love; we thought ourselves very learned; but were quite strangers to pity and kindness. The Vanjari was a quite illiterate and unqualified fellow and belonged to a low caste. Still he had love in his heart and asked us to eat the bread. In this way, he who loves other disinterestedly, is really enlightened; and I thought acceptance of his hospitality was the best beginning of getting knowledge. So very respectfully I accepted the loaf of bread offered, ate it and drank water. Then to! The Guru at once came and stood before us, "What was the dispute about?" He asked and I told him everything that had happened. Then he said, "Would you like to come with me? I will show you what you want; but he alone, who believes in what I say, will be successful." The others did not agree to what he said and left him; but I bowed to him reverently and accepted his dictum. Then he took me to a well, tied my feet with a rope and hung me - head downwards and feet up - from a tree near the well. I was suspended three feet above the water, which I could not reach with My hands, nor which could go into my mouth. Suspending me in this manner he went away, no one knew where. After 10 or 12 ghatakas (4 or 5 hours) he returned and taking me out quickly asked me how I fared. "In Bliss supreme, I was. How can a fool like me describe the joy I experienced?" I replied. On hearing my answer the Guru was much pleased with me, drew me near him and stroking my body with his hand kept me with him. He took care of me as tenderly as a motherbird does of her young ones. He put me into his school; how beautiful it was! There I forgot my parents, all my attachment was snapped and I was liberated easily. I thought that I should embrace his neck and remain staring at him always. If his image were not fixed in my pupils, I would like better to be blind. Such was the school! No one, who entered it once, could return empty-handed. My Guru became my all-in-all, my home and property, mother and father, everything. All my senses left their places and concentrated themselves in my eyes, and my sight was centred on him. Thus was my Guru, the sole object of my meditation and I was conscious of none else. While meditating on him my mind and intellect were stunned and I had thus to keep quiet and bow to him in silence. Among the four, one was a Karmatha (Ritualistic) who only knew how to observe, and abstain from, certain rites; the second was a Jnani, who was puffed up with pride of knowledge and the third was a Bhakta who surrendered himself completely to God, believing that he was the sole Doer. When they were discussing and arguing, the question of God turned up, and they, depending on their unaided knowledge, went in search of Him. Sai, who was Discrimination and Dispassion incarnate, was one of the four. Being Himself Brahman Incarnate, some may ask, "Why did He mix with them and act foolishly?" He did this for attaining the good of the public, and setting them an example to follow. Though an incarnation Himself, He respected a low Vanjari, by accpeting his food with the firm belief that "Food is Brahman"* and showed how those who rejected Vanjari's hospitable offer suffered and how it was impossible to get Jnana without a Guru. The Shruti (Taittiriya Upanishad) exhorts us to honour and worship mother, father and preceptor, and to study (learn and teach) the sacred scriptures. These are the means of purifying our minds and unless this purification is effected, self-realization is not possible. Neither the senses, nor the mind and intellect reach the Self. Modes of proof, such as Perception and Inference will not help us in the matter. It is the grace of the Guru that counts. The objects of our life such as Dharma, Artha and Kama are attainable with our effort, but the fourth object, Moksha (liberation) can only he had with the help of the Guru. * We think that this description of the topsy-turvy position in the well for 4 or 5 hours should not be taken too literally; for no one can be at ease and feel bliss if he be suspended with a rope-head down and feet up- in a well for hours together. On the contrary it might amount to torture. This seems to be a figurative description of the trance or Samadhi state. There are two sorts of consciousness; (1) Sensual and (2) Spiritual. When our senses and mind, which are created by God with an outgoing tendency meet their objects, we get the sensual consciousness in which we feel pleasure or pain, pure or mixed, but not bliss supreme of happiness. When the senses and the mind are withdrawn from their objects and are given opposite or topsy-turvy direction, i.e., when they are introverted and fixed on the Self, we get the other, i.e., spiritual consciousness in which we feel unalloyed joy or bliss which is ineffable. The words "In bliss supreme I was, and how can I describe the joy I felt?" So that the Guru put him in a trance and kept him above or aloof from the waters of the restless senses and mind.

 - It should not be thought that food is something quite different from the experiencer, or that matter is absolutely foreign to Spirit. Food is identical with the experiencer. Matter is only a phase of the Spirit. Food is only a manifestation of the Atman. One should adore food as the Atman (Maitra. Up. VI. 12). It is eaten and it eats all things (Taitt. Up. II. 2). I am food; I am the eater of food; I, who am food eat the eater of food (Taitt Up. III. 10). That the mind is influenced by the food that is eaten is mentioned in another place in the Chhandogya Upanishad: In purity of food there is purity of mind; in purity of mind there is established memory; in established memory there results the release from all the knots of the heart, (VII. 26). After a fast for fifteen days, Svetaketu lost his memory and could not recite the Vedas. But, when, afterwards, he ate food, he regained his memory and recited the Vedas. If one does not eat for ten days, even though he might live, he becomes a non-seer, a non-hearer, a non-thinker, a non-doer, a non-understander. But on eating food, he becomes a seer, a hearer, a thinker, a doer, an understander. Adore food! (Chh. Up. VII. 9). This is Sai's reinforcement of a Vedic concept the is twisted, terribly misunderstood and exaggerated in Puranic Hinduism. For, even the Bhagavad Gita makes this clear: There is no possibility of one's becoming a yogi, O Arjuna, if one eats too much, or eats too little, sleeps too much or does not sleep enough.

- The Taittiriya Upanishad says that is Brahma; from food all the creatures are born and having been born, by food they live, and having departed, into food again they enter.When an Atithi (uninvited guest) comes to our door at noon, it is our bounden duty to welcome him by giving him food. Just as varan (Pulse-soup) excels all other dishes, Anna-dana is the best of all merits. Baba required very little food for Himself and what little He wanted, was obtained by begging from a few houses. But when He took it into His mind to distribute food to all, He made all preparations from beginning to end, Himself. He depended on nobody and troubled none in this matter. Those who were accustomed to (take) animal food were given food from the Handi as prasad and those who were not so accustomed, were not allowed to touch it. He never created in them any wish or desire to indulge in this food. Baba at times proposed tests. For instance, on an Ekadashi day He gave some rupees to Dada Kelkar and asked him to go in person to Koralha to get mutton from there. So Dada Kelkar dressed himself and started for the place. Then Baba called him back and said, don't go yourself, but send somebody. On another occation Baba asked Dada just to see how the saltish Pulava' (mutton dish) was done. The latter said casually and formally that it was alright. Then Baba said to him - you have seen it with your eyes, nor tasted in with your tongue, then how could you say that it was good? Just take out the lid and see.Saying this Baba caught his arm and thrust it into the pot and then immediately added, take out your arm and taking a ladle, put some quantity in the dish without caring for your orthodoxy and without blustering. Baba, in a true motherly way pinched Dada Kelkar in this fashion. Really no saint or guru will ever force his orthodox disciple to eat forbidden food and defile himself thereby.

- This, the topic of meat eating, is probably one of the most grossly misunderstood and twisted topics in Puranic Hinduism, so much that in the present day it has gone so far as to create tussle between different faiths, public unrest and even cases of lynching and violence. The issue can be settled only if one takes a very deep, careful look at the topic from various scriptural sources. First, it is in the nature of Vedas and Sanatana Dharma, not to impose or forbid anything as a rule, but only suggests what is good for mankind. It is in this light that Brahma Sutras emphasise that one must avoid killing of animals, and may resort to eating any kind of food indiscriminately, only when in mortal danger. The Charaka Samhita gives medicinal and nutritional values of eating various kinds of meat, especially in tune with seasons. The Parashurama Kalpa Sutras and other authoritative texts on Sri Vidya describe the Vamachara Tantra involving Pancha Makaras, which include meat, but explicitly state that Shudras alone are entitled to it. This, one must take in conjunction with the Brahma Sutra, where one's Varnashrama is not determined by birth or profession but only by mindset. At the same time, as per the Sanyasa Upanishad, Sanyasis, especially of Avadhuta types are allowed to eat indiscriminately whatever they want. This is because, essentially, as Gita says, meat promoted Tamasic Gunas, but Avadhutas have far crossed that stage, to the very destruction of all illusion. This was what Sai followed too. He did not encourage our discourage the eating of meat, but had both vegetarian and non vegetarian fare cooked as part of the Handi, leaving people to choose as per their own mindset and the Varnashrama they identify themselves with. Furthermore Brihadaranyaka Upanishad in 6.4.18 gives the recipe of rice cooked with beef and veal for progeny of a well learned and respected son. While Puranic Hinduism, especially of the present day might find this jarring, it must be noted that the Upanishad specifies icy the male bull, that too of an advanced age, for this purpose. This does not amount to Go Hatya ie cow slaughter, neither does the Upanishad violate the Vedic Dictum of Go Avadhya ie forbidding cow slaughter, on the basis that cow is akin to a Mother, consuming lowly tasteless grass, and giving forth milk fit for human consumption just like a human mother, while also giving benefits out of its dung and urine as well. Since one male bull can father many calves, while each cow makes a distinct contribution by providing milk, the restriction of killing applies to the female cow and not to a male bull, and in fact, this allows for reasonable population control of cattle as well. Thus, one can see how Sai through the Handi system while have been controversially interpreted by half baked Puranic fanatics, nevertheless Sai sought to dispel all the Puranic misconceptions in this context. Related is the Brahma Sutra refuting any symbolic interpretation to Vedic Yajnas, with Vyasa clearly asserting that Vedic sacrifices positively involved killing of animals. This arises from the truth that all crayons being dream in nature, lack real value of life. Ultimately, this was the same aspect in which Adi Shankara was Himself defeated in Thiruvarur, being educated hence about the 16th stage.

- Sai disproves misconceptions about His illiteracy in Sanskrit, by giving the following exposition on Bhagavad Gita 4.34: It is not enough merely to prostrate before the Jnanis. We must make Sarvaswa Sharangati (complete surrender) to the Sad-guru. (2) Mere questioning is not enough. The question must not be made with any improper motive or attitude or to trap the Guru and catch at mistakes in the answer, or out of idle curiosity. It must be serious and with a view to achieve moksha or spiritual progress. (3) Seva is not rendering service, retaining still the feeling that one is free to offer or refuse service. One must feel that he is not the master of the body, that the body is Guru's and exists merely to render service to him. How is Jnana Upadesh, i.e., imparting of realization to be effected? Destroying ignorance is Jnana. (cf. Verse-Ovi-1396 of Jnaneshwari commenting on Gita 18-66 says - of ignorance is like this, Oh Arjuna, If dream and sleep disappear, you are yourself. It is like that.Also Ovi 83 on Gita V-16 says - there anything different or independent in Jnana besides the destruction of ignornace?* Expelling darkness means light. Destroying duality (dwaita) means non-duality (adwaita). Whenever we speak of destroying Dwaita, we speak of Adwaita. Whenever we talk of destroying darkness, we talk of light. If we have to realise the Adwaita state, the feeling of Dwaita in ourselves has to be removed. That is the realization of the Adwaita state. Who can speak of Adwaita while remaining in Dwaita? If one did, unless one gets into that state, how can one know it and realise it? Again, the Shishya (disciple) like the Sad-guru is really embodiment of Jnana. The difference between the two lies in the attitude, high realization, marvellous super-human Sattva (beingness) and unrivalled capacity and Aishwarya

Yoga (divine powers). The Sad-guru is Nirguna, Sat-Chit-Ananda. He has indeed taken human form to elevate mankind and raise the world. But his real Nirguna nature is not destroyed thereby, even a bit. His beingness (or reality), divine power and widsom remain undiminished. The disciple also is in fact of the same swarupa. But, it is overlaid by the effect of the samaskaras of innumerable births in the shape of ignorance, which hides from his view that he is Shuddha Chaitanya (see B.G. Ch. V-15)**. As stated therein, he gets the impressions - Jiva, a creature, humble and poor.The Guru has to root out these offshoots of ignorance and has to give upadesh or instruction. To the disciple, held spell-bound for endless generations by the ideas of his being a creature, humble and poor, the Guru imparts in hundreds of births the teaching - are God, you are mighty and opulent.Then, he realizes a bit that he is God really. The perpetual delusion under which the disciple is labouring, that he is the body, that he is a creature (jiva) or ego, that God (Paramatma) and the world are different from him, is an error inherited from innumerable past births. From actions based on it, he has derived his joy, sorrows and mixtures of both. To remove this delusion, this error, this root ignorance, he must start the inquiry. How did the ignorance arise? Where is it? And to show him this is called the Guru's upadesh. Unless the errors are exposed to his view, the disciple cannot learn what is God, jiva, world, body; how they are inter-related and whether they are different from each other, or are one and the same. To teach him these and destroy his ignorance is this instruction in Jnana or Ajnana. Why should Jnana be imparted to the jiva, (who is) a Jnanamurti? Upadesh is merely to show him his error and destroy his ignorance. Sai often involved in specific instructions and blessings to specific devotees, sometimes counter intuitive on first glance, but on deeper inspection, well aligned with their previous Karmas, promises etc. Through these specific instruction and treatment of devotees, Sai emphasised how Guru,bring the Self, was supreme, and that one must completely surrender and follow His instructions, if they were to benefit spiritually.

- The Upanishads have profoundly underlined the role of the guru. Mundak Upanishad says to realize the supreme godhead holding samidha grass in his hands one should surrender himself before the guru who knows the secrets of Vedas. Kathopanishad too speaks of the guru as the preceptor who alone can guide the disciple on the spiritual path. Term Upanishad derives from upa- ('nearby'), ni- ('at the proper place, down') and sad ('to sit') and it means 'sitting at the feet of a teacher to receive the sacred teachings'.

- Sai Baba expounded many a time Who this ME (or I) is. He said need not go far or anywhere in search of Me. Barring your name and form, there exists in you, as well as in all beings, a sense of Being or Consciousness of Existence. That is Myself. Knowing this, you see Me inside yourself, as well as in all beings. If you practise this, you will realize all-pervasiveness, and thus attain oneness with Me.

- Aitareya Aranyaka (II.iii.2.5) of the Rig Veda tells us that in man alone is the Atman ('Self') most manifest, for man is best endowed with intelligence and discrimination, and who knowing the higher and the lower worlds aspires to achieve immortality through mental things. Taittiriya Upanishad tells us that all should know Brahman as existing in the intellect in which, Shankara explains, are hidden – a) 'knowledge', b) 'the knowable' and c) 'the knower', as also enjoyment and liberation. The relationship between the Individual self and the Universal Self reveals the actual source of thought and action; it reveals Brahman; vichāra (reflection and contemplation) results in disinterest in that which is not the source of anything in this world.

- In true Yogic fashion, Sai has performed many deeds that have been recounted by the non initiates as miracles. Examples include His 72 hours continuous Samadhi as a means to get rid of an asthma attack. Conversing with animals, recounting the previous births with absolute clarity, sleeping on a wooden plank suspended with tattered cloth proving His remarkable stability of posture, subsisting on very little food, sleeping well after midnight to wake up very early in the morning, all these are the Siddhis acquired to Samyama that Sai showed through example.

- On the topic of getting smitten with lust, Sai teaches: why are you getting agitated in vain? Let the senses do their allotted work, or duty, we should not meddle with their work. God has created this beautiful world and it is our duty to appreciate its beauty. The mind will get steady and calm slowly and gradually. When the front door was open, why go by the back one? When the heart is pure, there is no difficulty, whatsoever. Why should one be afraid of any one if there be no evil thought in us? The eyes may do their work, why should you feel shy and tottering? Our mind is fickle by nature, it should not be allowed to get wild. The senses may get restless, the body, however, should be held in check and not allowed to be impatient. Senses run after objects, but we should not follow them and crave for their objects. By slow and gradual practice retlessness can be conquered.

We should not be swayed by the senses, but they cannot be completely controlled. We should curb them rightly and properly according to the need of the occasion. Beauty is the subject of sight; we should fearlessly look at the beauty of objects. There is no room for shyness or fear. Only we should never entertain evil thoughts. Making the mind desireless, observe God's works of beauty. In this way the senses will be easily and naturally controlled and even in enjoying objects you will be reminded of God. If the outer senses are not held in check and if the mind be allowed to run after objects and be attached to them, our cycle of births and deaths will not come to an end. Objects of sense are things harmful. With Viveka (discrimination) as our charioteer, we will control the mind and will not allow the senses to go astray. With such a charioteer we reach the Vishnupada, the final abode, our real Home from which there is no return.

- The Mahavakya Upanishad is a short text that discusses nature of Atman (self, soul) and Brahman (metaphysical reality), their oneness, and the nature of knowledge and ignorance. The text asserts that Yoga and introspection is the way to spiritual knowledge, with the help of a guru. The Upanishad is notable for characterizing Vedic rituals and chasing sensual pleasures as a mark of darkness within, that this darkness can be shed with the radiance of knowledge, the discovery of self as light.

- Through the incident involving Tembye Swami entrusting a coconut to a devotee asking to take it to Sai, with the result being the consumption of the coconut on the way. To the devotee feeling guilty for not executing Tembye Swami's orders, Sai explains: Now you need not worry yourself any more about the matter. It was on account of my wish that the coconut was entrusted to you, and ultimately broken on the way; why should you take the responsibility of the actions on you? Do not entertain the sense of doership in doing good, as well as for bad deeds; be entirely prideless and egoless in all things and thus your spiritual progress will be rapid."

- In the Kena Upanishad, is asked, By whom commanded and directed does the mind go towards its objects? Commanded by whom does the life–force, the first (cause), move? At whose will do men utter speech? What power directs the eye and the ear? Thus the disciple approached the Master and inquired concerning the cause of life and human activity. Having a sincere longing for Truth he desired to know who really sees and hears, who actuates the apparent physical man. He perceived all about him the phenomenal world, the existence of which he could prove by his senses; but he sought to know the invisible causal world, of which he was now only vaguely conscious. Is mind all– pervading and all–powerful, or is it impelled by some other force, he asked. Who sends forth the vital energy, without which nothing can exist? In the same Upanishad, Amma as Uma answers: "It is Brahman. It is through the victory of Brahman that ye are victorious." Then from her words, he (Indra) knew that it (that mysterious form) was Brahman. Uma replied to Indra, "It is to Brahman that you owe your victory. It is through His power that you live and act. He is the agent and you are all only instruments in His hands. Therefore your idea that 'This victory is ours, this glory is ours,' is based on ignorance." At once Indra saw their mistake. The Devas, being puffed up with vanity, had thought they themselves had achieved the victory, whereas it was Brahman; for not even a blade of grass can move without His command. Through this, there is the absolute refuting of any talk of free will whatsoever.

- Finally, in the Satcharitra we find the practice of Sai, of smoking Chillum filled with marijuana or Bhang, as is a typical custom of a NathYogi and also an Aghoris and other sects, extending all the way to Shiva Himself. This has been raised as a controversial point in Puranic Hinduism due to incomplete knowledge, especially by Vaishnava fanatics who go so far as to decry not just the practice, but Lord Shiva Himself, with the claim that this is not a Vedic deity. As a befitting slap right across their face, is provided the verse from Atharva Veda Samhita 11.6.15: "To the five kingdoms of the plants which Soma rules as Lord we speak. Darbha, hemp, barley, mighty power: may these deliver us from woe." 'भङ्ग' (bhang) or hemp refers to the cannabis plant. Atharva Veda not only mentions Cannabis to be one of the five sacred plants but signifies cannabis leaves as the guardian angel. In certain Vedic rituals, cannabis stems were thrown into the yagna (ritual fire) to overcome enemies and evil forces. According to Vedas; Cannabis is referred as a source of happiness, joy giver and liberator. Other references alluding to the ancient historical use of Cannabis in the ancient Indian culture can be found in Rig-Veda, Sushruta Samhita and the Mahabharata. Charaka Samhita too details recipes of smoking for various health benefits, while also cautioning against too little or too excess of smoking.

With this, the key incidents and teachings of the Satcharitra have been explored in light of the Shruthi ie Vedic and Upanishadic truths that they reinforce. In summary, Sai's teachings strictly adhere to the Sri Vidya Vedanta, conveying all the important points that have been explored in detail in the BrahmaSutra Bhasya, with the aim of taking all His devotees through the stages, to the final 16th stage. As an aspect of Amma itself as

Bala, Sai's playful and humorous side has not gone unnoticed either, since in the Satcharitra specifically in Chapter 36, we find a mention of these, with closer devotee Shama always being a favourite catch of Sai. In true Sri Vidya Vedanta spirit, the Satcharita asserts that Sai never favored harsh, self inflicting asceticism, but enjoyable and pleasurable living on earth, while also conscious and making efforts of one's ultimate goal being liberation, surrendering to the Guru to achieve this.

We now turn to the topic of Sai's birth and childhood. The Sanyasa Upanishad strictly prohibits a Sanyasa from talking about His Purvashrama or life before renunciation, and Sai undoubtedly strictly adhered to it. Thus, Sai directly has not revealed any details of His childhood, and even His birth date as 1838AD, was arrived at by Hemadpant only through inference. However, it would be plainly stupid to assume that Sai did not have any childhood, since even incarnations such as Rama and Krishna had. Some accounts believe that Sai Himself was born in the Rama Navami day, while Satcharitra confirms Hours passing away on the Vijayadashami or Dussehra day of 1918.

How then, could we know about the childhood of Sai? To this we resort to Das Ganu, one of the most trustworthy devotees of Sai who has composed the Sai Guru Charitra of 7 chapters. This book, just like the Satcharitra, has the express blessings and validation from Sai Himself. Das Ganu upon completion read out the 1st 3 chapters to Sai, and Sai gave His approval to the whole book. The book recounts Sai's birth in Pathri and childhood in Selu, which have also found mention in other places such as Sai Leelamrita, and affirmed in Satcharita itself as a footnote.

As per this account, Sai was born in a small village called Pathri, and then studied for 8 years under the tutelage or Ashram of Venkusa. This Venkusa was none other than an incarnation of Amma itself as Venkatesha, who had proved His mettle and austerity, taking out His own eyes at the slightest Temptations, with sight restored later. Other students, growing jealous of the loving relationship between Sai and Venkusa hatched a plan to kill Sai while asleep at night along with Venkusa, and did this by throwing a brick at Sai. Aware and protecting His disciple, Venkusa received the fatal blow on His forehead, while Sai, waking up to the commotion, nursed His Guru with a cloth. Realising that Venkusa was nearing His end, He fed Sai 3 liters of milk from a hitherto unmilked cow, symbolising Jnana, Bhakti and Karma Yogas. Sai got the blood stained cloth, which became part of His Kafni and the footprints of Guru Venkusa embossed on three brick, which He used as a pillow throughout His life. In the last ends of Sai's life, the Satcharita mentions the slipping and breaking of the brick while cleaning the mosque, and Sai passing away 3 days later.

The final instructions of Venkusa was that Sai was to go westward along the bank of the Godavari, and that Sai would be His representative henceforth. This was how Sai arrived in Shirdi. Das Ganu mentions that Venkusa ie Venkatesha was the formal Guru of Sai. Further Venkusa instructed that His body be cremated, but He would manifest as a Vigraha of Lord Venkatesha under a fig tree in Selu, and that, this was to be installed in a temple as His Samadhi.

However, by virtue of His mission to restore Dharmic Hindu and Abrahamic Muslim faiths to their Vedic roots, Sai was considered an incarnation of Kabir, whom Sai took as His Guru as well. The neem tree under which Sai meditated in Shirdi was adjacent to the Guru Sthan, which Das Ganu mentions, is one of the many Samadhis of Kabir, which are all the places where are interred the flowers that the saint's body transformed to after death. By some accounts, Sai also belonged to the Nath Yogi by initiation from Lahiri Mahasaya - His way of living and practices already have been explained pertaining to Sai as the Nath Yogi.

CHAPTER TEN

Trailokyamohanam

The first Avaranam of Sri Chakra is called Trailokyamohanam, or that which fascinates the three realms of existence, referring to humans, Gods and dead souls. Some systems consider this Avarana to be made of three concentric rings composed of 28 deities in total, yet in reality, there is only one ring consisting of ten deities, typically called Mathrukas, each of which being mapped to a superpower called Siddhi. Additionally ten Mudras described earlier are also mapped to these deities in systems involving 3 rings.

1. Brahmi – the one that creates, mapped to Anima Siddhi or atomic level perception required to build block by block. Desirous of performing a particular Yajna ritual benefiting the whole universe, Brahma once threw a slab of stone called Chitrashila, which landed in Thiruvarur eventually, and here Brahma established the sacred water source of Pushkar, called Kamalalayam, bringing together 16 oceans called Aadi sethu, Vinayaka sethu, Kumara sethu, Rudra sethu, Gauri sethu, Vishnu sethu, Lakshmi sethu, Brahma sethu, Vaani sethu, Soma sethu, Indra Sethu, Agni sethu, Indragni sethu, Durga sethu, Aditya sethu and Vanitha sethu for the purpose of Varuneshti rite.

2. Maheshwari – the Lord of greatness, mapped to Laghima Siddhi or lightness severing from all bondage, and dancing blissfully in space as Nataraja form. The form of Nataraja is geometrically sculpted from the Sri Chakra structure, and denotes the five sacred acts of creation, preservation, destruction, veiling and grace through the Damaru drum, fearless gesture, fire, right foot and raised left foot respectively, and this is the same philosophy reflected in Chidambaram as well, with historical narratives stating how the Nataraja of Thiruvarur and Chidambaram have been interchanged over time, with the real Chidambaram Nataraja now in Thiruvarur.

3. Kaumari – the one bestowing youthfulness, mapped to Mahima or greatness, due to this energy leading to performance of many activities efficiently. The form of Muruga or Kumara here is called Singara Velan, and is related to the episode where for slaying the demon Tarakasura who took the form of a mountain, Muruga threw His Vel weapon in Thiruchendur which finally landed in Thiruvarur, as Hatakeshwara, and caused the entire land to tremble and shake with its power, and to stabilize it, Muruga took the Singaravelan form along with help from Vinayaka called Nadukkam teertha Vinayakar, and then blesses even today in this form having settled down here itself with His Vel, even till today.

4. Vaishnavi – the one that pervades as divinity everywhere, mapped to Eeshitva Siddhi or the power of Lordship which one possesses if one's actions pervade everywhere universally. The arrival of Mahavishnu in Thiruvarur is related to the episode where the demon Bhaskali threatened and frightened Indra and the other Devas, upon whose request Vishnu manifested in Thiruvarur slaying the demon, along with His weapon as Chakrapani, in the reclining form called Jalashayina, which is the basis of the biggest reclining Vishnu found in Abharanadhari nearby, as well as historically established in Thiruvananthapuram as Ananthapadmanabha, after looting the wealth and Yantra Shaktis of Thiruvarur. As per His own promise, Vishnu spends the Chaturmasya period every year from Ashada to Krithika months residing solely in Thiruvarur, in penance, so much that He will not be found even in Vaikuntam or other places such as Badrinath, during this time. This is the same Vishnu who after manifesting in Thiruvarur, was the reason for the origin of Thyagaraja as well.

5. Varahi – the giver of excellence, mapped to Vashitva Siddhi or the ability to charm anybody and anything with excellence. Varahi was the chief of the Saptha Maathas manifesting in Thiruvarur to aid Durga in the killing of Mahishasura and to bless the Yajna of Brahma, even as they were commanded by Shiva to protect the place of Thiruvarur from mishappenings after the giant event of Vibhishana's time lead to upheaval and replacement of shrines.

6. Mahendri – the one that maximizes sensitivity of sense organs Indriyas, mapped to Prakamya Siddhi, or regulation of sensuality. Indra manifested in Thiruvarur after the formation of Hatakeshwara Jyotirlingam, and after Vishwamitra started to create a new heaven called

Trishanku, afraid of losing His position as the king of heaven, Indra worships Hatakeshwara which at the time is the giant tunnel called Naaga Bila, and later slays Vritrasura demon by praying here. Then after slaying the demon, Indra again manifests here to get rid of the Brahmahatti Dosha sin, and worships Hatakeshwara, and also covers the tunnel with a peak from the Mountain of Sumeru, called Raktashringa, so that nobody may access his power of ruling over heaven.

7. Chamunda – the destroyer of ignorance, mapped to Bhukti Siddhi or enjoyment that is attained with well informed actions resulting in success. Chamunda manifested in Thiruvarur as part of the Saptha Maathas, along with Varahi and others, and were also commanded by Indra to protect the place of Thiruvarur by creating the six vices of lust, wrath, greed, delusion, pride and envy so that people that are not qualified may not enter Thiruvarur.

8. Mahalakshmi – the one that blesses with attainments Labhyam of wealth and richness, mapped to Iccha Siddhi or growth of wishes and desires which usually manifest with wealth creation. Manifesting along with Vishnu, bringing with Herself the Shvetha Dveepam itself to Thiruvarur, Mahalakshmi got resolved of Her curse of an elephant face here given by Narayani or Madhavi, by praying to Brahma, and attained the Mahattva or position of greatness here.

9. Chakreshi – the one that manifests as the wheel of time, mapped to Prapthi Siddhi, or power of attaining anything if only one is ready to wait for appropriate time. This energy is manifest as the chariot of Thiruvarur, massive with 96 feet height and 300 tonne weight, called Aazhi Ther meaning the Chakra or Meru resemblance that moves in a sea of people, and the festival exists tocelebrate the killing of Tripurasura or three demons by Thyagaraja Shiva with a mere smile, even as the body of Ther is composed of all deities in different parts, such as the sun and moon being the wheel, the serpent Vasuki being the thread pulling the Ther and so on. The concept of the wood used in Ther forms the basis of the crucifix and carpenter theme of Christ, even as some accounts detail His final resting place in nearby Perumpannaiyur.

10. Nageshwari – the one that manifests as the force of reptilian brain, mapped to Sarvakama Siddhi or tendency to cultivate desires for everything. The manifestation of Nagas in Thiruvarur is related to vengeance towards a mischievous person Kratha who killed a Naga and after the entire place was ravaged, the place was rescued with the Mantra

chant of Naagaram by a thrice born Trijatha rendering the serpent venom poisonless here. Confused, a Naga attacked a woman Bhattika, losing its fangs, and being cursed to be born as a human, even as earlier, the same Bhattika was kidnapped to Kedarnath by Nagas, and as a result of all this Brahma pacified the Nagas giving them a place in Thiruvarur.

CHAPTER ELEVEN

Sarvashaparipoorakam

The second Avarana of sixteen petals is called the one that fulfills all hopes and desires, called Sarvashaparipooraka. These are sometimes mapped to sixteen forms of Lalitha called the sixteen Thihi Nithyas, each having a power and denoting one of the phases of the moon.

1. Kaamakarshini – the one that stimulates and controls love and lust, also known as Kameshwari Nithya, the Goddess of love. Manifest as Manmatha in Thiruvarur. Once, after the demon Tarakasura acquired the boon of dying only from a child born to Shiva and Parvathi,
   Devas prompted Manmatha to distract Shiva from a state of intense penance, as a result of which Manmatha was burnt to ashes in nearby Korukkai. Upon the prayers by His consort Rathi, Manmatha was brought back to life but without a physical body, suggesting how true love can never be achieved through two humans in physical form but only indirectly through each person loving God.
2. Buddhyakarshini – one that stimulates the intellect, mapped to Bhagamaalini the giver of fruits due to intelligent action. This is Aadi Buddha manifest during the episode of Tripurasura Samhara, commanded by Shiva and Vishnu to confuse the demons through intellectual polemics and confusing philosophies, so that their actions of merit will subside and they can soon be annihilated.
3. Ahankarakarshini – the one that stimulates and regulates ego or identity of Self, and mapped to Nithyaklinna, the ever wet denoting the ever aroused Yoni alluding to the ego forever in desire to achieve various things. This is manifest in Thiruvarur as Periyanayaki, which is the fundamental form of Mahakaali, as the consort of Muneeshwara known as Muneeshwari, and known as Aadya Shakti, as stimulating all of creation by building the Aham Bhava or I-principle in the mind of

Parabrahman.

4. Shabdakarshini – the one that controls and regulates all of sound mapped to Bherunda the one that causes fear, since fear of heights and fear of loud noises are the only natural fears that humans are born with. This is manifest as Raajamaatangi, who also known as Shyamala or Meenakshi, is the fundamental force of sound as music or Naadam, that arises as the collision between Prana Shakti the vital force and Jaataragni the fire that sustains life, and then spreads into different frequencies as music and speech. The Goddess is the dweller of Kadambavanam, which is the state of the grand cremation ground where all souls eventually reach after their lifetime, and are welcomed to the realm of sound by the Goddess.

5. Sparshakarshini – the one that controls and stimulates touch, mapped to Vahnivasini or heat generated as friction due to touch. This is manifest as Vaayu, the God of wind, who was born in multiple pieces called Marutha, to Diti the Mother of Asuras, even as Indra smashed the fetus in Her womb into multiple pieces before birth. They then manifest in Thiruvarur, to form the God Vaayu, who was then given the blessing of being the vital force of breath in sustaining life.

6. Roopakarshini – the one that stimulates and regulates form and appearance, mapped to Vajreshwari or power of lightning in illuminating things. This is manifest as Vishwakarma, who governs all of architecture, creating forms out of symmetry and breathing life into them as they are constructed materially to physical reality. Vishwakarma was commanded by Thyagaraja with the creation of Thiruvarur as a city and temple, destroying the forest of Daruka and bamboo Venu that was erstwhile existing.

7. Rasakarshini – the one that stimulates and regulates taste, mapped to Shivadooti the harbinger of auspiciousness as food that nourishes and gives positivity. This is manifest as Annapoorni along with Bhikshatana, which is a form by Shiva, made to be taken by Annapoorni to make Him realize the value of physical food and nutrition which is as important as the no physical spiritual realities that govern life. It is the same Bhikshatana form that Shiva later manifested in Thiruvarur along with Mohini to teach the sages of Thiruvarur a lesson in humility.

8. Gandhakarshini – the one that stimulates and regulates smell, mapped to Thvaritha or the one that gives fast results due to speed of wind in both energy channels of body. This is manifest in Thiruvarur as Bala

Tripurasundari, holding two flowers the lotus and lily to symbolize the solar and lunar energy channels of the two nostrils, which carry the sense and information of smell into the body. Bala Tripurasundari was born out of Lalitha during the killing of Bhandasura, and aided woth killing the thirty sons of Bhandasura, and later on She incarnated as Ashoka Sundari, the daughter of Shiva as the form of Kalpavriksha the wish fulfilling tree, to aid Parvathi in her loneliness, and later killed the demon Hunda through Her consort Nahusha, as he tried to abduct her.

9. Chitthakarshini – the one that regulates consciousness and awareness, mapped to Kulasundari, or the one that bestows beauty in the eyes of the beholder. Manifest as Sri Vidya Medha Dakshinamurthi who is none other than Sri Vidya Sastha, this is the position of principal Guru, teaching the merging of individuality Jiva into the Atma, symbolized by the Chinmudra gesture, to advanced disciples such as Sanaka, Sanatana, Sanandana and Sanatkumara.

10. Dhairyakarshini – the one that regulates courage and endurance, mapped to Nithya, the permanence of result available for those that are courageous. Manifest as Kalyana Veerabhadra as well as seven other forms, in total of eight locations to guard the temple of Thiruvarur, after having destroyed the sacrifice of Daksha filled with arrogance, in nearby Thirupariyalur, which lead to the immolation of Goddess in Her form as Sati.

11. Smrithyakarshini – regulates and stimulates memory, mapped to Neelapathaka, the blue bannered one, symbolizing the infinity of information and ideal memory. Manifest as the planet mercury or Budha who is known as the stimulator of brainpower and memory as Buddhikaraka. Budha was born of Chandra in an issue of adultery woth Thaara the consort of Brihaspathi.

12. Naamakarshini – regulates and stimulates identities such as name and word, mapped to Vijaya or victory achieved when mastery of speech is obtained as this leads to the Vidya superpower. Manifest in Thiruvarur as the Akshara Peetham, a formless orb of Aksharas or letters of the Sanskrit alphabet, whose manifestation is related to Shiva performing a Rudra Thandava dance of despair carrying the immolated body of Sati, which was then sliced by Vishnu using the Chakra weapon into 51 parts, which then fell all over the subcontinent creating various Akshara Peethas, all of them originating from this very Peetham in Thiruvarur.

13. Beejakarshini – regulates and stimulates the seed form that leads to growth of anything, mapped to Sarvamangala which means fully auspicious without any deficiencies. Manifest as Nirruthi, the God of disorder and Chaos, which in reality is simply any system that is extremely sensitive and dependent on its initial setup or seed, so much that even a very minute change in the initial condition of the system will lead to drastic changes in the results later on.

14. Atmakarshini – regulates and stimulates identity and experience of the Self, mapped to Jwalamalini – the formless fire or Jyoti symbolizing the self. Manifest in Thiruvarur as Hatakeshwara, the giant Jyotirlinga or pillar of fire that was formed after Shiva taight the sages of Daruka Vana in Thiruvarur a lesson of humility. This pillar of fire extended infinitely in height and depth, drilling its way all the way below to the nether worlds and creating a path for Nagas or serpent energies to infuse the place. A golden Lingam was consecrated by Brahma at the base of the tunnel, with gold symbolizing the color obtained by merging male and female principles symbolized by the white semen and red menstrual blood. Later on the tunnel was covered by Indra with a peak of the Meru mountain, even as Shiva asserts this Thiruvarur is the only supreme among 68 sacred places for worship, in the Naagara Khaandam. The energy for the Vel weapon of Muruga was taken from this Hatakeshwara Jyotirlinga, by Goddess Velnedunkanni and given to Muruga in nearby Sikkal, and after slaying the demon in Thiruchendur, the Vel was brought back here by Muruga and merged into the Hatakeshwara shrine. The source of the Hatakeshwara pillar of fire is indeed the Pranava Omkara itself, which is seen in nearby Swamimalai and is the wosdom of Atma itself, taught to Shiva by Muruga Himself, and this is the basis for the Hatakeshwara Jyotirlinga as well as Vel. For this reason, in the shrine of Hatakeshwara one sees a stone slab in which is engraved the Om in Tamil along with the interlocking of two triangles, a symbol of Muruga and Vel, signifying the joining of male and female.

15. Amrithakarshini – regulates and stimulates the divine elixir that transcends death, mapped to Chithra, which symbolizes perfection and variety of life. Manifest as Varuna, the God of water and rain, as that alone is the life giving force sustaining crops and hence, nutrition. Varuna was manifest in Thiruvarur after being summoned by Brahma to fulfill His Yajnam.

16. Shareerakarshini – regulates and stimulates the physical body, mapped to Mahanithya, the ever permanent form of the five elements. Manifest as Karuppaswami, who was the creation of Valmiki using the Kusha grass, when he got agitated once after finding Lava, the son of Sita missing, without realizing that Sita had taken the son out voluntarily. Later on, when meeting Rama, Lava passed the fire test while Kusha was charred giving the name Karuppaswami or black God, and given the position of protecting the physical bodily righteousness of people along with dignity, and often called Bhoothanatha or Sangili Bhoothathar, due to the body being made of the five elements of nature.

CHAPTER TWELVE

Sarvasamkshobhanam

The third Avarana consisting of eight deities is called Sarvasamkshobhanam or the one that agitates and excites a person, causing him to evolve and progress out of his comfort zone.

1. Ananga Kusuma – the one that flowers and blossoms. Manifest as Poongurathi, also known as Kathayi or Katyayani, as a protector and guardian of the Senkazhuneer Odai, a 35 acre water source exclusively dedicated for growing the Neelotpala flower for Thyagaraja. In a Yogic sense, Neelotpala alludes to the state of blossoming consciousness where the eye os neither open nor closed, where one is neither awake nor asleep.

2. Ananga Mekhala – the one that forms a restraining girdle. Manifest as Yama, the God of Dharma and righteousness who punishes wrong thoughts with suffering in hell, and hence governs death and afterlife. In thiruvarur, which iself is a place for those that graduated the Bhumikas beyond death, Yama assumes the role of Chandikeshwara, as the account keeper and prime devotee of Thyagaraja.

3. Ananga Madana – the one that deludes the mind. Manifest as Yakshini, also known as Isakki Amman the guardian of treasures of nature including truth and information, deluding the unqualified from accessing them. In Thiruvarur, She is shown to assist the Goddess Neelotpalamba, holding in Her hands the infant Skanda or Murugan.

4. Ananga Madanaatura – the one that goes beyond deluding. Manifest in the form of Rathi the Goddess of conjugal union and consort of Manmatha, who was manifest in Thiruvarur as Phalavathi, a daughter who married a Gandharva and engaged in sexual congress in the temple itself, later on punished by Her father and creating a war of words, bringing out the importance of the feminine and of love, and finally

being enshrined in the temple as a Goddess itself. This form of Rathi is known as Kamakhya or Kubjika.

5. Ananga Rekha – the one that creates a mark or footprint. Manifest in Thiruvarur as the Footprint or Paaduka of Goddess in twin forms of Amba and Vriddha. These were invoked by two queens of Kashi in a fire ritual in Thiruvarur after their husband king was slaughtered in battle. Along with the deities, hordes of Yoginis and Bhootha Ganas came and devoured the opponents, starting a chaotic period of animal sacrifices and alcoholic offerings to the Goddess, which was changed into a Mantra system by Shiva, who appointed a Rudra Kannika Goddess created from His heart for the same.

6. Ananga Vegini – the one that gives speed. Manifest in Thiruvarur as Garuda, who came here in search of Vishnu during the Chaturmaasya time, seeking help to find a suitable bridegroom for Madhavi, the daughter of his friend, who had initially gone to Brahma and by the time she returned, ages and eras had elapsed in earthly time.

7. Ananga Ankusha – the one that redirects the mind. Manifest in Thiruvarur as Bhuvaneshwari in the form of Visalakshi, along with Kashi Vishwanatha Shiva, who gave Darshan to 11 Rudra sages who had a fierce contest of who would arrive first to Thiruvarur to worship the Lord.

8. Ananga Maalini – the one that forms a garland of flowering results and benefits. Manifest in Thiruvarur as Vinayaki in the form of Ucchishta Ganapathi with consort Neela Saraswathi who is none other than Goddess Thaara, to give the benefit of liberation to people, Gods and demons alike.

CHAPTER THIRTEEN

Sarvasaubhagyadaayakam

The fourth Avarana of 14 triangles is called Sarva Saubhagya Dayaka or what bestows all auspiciousness.

1. Sarva Samkshobhini – the one that excites people. Manifest as Raudra Durga, the energy of Rudra, also called Erisina Kotravai, the term Rudra itself derived as one that makes others cry, especially the perpetrators of evil and wrongdoings.

2. Sarva Vidraavini – the one that liquifies and moves things. Manifest as Veeran or Madurai Veeran who took incarnation as a guard in the court of Madurai and was punished for loving the royal princess, only to be later vindicated and deciding to end his own life by severing his limbs and head to the Goddess Durga of Achaleshwara in Thiruvarur in search of a proper ritualized death.

3. Sarva Akarshini – the one that attracts and fascinates everything. Manifest as Raahu the north lunar node and shadow planet causing eclipses, Raahu was initially a demon that desired for the Amritham given by Mohini after churning of the milky ocean, and after the demonic identity revealed by sun and moon, got His head cut off, and cultivated desire in the form of seeking revenge on the sun and moon through eclipses.

4. Sarva Hlaadini – the one that gives happiness and bliss. Manifest in Thiruvarur as Neelotpalamba, the blue Goddess, which is the married form of Kamalamba as consort of Shiva with child Skanda, who later incarnated as Neela Devi, consort of Krishna better known as Radha.

5. Sarva Sammohini – the one that enchants and captivates the mind. Manifest in thiruvarur as Mohini also known as Kurukulla, the feminine form of Vishnu who accompanied Shiva in His form as Bhikshatana as He wandered after dejection at the death of Sati. Bhikshatana and

Mohini arrived in Thiruvarur, then called Daruka Vana and occupied by sages who were in arrogance of their Mantra proficiencies, and to humble them, Mohini enchanted them with Her beauty even as the naked Bhikshatana fascinated the wives of the sages into lust. Angered, the sages released a horde of animals including tiger, elephant, deer and snake, all of which were defeated and worn by Shiva, teaching the sages ultimately a lesson on humility and importance of surrender rather than arrogance on one's abilities.

6. Sarva Sthambhini – the force that stops happenings. Manifest in Thiruvarur as Pechi also known as Bagalamukhi, for the purpose of killing an evil king and preventing his newborn child from touching the ground and causing disaster to the world, thus exhibiting the force of stopping disaster alluding to the similar role in speech as well as Bagalamukhi.

7. Sarva Jrumbhini – the force that puts one to sleep and inertness. Manifest as Ashvarudhan, the energy of Tiraskarini Shakti also known as Mahanidra, with the role of the deity being twofold, charming the entire world in our favour, and revealing all the hidden intents and information to our sight.

8. Sarva Vashankari – the force that charms and enchants everybody. Manifest as Yogamaya also called Vishnu Durga, the energy of Vishnu created to create circumstances deluding necessary people favorable for Divine to enact the play in the world, and incarnated as the sister of Krishna named Vindhyavasini, and enshrined in Thiruvarur, after escaping the evil hands of Kamsa demon that tried to kill the Goddess.

9. Sarva Ranjini – the giver of delight in everything. Manifest as Chandra the moon deity, which in Thiruvarur is the chief consort of Valmikanatha or Shiva as Somakulambika referring to the Soma plant called Tulasi, whose extract can cure all disorders and give freshness, rejuvenation and mental stimulations. Chandra manifested here to get rid of a curse by father in law Prajapathi, after having shown partial treatment to Rohini alone, the star among all 27 Nakshatra or star Goddesses whom he had married.

10. Sarvonmaadini – the one that makes the mind intoxicated like a drunkard. Manifest in Thiruvarur as Kethu, the descending lunar node, manifest as comets. As the severed body of Raahu attached to a serpent head, Kethu denotes mindlessness, and was raised by Jaimini and later honored as a planet among the Navagrahas.

11. Sarva Artha Saadhini – the one that makes means to resources possible. Manifest in Thiruvarur as Shankara Narayani also known as Madhavi, or Kamalathmika or Padmavathi, and manifest in the episode of incarnating as the daughter of an acquaintance of Garuda and seeking his help in finding a bridegroom, following which Garuda took her to Brahma only in vain, with ages and eras having elapsed in earthly calendar, and returning to Thiruvarur to seek the help of Vishnu, who honors Her purity by marrying Her Himself, which only enrages Lakshmi causing the latter to curse Madhavi to acquire a horse face, even as Madhavi Herself retaliated and cursed Lakshmi to acquire an elephant face. Madhavi resolved the curse and was then born as Subhadra, the sister of Krishna and Balarama.

12. Sarva Sampatti Poorani – the one that fulfills our wealth and resources. Manifest in Thiruvarur as Kubera as well as the twin form of Shankhanidhi and Padmanidhi forming the Dwarapalakas or gate keepers to Kamalamba. In a later episode, Kubera enters an friendly arrangement with Thyagaraja known as Bhaktha Katchi Utsavam, where to match each step taken by Thyagaraja, Kubera pours out His gold coins, and soon, He runs out of the entire Divine treasure.

13. Sarva Mantra Mayi – the one that is of the form of all mind stimulating chants. Manifest in Thiruvarur as Gayathri who is the deity of the Gayatri Mantra, the core of all Mantras in Sanatana Dharma, that stimulates the mind towards positivity and divinity, such that Varivasya Rahasya states that each Kuta of the Shodashi Mantra itself is a Gayathri Mantra.

14. Sarva Dvandva Kshayankari – the one that dispels all duality and confusion. Manifest in Thiruvarur as Adithya, the form of Surya or Sun God, denoting non duality as the number one, and sole energy producer of the solar system. Energized with the Gayathri Mantra by Yajnavalkya, the Aditya in Thiruvarur is known as Pushpa Aditya, after a merchant Pushpa who worshipped here after being wrongly accused and punished of theft by a greedy merchant. As a revenge, Pushpa took on the disguise of the miscreant, turned the mob crowd against him and killing him, and then enjoying a lifestyle with his wife, in disguise as the merchant, eventually revealing the truth as well as the power of Pushpa Aditya.

CHAPTER FOURTEEN

Sarvaarthasaadhakam

The fifth Avarana composed of ten triangles is known as Sarvartha Sadhaka, the means towards wealth and resources.

1. Sarva Siddhi prada – the one that yields all accomplishment. Manifest in Thiruvarur as Siddhi Vinayaka also known as Muladhara Vinayaka, created by Parvathi Goddess to pray to Vinayaka for incarnating as Her child. Established to activate the root life force lying dormant at the base of the spine, known as Moladhara, with Thiruvarur being the Muladhara Kshetra.

2. Sarva Sampath Prada – the one that yields all earnings and wealth. Manifest in Thiruvarur as Brihaspathi, the preceptor to Gods and planet of Jupiter, which is known as Guru, meaning gravity, de to its ability to grant powers of accumulation and abundance.

3. Sarva Priyankari – the one that gives love and affection powers. Manifest in Thiruvarur as Krishna, with certain accounts narrating how the original form of Krishna in Mannargudi is interchanged with the form worshipped as Sundaramurthi in Thiruvarur. Manifestation of Krishna is associated with the episode of Kalayavana, an attacker and demon from a foreign land, to slay whom, Krishna devised a plan and ran to Thiruvarur, prompting a chase by the Divine, with Krishna entering a cave in which the Muchukunda king was asleep, after helping Indra win a war and establish Thyagaraja in thiruvarur, and getting a boon that anybody that wakes him will be burnt to death. Knowing this, Krishna ran into the cave and hid himself, with Kalayavana chasing in hot pursuit, and mistaking Muchukunda to be Krishna, and waking him violently, only to get burnt to death, after which Krishna blessed Muchukunda with liberation called Moksha.

4. Sarva Mangalakaarini – the one that bestowd auspiciousness. Manifest in Thiruvarur as Angaaraka or the planet Mars, also known as Mangala, born of the Earth through the energy of Shiva Himself.

5. Sarva Kaama prada – the one that fulfills all desires. Manifest in Thiruvarur as Kamadhenu, the divine wish fulfilling cow, residing in the Ashram or residence of Jamadagni, Renuka and Parashurama, and later kidnapped by a demon Karthavirya Arjuna, only to be rescued by Parashurama after killing the demon.

6. Sarva Dukha Vimochini – the one that removes all sadness. Manifest in Thiruvarur as Jyeshta Devi, the elder sister of Lakshmi, also called Dhumavathi and Paathaala Jyeshta. The manifestation is related to the episode of milky ocean churning done by Gods and Demons, where due to not worshipping Vinayaka prior to the act, led to poison being released by serpent Vasuki, which later was drunk by Shiva. However, before neutralizing the poison, it started to take its toll on the ocean and life forms in it, and with none willing to clean it, Jyeshta took it on Herself, and cleaned the ocean, being affected with weakness, and appearing disheveled, old and rejected by Devas when She appeared out of the ocean, with Shiva Himself taking the form of Shanishwara and marrying Her, restoring Herself to former glory, where She is seen with Her two children, the son Maandhi known as Kapaleeshwara and daughter Pralayambika.

7. Sarva Mrithyu Prashamani – the one that averts untimely and gory death. Manifest in Thiruvarur as Kaala Bhairava who incarnated along with Bhairavi Kelishwari, for the purpose of killing a demon Andhakaasura who approached Parvathi with attitudes of lust and adultery. Surrendering at the last minute, Andhakasura was transformed into Bhringi, one of the Bhutha Ganas of Shiva.

8. Sarva Vighna Nivaarini – the one that removes obstacles. Manifest in Thiruvarur as Maha Ganapathi or Vinayaka, also known as Vathapi Ganapathi, mistakenly identified to be brought from the kingdom of Vathapi. Was established by Devas as the chief of Shiva Ganas or attendants of Shiva, and controller of astral travelling, called Vimanas.

9. Sarva Angasundari – the one tht makes all organs beautiful. Manifest in Thiruvarur as Pachai Amman or Parvathi Devi, to perform penance and win the hand of Shiva in marriage. Also called Aparna Devi.

10. Sarva Saubhagya Dayini – giver of all fortune and auspiciousness. Manifest as Rajarajeshwari Akhilandeshwari, also known as Kshemakari

Devi, installed by Naga Raivatha to get rid of the curse obtained by kidnapping a woman Bhattika to Kedarnath.

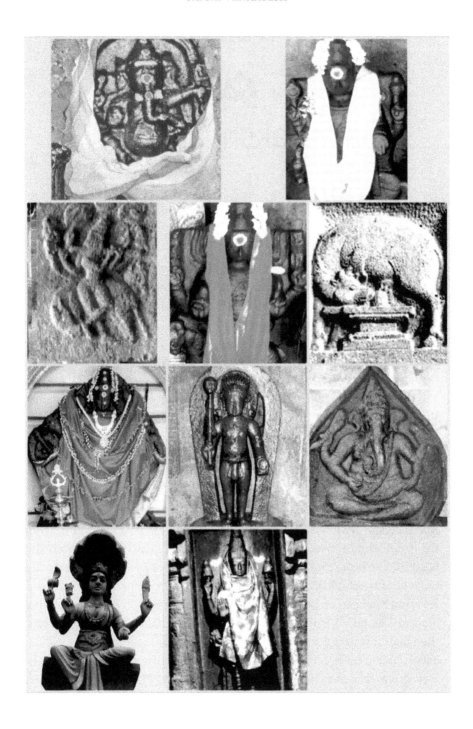

CHAPTER FIFTEEN

Sarvarakshaakaram

The sixth Avarana consists of ten triangles and called Sarva Rakshakara or the one that gives complete protection.

1. Sarvajna – the knower of everything. Manifest as Saraswathi, related to the incident of established by Vasishta to cure the dumb son Ambuvichi born to the ruling king of the region, and later on being installed in Kashmir as well in the same form.

2. Sarva Shakti – the all powerful. Manifest as Hanuman or Anjaneya, who is none other than Rudra Himself, related to the episode where Dasharatha the father of Rama established certain shrines in Thiruvarur, and this caused the halting of Pushpaka Vimanam in Thiruvarur carrying Rama with Lakshmana, Sita and Hanuman on His way back from Lanka, and on this account, Raama asked Hanuman to survey the land, which He did and reported the presence of these shrines.

3. Sarva Aishwarya Prada – the bestower of all auspicious fortunes. Manifest as Shiva in the principal form of Lingam in Thiruvarur as Valmikanatha, with the origin story being a Yajna conducted in Kurukshetra, with Vishnu winning the prize of a bow emerging from the fire. Vishnu arrived to Thiruvarur and feigning arrogance, rested His head on the bow, even as Devas by the advice of Brihaspathi, took the form of ants establishing an ant hill, snapping the string of the bow and severing the head of Vishnu. Then to agitated prayers by Lakshmi, Shiva blessed Vishnu with a horse head, for the incarnation of Hayagriva and then manifest in the ant hill called Valmikanatha.

4. Sarva Jnaanamayi – the one of the form of wisdom. Manifest as Hayagrive, related to the incident of Vishnu losing His head and replaced with a horse head by Valmikanatha, this incarnation being of the form of Jnaana Anandam or blissful wisdom, who rescued the Vedas stolen by a

demon under water, killing the demon. As the primordial form wih the bow, it is this form that later took on the form of Raama as well.

5. Sarva Vyaadhi Nivaarini – the one that cures all diseases. Manifest as Jwara Deva, with three legs denoting the body Doshas or qualities of airy Vaata, fiery Pitta and slimy Kapha, balance or lack of these that causes health and disease. This form was created by Shiva as part of the Virabhadra incarnation to destroy the arrogant Yajna of Daksha.

6. Sarva Aadhaara swarupa – the one that is the basis of everything. Manifest as Varaha the boar incarnation of Vishnu coming out of the nose of Brahma, which established order in the earth which had sunk into chaotic waters due to the demon hiranyaksha, with Varaha stabilizing earth in current orbit around the sun, thus creating seasons and progress of time itself, and it is for this reason, that the current solar system era is called Shvetha Varaha Kalpa.

7. Sarva Paapa Hara – the one that eradicates all sin and evil. Manifest as Pidaari or Chandika form of Durga, in the incident of a demon Chitrasharma who was cursed by Durvasa to take the form of a bull headed demon Mahishasura, who after tormenting people and Gods was finally defeated by Chandika, even as he surrendered to the Mother in the last moments of his life, which She acquiesced by holding his head for all eternity without killing him.

8. Sarva Aanandamayi – the one that is of the form of pure bliss. Manifest as Nandi, the chief of attendants of Shiva, who was born as son of the sage Shilada and exhibited exemplary excellence in devotion to God.

9. Sarva Raksha Swarupini – the one that is the form of protection. Manifest as Raaja Durga, the term Durga meaning fortress, who protects from all attacks and threats, and installed by Raama prior to His was in slaying the demon Ravana.

10. Sarvepsitha Phala Prada – the one that gives fruits desired for. Manifests as Shani, the planet Saturn, in the incident where Dasharatha the father of Raama had a confrontation with Shani over affecting children below the age of eight, and subsequently Dasharatha installed the energy of Shani in Thiruvarur, which was later worshipped by Nala to get rid of his troublesome affliction which then happened in nearby Thirunallar.

CHAPTER SIXTEEN

Sarvarogaharam

The seventh Avarana has eight triangles known as Sarvarogahara, the remover of all diseases and afflictions.

1. Vashini – the fascinator of all. Manifest as Sastha, also known as Vishnu maya or Chathan, with Sastha considered a form combining Shiva and Vishnu, born to Shiva as Bhikshatana and Mohini when they visited Thiruvarur Daruka Vanam.

2. Kaameshi – the controller of love. Manifest as Kamakshi, the form taken by Mother Goddess to restore life to Manmatha after being burnt by Shiva, with the Goddess taking control of his weapons namely the sugarcane bow denoting mind and five flowery arrows denoting the five senses. Later, this form was taken to slay the demon Bhandasura in Kanchipuram.

3. Modhini – the enjoyer of all. Manifest as Shukra, the preceptor to demons and the planet Venus, who denotes indulgence and enjoyment in physical pleasures.

4. Vimala – the purest form. Manifest as Kamalalayam the sacred temple tank or Pushkar created by Brahma which is the biggest ever existing at 35 acres, as big as the temple itself, whose waters are believed to purify one and all, and the tank itself consists of 64 stepways or Ghats, where donation of different kinds of gifts are said to yield different kinds of benefits, and dipping into the waters are said to remove all kinds of Doshas or ill effects.

5. Aruna – the fiery red one that dissolves and destroys all Runa or bondages. Manifest as Agni after being pacified by all Gods, due to Agni earlier getting enraged by the offering of the meat of a dead dog in the purified sacrificial fire.

6. Jayini – the victorious one. Manifest as Narasimha, to save the devotee Prahlada and destroy the demon Hiranyakashipu, while taking a form that is neither animal nor man, during twilight between day and night.

7. Sarveshi – the Lord over everything. Manifest as Sharabheshwara, the form taken called Akasha Bhairava to tame the uncontrollable anger of Narasimha, after completion of the incarnation, accompanied by Shaktis called Shoolini and Prathyangira.

8. Kaulini – the regulator of all movements. Manifest as Kundalini or Nagakanni, the form of the primal life force viewed as a dormant serpend at the root of our spine, and activated by Yogic practices or devotion, on its journey upwards to reach the crown of the head.

CHAPTER SEVENTEEN

Sarvasiddhipradam

The eighth Avarana is the central triangle of the Sri Chakra, consisting of three deities at its three vertices, and called Sarva siddhi prada, the one that bestows all superpowers. In some systems, the three deities are seen in the space between avaranas 1 and 2, along with the Kameshwara aspect of 9th Avarana seen as Thuriya or the fourth beyond the 3 deities of 8th Avarana.

1. Maha Kameshwari – the fulfiller of everything desired. Manifest as Shitala Devi Maha Mariamman, also called Magamaayi or Mahamaya, the form taken by Adi Shakti, particularly as a Mother to fulfill the desires of all her devotees by changing or transforming situations, and hence the Mari name.

2. Maha Vajreshwari – the one that bestows invincibility like a diamond. Manifest as Renuka Devi known as Ellaiamman, and in reality the Mahavidya Chhinnamasta also known as Vajra Vairochani. Incarnating as the Mother of Parashurama, Renuka once let Her chastity slip Her concentration by observing and getting distracted by a group of Gandharvas in a river bank, as a punishment of which Jamadagni Her consort instructed Parashurama to cut off Her head, but was brought back to life on the insistence of Parashurama.

3. Maha Bhagamaalini – the one primordial Yoni or creatrix that is garlanded and adored. Manifest as Bhadrakali also known as Angalamman, Her original form is Kannaki, who exemplified the height of chastity by burning down the city of Madurai to avenge wrong accusation and killing of her husdand Kovalan. After settling down in Thiruvarur, She took the form of Bhadrakaali when commanded by Shiva to destroy the Yajna of Daksha. Later, a demoness Daruka brought her forest to the region of Thiruvarur, and tormenting people, and She was killed by Bhadrakali. The form is the basis of the Bhadrakali enshrined in

Kodungallur and worshipped all over Kerala.

4.

CHAPTER EIGHTEEN

Sarvaanandamayam

The ninth Avarana is the central dot of the Sri Chakra known as Bindu and called Sarvanandamayam, which is of the form of pure bliss seen in everything. This Avarana enshrines Lalitha Herself in the form of Kamalamba, seated upon a Peetam or cot which is of the form of Sadashiva Kameshwara, enshrined in Thiruvarur as Thyagaraja.

1. Kameshwara Kameshwari – the exemplary ideal of love between Atma and God. Manifest in Thiruvarur as principal deity Thyagaraja, who is of the form of Somaskanda consisting of Shiva, Shakti and Skanda, with a single plait of hair in the rear side. The manifestation is related to the desire of Vishnu to have a child, for which purpose a fire sacrifice

was created and Thyagaraja coming out of the fire, and was worshipped by Vishnu placing Thyagaraja on the chest and letting the deity dance in tune with his breath called Ajapa Natanam, and going to Nirvikalpa Samadhi by meditating on the breath. At a later time, Vishnu presented the Thyagaraja to Indra, who then, due to attacks from demons sought the help of king Muchukunda in fighting them, which was successful. After the war, as a reqard, Muchukunda asked for the Thyagaraja of Indra, which reluctant to part with, Indra created six copies each with its own dance style, asking muchukunda to find the original, which he successfully did. Then all seven Thyagaraja were presented to Muchukunda which were installed in seven places in and around Thiruvarur namely Thiruvarur Ajapa Natanam, Nagapattinam Tharanga Natanam, Thirukuvalai Bhringa Natanam, Thirunallar Unmatta Natanam, Thirukarayil Kukkuta Natanam, Thiruvaimur Kamala Natanam and Vedaranyam Hamsapada Natanam. The worship of Thyagaraja is carried on in a grand scale in Thiruvarur everyday, and the system of the same has been established by Durvasa. Of the 364 Leelas or divine plays enacted by Thyagaraja, here are some key ones. The first 50 Leelas of Thyagaraja mainly concern with the divine world, among which important Leelas include establishing the Thiruvarur city (2), marrying Paarvathi as Kamalaamba (5-6), establishing the Aadi Chola king (8), restoring power to Brihaspathi and Kubera (11,13), saving Navagrahas (19) and bringing the Ganga to Kamalaalayam (21). Leelas 51 to 130 are Uttaraayana Leelas (January-June months). Chief among them are Restoring offspring killed due to Guru's curse (55), restoring sight to Vaishya (60), saving yaaga by preventing rains (64), changing face from wolf (68), saving and gracing parrot and hunter (72), saving from famine and drought (75), honoring Guru Upadesha (81), inflicting the Vaidya with disease (82), walking on water (83), lighting lamps with water (85), restoring life (86), accepting jail imprisonment for sake of Bhakta (87), protecting the king by disguising as a blind man (94), saving Bhakta from fire (98), ability to fly (101), bestowing progeny (108), restoring sight to the blind (109), speech to the dumb (110), sound to the deaf (111), movement to the crippled (112), drinking molten metal like water (118), roaming in the streets as a Vaidya doctor (120), bending a coconut tree (124), saving life by providing water in the middle of forest (126) and bearing sand for building tank (127). Leelas from 131 to 364 are Dakshinaayana Leelas (June-December months).

Chief among these are converting honey to water (132), disappearance of wealth (133), removing of poison (137), protecting an orphan boy (139), walking of stone elephant (140), displaying His form to lady who served three mouthfuls of rice (142), displaying the truthfulness of Guru-Patni (144), growing a stumped tree (146), sounding the musical instrument (150), lighting lamp (151), obtaining golden parrot (155), drying up of Hamsa Teertha (157), Granting Guru Dakshina (160), protecting a cow (170), curing insanity (171), rising the sun at night (179), losing eyes (180), preventing marriage by offering Jada hair (182), protecting chastity (187), turning snakes into flowers (192), sand into Pooja items (193), crowning Sannyasi (196), turning sand into gold (211), granting kingdom to boy (212), removal of serpent curses (222), making of rope from sand (223), creating eyes in legs (238), writing Beeja Akshara in tongue (240), withering of fruit (250), exposing a robber through pearl necklace (252), protecting boy through lion (253), preventing flower from withering (258), granting wealth to the poor (260), opening the doors through Vedas (269), providing food (271), floating of stone (277), closing of door (283), curing of skin disorder (287), bestowing of auspiciousness (289), inflicting fever on one who rebuked Bhakta (292), talking of sand doll (295), providing fruit (298), appearing as son (302), drying up of water using fire (303), turning iron into gold (310), Darshan in forest (317), hearing of Veena music (322), joining of head and body (329), appearing as snake charmer (326), digestion of poison as food (341), waking of 3000 people (346), eating of food fed by boy (352), teaching (353), singing in dream (354), feeding milk through finger (356) and saving the knife from falling (358). However, spiritually, the most interesting Leela is the 77th, where the Lord gave darshan to Shishyas of Gautama Rishi, who were simultaneously and independently performing austerities, prayers and penances in various ways, including Sankha Vedika Aatma Jnaana, Daanam (charity), Panchaakshara Japam, Homam, Archana, Maanasika prayers, Gopura Darshanam, Dhyaanam, and Paada Sharanaagathi. The Lord manifested simultaneously as Shiva, Shakti, Narayana, Surya and Nirguna Parabrahman, according to each devotee's way of worsarahip.

2. Para Bhattarika – the Mother Goddess has been enshrined as Kamalamba by Agastya, and is made of the only existing Chinthamani stone, which continuously absorbs and emits vibrations of Omkara. While the presence of Goddess in Thiruvarur is basically timeless, Agastya invoked the Kamalamba form of Goddess for energy of Soshini Devi required to swallow the ocean near Kanyakumari under which demons were hiding. Enshrining Thiruvarur as the Bindu of the Sri Chakra, Agastya enshrined 25 different towns from Kanyakumari all the way to Thiruvarur as 25 concentric corridors or Prakaras, described together as Manidweepam, with those 25 towns all being Parivara Devatas or accompaniment shrines to

the Kamalamba of Thiruvarur. These 25 are Mahakali Mahakala in Kanyakumari, Ashwarudha in Therikadu, Bhavani Parvathi in Shankarankovil, Prana Shakti Vayu in Chathuragiri, Kaumari in Palani, Bagalamukhi in Thiruparankundram, Raajamaangi in Madurai, Siddhiswari in Anaippatti Dindigul, Chamunda in Manapparai, Chhinnamasta in Karaikkudi, Bhairavi in Vairavanpatti, Nageshwari in Peraiyur, Annapoorni in Sittannavasal, Indrani Sampatkari in Manachanallur, Vaaraahi Akhilandeshwari in Thioruvanaikaval, Brahmi in Kumbakonam, Vaishnavi in Thiruncherai, Maheshwari in Kodavasal, Thaara in Koothanur, Vaaruni Amritha in Ambagarathur, Kurukulla in Srivanjiyam, Surya Madhumathi in Nannilam, Chandra Soma in Achuthamangalam, Rathi Manmatha in Melavasal, and Sadashiva in Kilvelur. These are reflections of the respective deities inside Thiruvarur Sri Chakra formation. Furthermore, the Goddess who is seen in a posture of penance towards marrying Thyagaraja, is described as all powerful in Naagara Khaandam with various Mantras prescribed to be chanted in this location to get various effects as follows, where one day of chanting gives what one year of chanting elsewhere would bestow. Pullinga japam for progeny, Shatarudriya for destruction of enemies, Vaamadevya Saaman for protection from evil spirits and ghosts, Ko Adat Rig Japam for fast marriage, Imam Deva for favour even from greatest of kings, Tam Patnibhih for harmony in the family, Aditi Japa for affection from people, Sri suktam for abundance of wealth from all directions, Bhoomi Saaman for position of emperor, Rathantaram Saaman for fast vehicles, Ganaanam Tvaam for hordes of elephants, Na Tadrakshya Mantra for unconditionally strong security, Saptarishaya Mantra to destroy all physical and mental ailments, Yadubhi Mantra to turn malefic planets favorable, Brihat Saman to turn even Yama into a friend, Shakuna Sukta for successful journey, Sarpa Sukta to keep serpents at bay, Utthishta Mantra Japa to destroy poison, Vyaaghra Saaman to turn tigers and pythons gentle, laangalaani with Devavrata Mantra Japam to destroy calamities, Samsrishtam Mantra to win arguments, Kaali Karaali Mantra Japam to yield anything desired, and finally chanting Japams such as Damstrambhyam, Vishnusamhita, Kushmandih, Prajaapatya, Vaaruna and Rudrashiras to destroy and delude sinners, thieves and enemies. In yogic significance, Kamalamba is known as Manonmani and is venerated by Siddhas as Vaalai Manonmani.

CHAPTER NINETEEN

Trividha Upaasana

For a person to graduate through the Bhumikas, and attain the powers of Sumeru and Srimannagaram, it is possible only if all the energies of the person are perfectly regulated, and in this context, every person can be said to have three bodies called Thrayathmaka. These three are the physical or Sthoola Sharira consisting of the biological human body with all its organs, the astral or Sookshma Sharira consisting of the seven energy centers with concentration in the form of Kundalini serpent journeying through them, and causal or Kaarana Sharira consisting of the mind and all the ideas generated which run the dream creation. The regular exercise to keep the energies in perfect balance and regulation is known as Trividha Upasana. Of these the Sthoola is regulated by the practice of Kaamakala, also called Kaayaka Upaasana, and the Sookshma is regulated by Kriya Yoga, also called Maanasa Upasana, while the Kaarana is regulated by music or Sangeetham, called Vaachaka Upaasana. These three practices will be explored in this chapter.

KAMAKALA:

This Puja, done unclothed in private, or in the bedroom, consists of viewing himself as Shiva (or Krishna) unclothed with all Divine radiance, and as having intimate physical relationship with Shakti (or Radha), equally radiant and unclothed. This applies if the performer of the Puja is male. If female, then performer visualises herself as Shakthi, having intimate relationship with Shiva. In the process the visualising may be accompanied with corresponding physical movements as well. Also, one can modify the procedure to same gender scenarios as well, ie male-male (such as Chaitanya Mahaprabhu and Krishna) and female-female. To do this, one must replace the corresponding parts of the female organs by male, if pursuing male-male, and vice versa if female-female.

In reality, one is indeed Atma, and hence one is indeed Divine. This is the Vedantic truth, and any thought that one is human is nothing but the imagination of Maya. This must be clearly understood, asserted and affirmed by the performer before starting the Puja. During the entire worship, any thoughts of being human must be thrown away as figment of imagination - you are not a human visualising yourself as Divine, but rather you are the Divine with a mind creating illusions of human identity.

This Dhyana of Linga and Yoni must be done with utmost respect, and more importantly love, and one is to be fully unclothed. It is the foreplay that is paramount here rather than the actual physical union. The following Excerpts illustrate the reverence and sanctity of the organs.

"Worship carefully a woman or a maiden as she is Shakti, sheltered by the Kulas. One should never speak harshly to maidens or women." (Kaulajnananirnaya, Patala 23)

"In Kaula every woman is thought of as a manifestation of the Goddess. No man may raise his hand, strike or threaten a woman. When she is naked, men must kneel and worship her as the Goddess. She has equal rights with men on all levels." (Occult World of a Tantrik Guru, Values Vol. IX)

"Devi is at the base of the yoni and Naganandini is in the yoni. Kali and Tara are in the yoni chakra, and Chinnamasta in the hair. Bagalamukhi and Matangi are on the rim of the yoni. Mahalakshmi (Kamalatmika), Shodashi (Tripura Sundari), and Bhuvaneshvari are within the yoni. By worshipping the yoni one certainly worships Shakti." (Yoni Tantra, Patala 3)

"For the sadhaka who says 'Aim Aim' at the time of worship, the yoni is fortunate and gives both enjoyment and liberation. A yogin is not a bhogin (seeker of pleasure) and a bhogin is not a yogin, but if one worships the yoni, one is a Kaula, a person who has both yoga and bhoga (enjoyment). All worship is pointless without worship of the yoni, O Durga." (Yoni Tantra, Patala 3)

"Liberation is achieved through enjoyment. Happiness is gained through enjoyment. Therefore, by every effort, a sadhaka should become an enjoyer. The wise man should always avoid blame, disgust, or shame of the yoni." (Yoni Tantra, Patala 6).

Thus, in essence, Inner Linga yoni puja implies that we must as clearly as possible visualize the living form of a yoni and Linga and contemplate it as long as possible with devotion and reverence.

This established, one must first visualise Shiva's Linga (in oneself if male, in the beloved Shiva of female), and worship it in the manner mentioned in the Kaulajnana Tantra.

This linga, the cause of both creation and dissolution, worshipped by siddhas, shining by its own light, pure, eternal, completely immeasurable, like lightning in the sky.

This linga is eternally erect, a vajra linga, and my not be destroyed by anything. Worship the Linga employing mental flowers and sweetly scented incense.

Next, visualisation of the Yoni and other female parts of Shakti is done (in the beloved if male, in own self is female).

Next, one must perform the foreplay and amorous activities between oneself and partner, as Shiva and Shakti.

This is done in 9 parts, corresponding to the nine Avaranas of Sri Chakra.

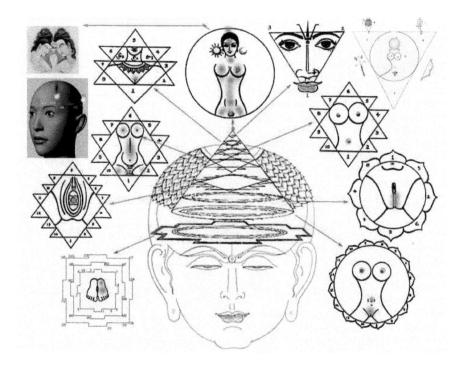

The 9 body regions corresponding to the nine Avaranas, in order, are as follows.

- Feet and soles
- Caressing of the breasts, navel and genital areas.
- The labia and vulva
- Vagina and clitoris
- Caressing gently on the breasts, navel genital areas and inner thighs
- Breast nipples and navel.
- Caressing the neck and breast cleavage.
- The face, especially the mouth and kissing.
- Caressing the entire body from face downwards till genital regions, leading to intercourse.

In each of the 9 visualisations, one must visualise the foreplay of Shiva with the corresponding parts of Shakti. In the 9th visualisation, ie Bindu, one must visualise the whole form of Shakti (or Shiva if female), beautiful and radiant. The below illustrates a male and female, in this state of Dhyana, their physical organs aroused.

After this 9th Avarana Dhyana, is the actual intercourse between Shiva and Shakti. This will eventually result in synchronous culmination of male and female, which will be physically reflected as an orgasm. The posture of intercourse will be with the male on top and the female on bottom, as already illustrated in the earlier section of love making. It may be necessary to use as aid, some phallic shaped objects, or even carrots etc if female.

In the first few days of doing this worship, due to the erstwhile prevailing lust and its strength, one may reach physical climax even before finishing the 9 visualisations. One can finish nevertheless the remaining Avaranas even after climax. Correspondingly, one can plan by speeding up the visualisations in forthcoming days, so as to bring it in sync with physical culmination. Once that is achieved, one can slowly and gradually in small steps, increase the length of visualisations, thereby increasing control. If one is able to do the entire process in lasting for half an hour, without physically culminating until the end, then one has achieved significant removal of lust.

The Linga Yoni Dhyana may be done by anybody, having received verbal instructions from Diksha or Guru. There are no time or day restrictions for this. While Kaulachara Puja must be discontinued once removal of addictions are achieved, Linga Yoni Dhyana may be continued for as long as one pleases, and may even be done alongside with Shodashi or Sri Chakra Puja. The Kamakala Dhyana must be taken as an extension of Bhakti Yoga, among the Sapthangas, as a system of taking to the physical level, the relationship that one experiences in Thithi Bhakti.

Thus, Kamakala should not, at any cost be seen as just the physical or Kama part, without the Kala, ie love aspect. Kamakala is not by any means, just a half hour pleasure session for the creative organs. Rather, Kamakala is a continuous, ongoing romance affair, as Kameshwara and Kameshwari, each viewing the other in everything, visible and invisible, and this intense love affair must be a complete one, with proposal, wedding, honeymoon, and of course the physical consummation as well.

For those unable to come out of viewing Devi as Amma, must take example of Vallabha Ganapathi as how Devi can at the same time be both Mother and Lover. To these souls, the following instructions are given: You have a responsibility, a mission in the world, which needs you. You can't be a child forever, that position is one of irresponsibility. So grow up, take charge. In Tamil there's a saying "thol mel valarndavan thozhan" - parents to treat children as friends once they reach shoulder height. So Devi will be your friend. Ie girl friend.

To illustrate this concept, there is no better example than Ganesha, who is shown in the specific amorous form as Ucchishta Ganapathi, along with Neela Saraswathi Thara, who is none other than a form of Parvathi Herself, ie His own Mother.

It has been observed that performing Kamakala, as mentioned above, gives physical strength to a person due to the Atma Bhava or identity at the Atma level. The Sattva Guna of Kamakala as a Divya Sadhana, coupled with this added Atmic strength reflects in physical aspects, such as for example the weights one is able to lift, in gymnasium workouts, as well as a decreased level of tiredness.

The basic premise of Kamakala, is about tapping into the concentrated energy of Muladhara through Kama, which then reflects as increased strength throughout, in all areas of life. But that is possible only through removing Rajasa and Tamas, and adhering to Satva. Satya is Satva, and in this case is indeed the Atma alone. Here maintaining a vegetarian diet, and praying to Amma to purify every single food item before we eat, helps to accelerate the Sattvic progress even further.

Furthermore, the Atma Bhava or identity that one adheres to during Kamakala Dhyana, takes the person towards throw ultimate truth or Satya, which is indeed Atma. Where there's Satya, there's Sattva Guna. Thus, physical emissions by male or female during Kamakala are all seen as Sattvic, and free of Doshas of Rajasa or Tamasa. In the case of females, this also all applies to menstrual discharge called Rajasvala, which becomes Sattvic in Kamakala, as opposed to Rajasic without Kamakala. Thus, by making Rajasvala Sattvic, the female is eligible to perform Sri Chakra Puja, Japas and other such rituals even during the menstruation periods.

KRIYA YOGA

As a daily routine, the following is recommended. Kriya Pranayama, one Pranayama consisting of visualising all 7 Chakras up and all 7 down, maintaining Shambhavi Mudra. 24 such Pranayamas to be done, which would typically take 8-10 minutes. Focus on the last part of exhalation on the stomach going in and the sweet feeling arising thereon when the muscle is relaxed after full exhalation.

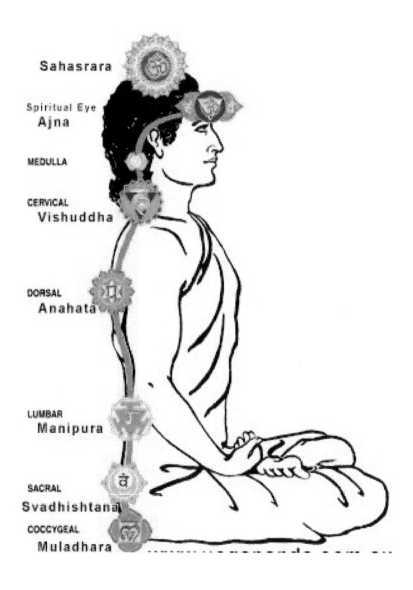

Sahasrara

Spiritual Eye
Ajna

MEDULLA

CERVICAL
Vishuddha

DORSAL
Anahata

LUMBAR
Manipura

SACRAL
Svadhishtana

COCCYGEAL
Muladhara

Sit facing East. Mouth and eyes are closed. Feel that the center of your awareness is located at Medulla while the inner gaze converge effortlessly on Kutastha.Inhale deeply through the nose producing an unvoiced sound in the throat. To make certain the sound is correct, concentrate only on increasing the friction of the air flowing through your throat. A muffled sound will originate. Increase its frequency. If the surroundings are perfectly still, a person could hear it within a 4-5 meter radius – by no means outside it. Kriya Pranayama is to be practiced with a deep abdominal breathing. This means that, during inhalation the upper part of the thorax remains almost immobile while the abdomen expands. Shoulders are not raised. During exhalation, the abdomen comes inside. Practice 24 breaths. Gradually increase by 12. Mentally chant Om in each Chakra. Enjoy the breathing process.During inhalation, Om is mentally chanted (or, more simply, "mentally placed") in each one of the six Chakras from Muladhara to Medulla. During exhalation, Om is mentally chanted in the Medulla and in all the other Chakras coming down to Muladhara. Don't lose the focus of your inner gaze on Kutastha. It is clear that going up and down the spine producing the throat sound and at the same time placing Om in each Chakra is difficult. Enjoy the beautiful feeling of fresh air that seems to come up through the spine and pierce each Chakra, enjoy the warm exhaled air permeating each zone of the body from top to bottom. Merge your awareness with the beauty of this deep breathing. A short pause between inhalation and exhalation and between exhalation and inhalation comes naturally. The pause do no last more than 2-3 seconds. Each pause is a moment of comfortable peace.

Perceive the energy moving through the spine. After regular practice, during inhalation, you will perceive a cold current coming up through the spine – or simply a diffused fresh sensation. During exhalation you will perceive a lukewarm sensation in the spine. Exhalation could be longer than inhalation. During the last part of the exhalation, there is a clear perception of the navel moving in toward the spine. By refining this experience – being more aware of the navel moving inward and of the action of the diaphragm muscles – you will feel an ecstatic sensation. Make the sound of the breath subtler and subtler. The exhalation arising in the nasal pharynx has a fine sound like a faint whistle. That has the power to cut out any external distracting factor. This sound is produced in the upper part of the nasal pharynx. If you feel it you have only one duty more, letting that this sound absorbs your mind completely.

Shambhavi Mudra is the act of concentrating on the space between the eyebrows, bringing the two eyebrows toward the center with a slight wrinkling of the forehead. Alternatively The eyes look upward as much as possible as if looking at the ceiling but without any head movement. The light tension perceived in the muscles of the eyeballs when closed gradually disappears and the position can be maintained rather easily. A bystander would observe the sclera (white of the eye) under the iris because very often the inferior eyelids relax. Through this Mudra all one's Prana collects at the top of the head. You will eventually have the impression of crossing a mental state, which is like falling asleep, then suddenly returning to full awareness and realizing you are basking in a spiritual light. It's like a plane emerging from clouds into a clear transparent sky.

Manasika Pranayama of visualising the melting of Chakras from Muladhara to Sahasrara and back to Muladhara. This must be done atleast 3 times. Focus on the sweet feeling arising when each Chakra melts. Do not force the Chakras into melting or even keep reinforcing the thought that it will melt. Just with an initial thought that a Chakra will melt, focus on the Chakra and passively observe it.

- When you are listening to somebody and get bored, the attention slowly slips away and the person or thing in focus slowly blurs away and you drift into sleep. The moment of drift into sleep gives the same sweet feeling that is obtained during melting of Chakras. The state of pure bliss that is Brahman is indeed experienced by everyone during sleep, except that one is not aware of it. The whole idea of Samadhi is experiencing this feeling while being aware of it, for which Manasika Pranayama offers a means. Whether the meditation before such a Samadhi involves thoughts and forms or doesn't determines whether the Samadhi achieved is Savikalpa or Nirvikalpa. After wisdom that entire creation is unreal, an inherent boredom arises towards the world. Because of this wisdom, a person naturally starts to see everything as blurred and without substance, and because of this, that sleepy happiness occurs at all instances, and at will. This is Sahaja Samadhi. Since Manasika Pranayama opens up that sweet feeling or happiness, which becomes a continuous thing in spiritual advancement, Manasika Pranayama is called Uttama Pranayama.

Even a non Yogi experiences the Samadhi state in the everyday activity of deep sleep, and astral travelling in the dream state. Yet, he is not consciously aware of these experiences. A Kriya Yogi on the other hand consciously experience ms these Samadhi states as Manasika Pranayama and goes forward to various Samyamas as given here. One finds that the refreshment and rejuvenation got through Samadhi state is often comparable to sleep, if not even better. Thus, some Yogis have known to regulated sleep accordingly, while others have given up sleep altogether, getting all their refreshment from Samadhi itself.

Ajapa japa is a complete sadhana and through it one can have direct experience of Nirvikalpa samadhi. In order to attain samadhi, in all the other yogic practices one has to have complete control over the breath, the reason being that in samadhi the breath is suspended and kumbhaka takes place spontaneously. However, in the practice of ajapa japa, due to the continuity of breath and mantra, the breathing remains normal throughout, and even in samadhi there is no change.

In Yoga Philosophy, Paramaatma is described as the form of Purusha and Kala (time). Purusha is Antaryami of the upasaka. The Universe which is the projection of Paramaatma for his divine sport. To continue his divine sport (pravritti) with universe, paramaatma takes the form of Kala (time). The entire creation is under the control of this Kala. Unit of Kala is measured in terms of One Year in Veda which is 360 days. This is also the time taken by the Sun to enter into all the 12 raasi chakras. Time taken by the sun to pass one zodiac sign is 30 degrees. Hence, to enter into all the 12 raasis, it would take 30 degree x 12 = 360 degrees. Each degree is measured in terms of 60 liptaas ie., 360 degrees is equivalent to 12600 liptaa kala parimana. The number of breaths per day of an individual is 21600. These are called "Hamsa". Because, while exhaling "Ham" sound is produced and while inhaling "Sa" sound is produced. This is in the form of Ajapa Gayatri. When this 21600 hamsa are divided with 60 lipta, it comes to 360 degrees This 360 degrees is divided in the 6 chakras of pindanda of the jiva as follows: Mooladhara : 56 degrees, Manipura : 52 degrees, Svadhistana : 62 degrees, Anahata : 54 degrees, Visudhi : 72 degrees, Ajna : 64 degrees with a grand Total of 360 degrees, and this is how space is mapped to time.

From Mooladhara to Manipura, devi is called Agni Kundalini, from Svadhistana to Anahata, devi is called Surya Kundalini and from Visudhi to Ajna, the devi is called Chandra Kundalini. One can see that kala chakra of 360 degrees is divided in shat chakras as Agni, Surya and Chakra Kundalinis. Since, the Devi resides at Sahasrara which is beyond these 6 chakras and hence, cannot be reached by this kalachakra swarupa. Hence, she is called "Desa Kalaa Parichinna".

During Rasmi Mala Parayana, the following numbers of Hamsas are distributed in the 6 chakras of body: Mooladhara : 600 hamsas to Ganapati, Manipura : 6000 hamsas to Brahma, Svadhistana : 6000 hamsas to Vishnu, Anahata : 6000 hamsas to Rudra, Visudhi : 1000 hamsas to Jivatma, Ajna : 1000 hamsas to Paramatma, Sahasrara : 1000 Hamsas to Guru, totaling 21600 hamsas of ajapa in a jiva.

Ajapa japa is a complete practice in itself. Those who have read the Yoga Sutras of Patanjali know that first of all one has to concentrate on a concrete object. When the concentration on a concrete object is complete with open eyes, one must meditate on the same object with closed eyes. This is concentration on a subtle object. One must concentrate on the simple awareness of its presence. By practising ajapa japa both stages of concentration can be achieved. Therefore, it is a complete practice in itself and through it one can enter the spiritual realms.

In ajapa japa the three important points are: deep breathing, relaxation and total awareness. During the practice you must maintain complete and unceasing awareness of what you are doing. Not a single breath should go unnoticed. There should be no automatic breathing. You must have unceasing awareness of every ingoing and outgoing breath. Automatic breathing goes on at night when you are asleep also; it is not ajapa japa. You must consciously notice every ingoing and outgoing breath, like a watchman, observe the continuous rhythm of the two breaths.

Lie down and feel as if you are going to sleep. Breathe deeply like a person in deep sleep. After a few days practice, your breathing will be completely relaxed, rhythmic and proportionate. The normal rate of inhalation is 15 times in a minute, 900 times in an hour, and 21,600 times in 24 hours. Thus a person who has perfected ajapa japa will do 21,600 rounds of japa per day, effortlessly.

As and when the concentration becomes deep, the breathing will become slower. Instead of 15 breaths per minute, you will breathe 10. In the practice of ajapa japa you make the breath as long and as deep as when you are snoring, but there is no audible sound. By conscious breathing and prolonging the breath, longevity is increased.

Next synchronize the mantra Soham with the breath. The sound So joins with the ingoing breath and the sound Ham joins with the outgoing breath. Maintain unceasing awareness of the breath and mantra. Feel that you are introspecting upon Soham.

There should be continuous awareness of the ingoing and outgoing breath and Soham. If you prefer, you can also adjust your personal mantra with the breathing process. If you practise with Soham, you need not think of the literal meaning of this word at all. It is not ahamgraha upasana. So is the introspective sound of the ingoing breath, while the vibrations that are created by the outgoing breath sound like Ham. Soham merely indicates the complete circuit of introspection upon the ingoing and outgoing breath.

Whenever your mind, your consciousness, your awareness dissipates, be alert. No mental activity should go unnoticed. You should never be unmindful of the process of concentration. This is the fundamental and the only point in meditation to be remembered. If you fail to remember or understand this most important point, you will never get success in meditation, even if you meditate for a century.

It is a psychological fact that when you want to control the mind, it will wander ruthlessly and you will fail to control it. But if you quietly watch the mental activities, they will immediately stop. by just watching the breath continously, you will reach the same state of Samadhi as you had with the Chakras melting. This is Nirvikalpa Samadhi.

The throat as the windpipe supplies air to all organs below it, while its endocrine Gland the Thyroid principally controls the intensity of Hunger and thirst, and with the appropriate Kriya, one can quench this Hunger and thirst using nothing but the air inhaled. To achieve this, close your eyes and watch the rise and fall of the abdomen during breathing. Slowly, shift your attention to the throat area and visualise it. With each inhaled breath, visualise the throat materialising a fruit. Continue until Samadhi. After about a quarter hour one may begin to experience slight Belching up finish off any previous diatom, after which a continual secretion of sweet taste by the throat into the Saliva can be felt, indicating the success herein. Interestingly, the sweet taste is seen as a symptom of reduced Thyroid activity and thus reduced Hunger, while at the same time, other diseased effects of hypothyroidism will not be seen. In this as well as the regulation of body temperature the effects of the exercises done last till whenever one sleeps for the day. Also within the day, when one eats, the sweet secretion will decrease, and will automatically increase after Digestion of the eaten food occurs. Furthermore, the intensity sweet secretion is directly connected to one's level of happiness, since it is the mind that has enabled this secretion. This is what is referred to as Amritham in Vedic literature.

Astral Travel: In a comfortable position, preferably reclining or lying down, close your eyes, and take 2-3 deep breaths. Visualise the destination you want to travel to. Focus on the space between the eyebrows. Mentally Paint a picture of the destination based on what you last saw it or how you think it would probably appear now. Start with the focus point between eyebrows, but then continue painting on either side, eventually covering your entire field of vision. Gaze at the painted picture and visualise yourself in the location, far removed from your residence. If there be doubts that you have not travelled anywhere but are simply imagining, clear the doubts using the following justification: it is Amma's will that you must travel now, which is why you visualize the destination, and Divine Will is always infallible. Thus, any sounds or thoughts you might have suggesting that you are not travelling cannot be true, but rather is your own dreamy mind experiencing some kind of home sickness. Ignore it and move on with the astral travelling. After having mentally painted it, just admire the location all around. Keep gazing and admiring. In due course, you would get sleepy, but will soon automatically wake yourself Up. If you see a blank on waking up, recreate the visualization again. In these moments of transition between sleep and waking up, you will get the experience of the astral travel, seeing and experiencing various things in the destination, thus enjoying this as one would in normal travel. One can continue this as long as one likes.

Astral Information Access: Close your eyes and look at the point between the eyebrows. Fix your attention there. Visualize Amma and attest to yourself that Amma through this technique will give what is sought. Think about the thing on which you seek information, with a quick mental visualization either by your last seeing it, or by a guess of what you feel it would be like. Close your eyes and see the blackness that is formed. If done in the presence of sunlight, a flesh coloured hue will be seen instead of full darkness. Blankly gaze at it. Occasionally gently remind yourself of the object you seek. After a while the darkness or redness slowly clears up. You may then see the desired object directly or the sought information as a colour. Continue with the exercise of seeing the object until a sleepy feeling takes over. You will automatically wake yourself up. That sleepy feeling is Samadhi and at that moment, time becomes meaningless, and that is when Samyama is achieved. There are few signs that one has reached Samyama or full focus in thinking. First, one's full attention span will center on the object whose information is being sought, and for that brief moment, one would be inattentive to any other sound or thought going around him. Second, if one is standing, at the moment of Samyama, one will lose balance and the legs will shift position. Third, after opening the eyes, one's vision would take time to set, just like it happens during waking up in the morning.

SANGEETHAM

The basis of everything, as the fundamental creation, which are the 16 stages, represented as Shodashakshari, is also seen in the Guru Tharaka Mantra of "Saayiñ Raam" साई॑ राम् are given as follows.

1. "Saa" of Sai Ram translates as He/She, God as the subject performing all actions.

2. "Ar" obtained by reversing Raa in Sai Ram is the Bija or root of Arhant, the one victorious over Karma cycle.

3. "Ayim" got by splitting the long sound in Saayiñ is the Ain Sof, which is the name of God simultaneously as everything and as nothing, add the unity behind all the variety.

4. "Eem" of Saayiñ is among the phonemes the Kamakala Bija representing the Shiva Shakti principles uniting to produce Ganesha. Ee as the Eeshini Devata invokes perfection and balance, overcoming all emotions.

5. "Maraa" from Raam denotes death, particularly of the unworthy misalignments.

6. Sa translates to Tat or that, which is Parabrahman, with all its characteristic essence of bliss, love, wisdom and beauty.

7. "Aa" of Sai Ram is the Atharvani Akshara, which represents fire, along with its powers of Illumination, and is the seed letter of Adithya Surya.

8. "Am" obtained by splitting Raam denotes perfection and Amrit or nectar of immortality, which is nothing but enlightenment, since wisdom alone has the power to take one beyond the cycle of birth and death.

9. "Aayi" of Saayiñ addresses the Divine as the Mother, who gave birth to the perishable universe and is thus beyond its birth and death.

10. "Maam" from Sai Ram is the variant of the most supreme among Bijas, Aham which denotes the Real Self, metre repitition of which takes one's mind to the source from where all thoughts arise, eliminating these thoughts on the way.

11. "Raama" is the most supreme among Mantras, and is no different from the Pranava Om.

12. "Raa" of Raama is the essence of the Narayana Ashtakshari Mantra, without which the name Narayana would read as Na Ayana meaning no path to salvation. Ra of the Bija of fiery passion as also of Rakthi or Raga, the divine passion from the heart of Amma to unite with Her child, which is the very fuel and motive of Divine Will.

13. "Eesaa" obtained by reversing Saayi is the Mantra, the very name of Christ who is none other than the Divine Consciousness within us, which kills the sense of ego by sacrificing the body consciousness.

14. "Ma" of Raama is the essence of the Panchakshari Shiva Mantra without which the Mantra would read Na Shivaya or Shiva as non existent. Thus, it is this Ma that asserts Shiva or the consciousness of pure existence, which gives correct perception of Reality and the Dreamy world.

15. "Amara" from Sai Ram denotes the state beyond death and birth, completely and effortlessly blissful without a trace of the fear of death.

16. The inherent playful nature of Amma is the reason for the name Lalitha, and this is the sixteenth stage, of the playful Jeevanmukthi. The Sai Ram Mantra in its entirety is no different than Sai Baba as the Guru form who in turn is no different than Venkatesha as Bala Amma.

The seven notes or 'swaras' in the Music were conceived from the sounds of the nature. The seven swaras as we all know are- Sa, Re, Ga, Ma, Pa, Dha, Ni. Represented by: Shadaja (Sa); the rapturous sound of the peacock when rain clouds gather in the sky, Rishabha (Re); the bellowing of a cow when her calf is separated from her, Gandhara (Ga); the bleating of a goat in a flock, Madhyama (Ma); the cry of a heron, Panchama (Pa); the sound of the Indian Kokila (nightingale) in spring, Dhaivata (Dha); the neighing of a horse, Nishada (Ni); the trumpeting of an elephant.

An interesting thing that is noted in the swaras is Sa, Ma and Pa are sounds made by birds whereas Re, Ga, Dha and Ni are sounds made by animals. If we get into too deep into these swaras then these swaras further have divisions. Ragas are nothing but different combinations of these swaras where any swara can be repeated or even omitted.

While music is based from the fundamentals of sound energy with Its various features such as frequency, timbre etc, it has been accessible to human civilization for tens of thousands of years. However, the oldest system of music, extant today, directly deriving from the Vedic system is Indian music. Based on its sheer age heuristically, as well as incidents of curing, stimulator nature etc, one can conclude that this system is the most efficient system of music, that can yield effect. Other systems of music, such as Chinese or Tribal music do not have substantial repertoire of notes which can cover the entire variety music has to offer, while other systems such as Arabic or Western are too fast paced for every note to produce its intended effect on nature and in humans.

Swara is the most fundamental concept in Carnatic music. It plays a similar role to that of a 'note' in western music, but has a distinct character. There are seven swaras in Carnatic music: S for Shadja (sung as Sa), R for Rishabha (sung as Ri), G for Gandhara (sung as Ga) , M for Madhyama (sung as Ma), P for Panchama (sung as Pa), D for Dhaivatha (sung as Da) and N for Nishadha (sung as Ni). The ascending order of the swaras, i.e. SRGMPDN, is called aarohana and the descending order, i.e. SNDPMGR is called avarohana. Aarohana and Avarohana together make a moorchana.

Nishada is followed again by a Shadja from the higher octave. The frequency of higher Shadja is twice that of the Shadja. An octave spans all the swaras from Shadja until, but not including the higher Shadja.

Shadja and Panchama are achala (immovable) swaras. The other five swaras, viz Rishabha, Gandhara, Madhyama, Dhaivatha, Nishadha are swaras with two or three variations each. The variations are listed below:

- R has 3 variations: shuddha (Ra or R1), chaturshruthi (Ri or R2), shatshruti (Ru or R3)
- G has 3 variations: shuddha (Ga or G1), sadharana (Gi or G2), antara (Gu or G3)
- M has 2 variations: shuddha (Ma or M1), prathi (Mi or M2)
- D has 3 variations: shuddha (Da or D1), chaturshruthi (Di or D2), shatshruti (Du or D3)
- N has 3 variations: shuddha (Na or N1), kaishiki (Ni or N2), kaakali (Nu or N3).

Sa and Pa, the only two notes that do not accept of any variations, act as the fulcrum points of an entire scale. The relation between Sa and Pa itself, if such that the sound frequency of Pa is 1.5 times that of Sa. This is called a harmonic relationship, and is called a fifth, due to Pa being the 5th note from Sa. However, just like Sa, each Swara has its own fifth Swara pair. For example, Ra, which is one place away from Sa, has as its fifth, Da, which in turn is one place away from Pa. The list of fifths of all keys are as follows: Sa Pa, Ra Da, Ri Di, Gi Ni, Gu Nu, Ma Sa, Mi Ra, Pa Ri, Da Gi, Di Gu, Ni Ma, Nu Mi.

Similarly, the fourth, such as Sa and Ma, are also a very harmonic pair of notes, and when sounded together or in succession, sound very consonant and pleasant, due to the frequency of Ma being 4/3 times that of Sa. All such fourth pairs are as follows: Sa Ma, Ra Mi, Ri Pa, Gi Da, Gu Di, Ma Ni, Mi Nu, Pa Sa, Da Ra, Di Ri, Ni Gi, Nu Gu.

The concept of fifth and fourth notes giving consonance is referred to as Samvadi. Thus, in a musical scale, if for any given note, its fifth or fourth note pair is also present in the scale, then the former note is called a consonant note.

Carnatic raga refers to ragas used in Carnatic music. A Carnatic raga has several components - primordial sound (nāda), tonal system (swara), pitch (śruti), scale, ornaments (gamaka) and important tones.

Janaka ragas or Sampoorna ragas are parent ragas from which more ragas are derived. Sampoorna ragas as the name suggest are those in which all 7 swaras are present. They are also called Melakarta ragas. These ragas have all 7 swaras or [notes] in their scales (only one of each swara, Sa, Re, Ga, Ma, Pa, Dha, Ni), following strict ascending and descending scales and are sung in all octaves. Example of melakartha ragas are : Shankarabharanam, Kalyani, Natabhairavi, Chala Nattai, Harikambhoji, Kharaharapriya, Mayamalavagowla, Chakravakam etc. Janya ragas are ragas that are derived from Janaka ragas (Melakarta ragas). They may have less than 7 notes in their scales, or have additional notes in them, zig-zag (vakra) notes that step up and down, asymmetrical scales, etc. Janya raga is also called as Upanga raga. Example of Upanga ragas are : Malahari, Mohanam, Begada, Shriragam, Hamsadhvani, Bilahari, Vasanta, Kambhoji, Janaranjani, Hindolam, Todi etc.

However, there are only some combinations that are allowed as for instance Shatshruthi Ri can combine with Antara Gandhara and Chathushruti Rishabha can combine with Sadharana and Antara Gandhara only. Likewise the same principle holds good for Da and Ni.

There are 72 combinations of melakartha ragas giving rise to a huge variety of musical flavours. Any sampurna raga is present in this 72 melakartha cycle. From these 72 melakartha ragas, there are more than a thousand janya ragas that contain more beautiful musical notations.

Vakra ragas are janya ragas that have swaras arranged in a zig zag manner. For e.g. Raga Sri has the following arohanam and avarohanam : S R M P N S. S. N P M R G R S. Such a raga is called vakra raga.

Auḍava rāgas are janya ragas that have exactly five notes in ascending and descending scale (arohana and avarohana). Examples are :
1)Mohanam (S R G P D S. S. D P G R S)
2)Hamsadhwani (S R G P N S. S. N P G R S).

Shaḍava rāgas are janya ragas that have exactly six notes in ascending and descending scale (arohana and avarohana).

A Carnatic raga consists of an ascending and descending scale pattern (known as aarohana and avarohana respectively). Both ascent and descent should have at least five tones, although rarer ragas contain fewer tones. Scales establish rules for all performers to adhere to in melodic performance, and provide a tonal boundary. Typical scale features also act to help listeners identify ragas.

Saama Sangeetham is a short 2-minute exposition in the original Saama Raaga of the Vedas. This would correspond to Kharaharapriya in Sampoorna and Shree Raaga in Asampoorna system of Carnatic Music, Khafi Thaat of Hindustan Music, Dorian Mode in Greek and Western music, and Maqam Rast in Arabic music. The udgātṛ was a chanter of hymns set to melodies (sāman) drawn from the sāmaveda. This was a specialized role in the major soma sacrifices: a characteristic function of the udgātṛ was to sing hymns in praise of the invigorating properties of soma pavamāna, the freshly pressed juice of the soma plant.

The Saama Sangeetham is always a vocal activity, has to be sung aloud. Instruments can only help so far as to help one familiarise with the pitch and exact frequency of the notes used. Saama Sangeetham cannot be performed on an instrument.

In the Vedas, Sama Veda has taken almost all of its lyrical content from the Rig Vedic verses as is, and added musical notations to those. Thus, it is clear that the tune plays a more critical role then the lyrics. In the Saama Sangeetham, the lyrics will be set to the Guru Nama SaiRam SaiRam, since that, containing all the 16 stages, is the zenith as Tharaka Mantra for all Vedic wisdom.

Due to convenience and compatibility with today's technology of phones etc, the keyboard shall be used as the instrument for pitch reference and familiarise with the notes. The key positions of the Swaras are as follows.

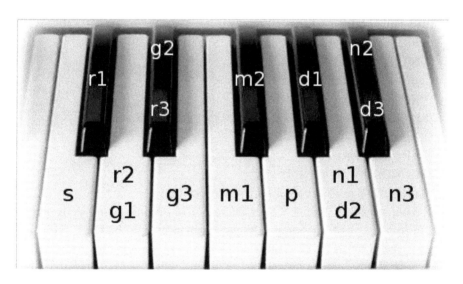

These key positions expand in both the left and right directions following the same pattern. One must first familiarise oneself with these key positions.

The Saaman Raaga contains the following notes. S,r2,g2,m1,p,d2,n2,s. Thus is represented as sa ri gi ma pa di ni sa.

The Saaman tune can be formed as a simple expansion on this scale as follows with lyrics given in brackets below each line.

The Saaman consists of two components, the first being a Sama pattern around Sa. The second is a Sama pattern around Pa. Between the 2, there is a transition line, and after the second component, there is a transition line to higher Sa, and all the way back to original Sa.

A Sama pattern refers to a specific order of notes centring around a note. The order followed is, one note higher, one note lower, two notes higher, two notes lower, and so on.

SaSa RiSa NiSa
(SaiRam SaiRam SaiRam)
RiGiRiSa NiDiNiSa
(SaiRamSaiRam SaiRamSaiRam)
RiGiMaMa GiRiSaSa NiDiPaPa DiNiSaSa
(SaiRamSaiRam SaiRamSaiRam SaiRamSaiRam SaiRamSaiRam)
RiGiMaMaPaPa
(SaiRamSaiRamSaiRam)
PaPa DiPa MaPa
(SaiRam SaiRam SaiRam)
DiNiDiPa MaGiMaPa
(SaiRamSaiRam SaiRamSaiRam)
DiNiSaSa NiDiPaPa MaGiRiRi GiMaPaPa
(SaiRamSaiRam SaiRamSaiRam SaiRamSaiRam SaiRamSaiRam)
DiNiSaSa
(SaiRamSaiRam)
SaSa NiDiPaPa MaMa GiRiSaSa
(SaiRam SaiRamSaiRam SaiRam SaiRamSaiRam)

Having mastered Saama Sangeetham in the original Sama Veda Raga, One may take any of the popular Ragas, given earlier in the book, with the forms invoked by them. One can also form one's own Raga by creating the ascending and descending Swara patterns to form a scale. Of course, the forms invoked by this new Raga can also be calculated by following the rules and examples mentioned earlier.

Next, for the Raga taken up, one must play the scale pattern up and down a few times to get familiarised with the keys and patterns. As a general rule of thumb, one can set the playing range from Pa of the lower octave, onward to Sa and the current octave fully, and further onwards to Sa of the higher octave.

Familiar with the Saama patterns, one can apply this to the Raga, keeping in line with the Raga scale structure. The white and black notes appropriate to the Raga scale must be used. Some Ragas called Varja may omit Swaras in ascending, descending or both, or some Ragas may have a crooked arrangement of Swaras. The Saama must be modified to align with all of this. A few examples are given here.

1. Mohanam, scale sarigupadi sadipaguri:

Sasa risa disa rigurisa dipadisa

Rigupapa gurisasa didipapa didisasa

Rigupapa

Papa dipa gupa disadipa gurigupa

Didisasa

Sasa dipa guri sasa

2. Bilahari, scale sarigupadi sanudipamaguri

Sasa risa nudi sasa

Rigurisa nudipapa disa sasa

Rigupapa magurisa nudipapa disa sasa

Rigupapa

Papa dipa mapa disa nudi papa magu riri gupa

Disa sasa

Sa sa nudipapa magu gurisasa

3. Begada, scale sagurigumapadinidipa sanidipamaguri:

Sasa gurisasa nidipapa sasa

Guriguma gurisasa nidipapa papasasa

Guriguma papa

Papa dipa mapa dinidipa magumapa

Dinidipa sasa nidipapa maguriri gumapapa

Dinidipa sasa

Sasa nidipapa maguriri sasa

One can set these Saamans for any selected Raga to a repetitive loop.

One may also, if interested start improvising on the Raga. Let the fingers glide up and down the patterns following the flow of the mind. One can start initially from the base Sa, drift towards the downward Pa and back to Sa,a few times in various patterns, occasionally involving higher notes. For example, if the chosen Raga is Shivaranjani ie Sarigipadi sadipagiri,one can go sds,dpds,pdps,drsdp,dsrsds.

Then, starting from s one can go onwards to pa. Such as, rgegsrdsrg, srgpgrs,rgrsrgp, gpgrsgr, sgrsdrs,dpdsrgrs,rgpd.

Then one goes further up towards higher Sa. Dpgrgp, grgpdpds, pdpg, gpgrsr,srgr,gpdp,pdgp, pdsds.

Then even higher into higher pa, finally returning back to the base Sa.

Dsrsdp, pdsrdrs, dsrsdpd, pdsrg, grdrs, rsdpds, pdsrgr, srgpgrs, grsdr, srgrsdpd, odrsdpgp, pdgrsds, pdrsdpd, sdpgdp, gpdsdp, gpdpgrsr, gpdpgd, pdpgrsrgr, grsds, rsdpdp, pds, pdgr, grsdrs.

In this way, as short phrases put together as the mind flows, one can elaborate and improvise on a scale, to bring a Raga to life, and invoke the corresponding forms.

One can also embellish the rendering with Gamakas, or oscillatory adornments. The key to continuity, is to choose an instrument of good key sustenance, such as violin etc, and to get continuity of note transitions, press the second note key before releasing the first key, so that, for a very brief moment, both notes are sounded, and then release the first note key. This will sound a smooth "slide transition" between notes, called Jaaru. One can also do quick transitions, such as for example rgr, where the g is very very short, with the r's long, the result being an oscillatory effect on r. Further, it can be observed that in some Ragas such as Thodi, one always sings certain notes, g in the case of Thodi, from a lower note. Even in instruments such as Veena, the Gi is played in the area of Ri itself, with oscillation or pulling the string. In keyboard this can be achieved. In ascent, never sound gi plain, but always as a slide from Ra. In descent though, whenever gi is to be played, start from ri. Play ri very shortly, and do a slide transition to gi. One can also oscillate between Ri and gi, two or three times, both notes sounded shortly.

In this manner, Gamakas can be rendered as well wherever they are found to be necessary.

Learning this, and with a little practice, one can easily bring to life many Ragas, existing or new, and invoke the corresponding forms. All the while, one must play to the lyrics SaiRam, SaiRam, SaiRam. .... that is, every pair of notes struck would sound Sai Ram.

One can, proceed further, and start singing along with the keyboard to get the note pitches correct. With enough practice, one can master singing as well, and then can use vocal for invocation, again with the lyrics SaiRam, SaiRam.

This is indeed music at its purest, as Manodharma, giving a free rein to the mind, letting Amma as Atma speak through the mind, in the form of notes. This, especially in one's own home or temple, was indeed the way music was handled in the early days, and was the way by which Muthuswami Dikshitar, Thyagaraja and other great stalwarts excelled brilliantly. In their times, there were harshly many predecessor compositions to learn. It was only in the later days, after the Trinity, that the format of concert came into being, and with it, a heavy focus on rendering already composed pieces, limiting, and in some unfortunate, almost eliminating Manodharma, violating the very purpose for which music exists. The same trend exists in the western world of music as well, shifting from original composing of symphonies by Bach, Beethoven etc, to today's large orchestras fundamentally rendering composed pieces rather than composing new ones.

However, with this given procedure, one can revive the original purpose and temperament of music, and its incredible powers of invocation. So too, in Saama Sangeetham, even though the notes and patterns are fixed, depending on the current mindset, the particular note coinciding with Divine Will at any point, will be highlighted, and this will repeat, everytime the note is touched, since Saama Sangeetham is sung as a loop.

CHAPTER TWENTY

Conclusion

In this book the real wisdom of Sri Vidya has been given and explored in considerable detail with its various intricacies. Yet, Sri Vidya in itself is an ocean, as is any book on the topic, since a lot of wisdom emerges, reading in between lines of the text, and it is with this understanding that one must approach the text, where the base structure and content are quite firm and established, but inner details and nuances may always emerge, every day, every moment of living. The end aim of Sri Vidya and all of the message conveyed through this book is only one – a life of pure, blissful, intense love, every moment, living happily as a infant in the lap of the ever loving Amma, where the love in intense moments becomes romance between Atma and God, the most ideal lovers ever to exist.

Amma! Amma! Ammaaa!

Milton Keynes UK
Ingram Content Group UK Ltd.
UKHW020941280923
429557UK00013B/476

9 798887 725253